PSYCHOLOGY AND VISUAL AESTHETICS

'Driving out the Demon'

by Yoko Tatehana, a girl aged 8 years in the 4th year Grade of Rikkyo Togakuin (St Margaret's Primary School), Tokyo, Japan.

The picture is part of a calendar for 1968, illustrated by pupils of St Margaret's Primary School for girls and St Paul's Primary School for boys (Rikkyo Primary School). This is the illustration for February, and, according to the 1968 calendar, the 4th of February was 'the day before the beginning of Spring'. The Japanese call this day *Setsubun*. On the eve of spring time the Japanese have a long established custom to scatter dried beans about in the house to drive out the evil spirit, crying, 'Happiness, stay here; Demon, get away!' The red demon with a club is being driven away by the beans scattered from the child's hands. (These notes were kindly provided by Professor W. A. Sakow.)

Psychology
and Visual Aesthetics

R. W. PICKFORD

*Professor of Psychology
in the University of Glasgow*

HUTCHINSON EDUCATIONAL

HUTCHINSON EDUCATIONAL LTD
3 Fitzroy Square, London W1

London Melbourne Sydney Auckland
Wellington Johannesburg Cape Town
and agencies throughout the world

First published 1972

72 - 193824

8/11 *Black. 1-8-75 (Cancel)*

*This book has been set in Imprint type, printed in Great Britain
on smooth wove paper by Anchor Press, and
bound by Wm. Brendon, both of Tiptree, Essex*
ISBN 0 09 110820 9

To *The International Association of Empirical Aesthetics*
in Commemoration of the Publication of Fechner's
Vorschule der Aesthetik, Leipzig, 1876, and of
his earlier papers on Experimental
Aesthetics

Contents

Illustrations

Preface

The aim of this book is to present a study mainly concerned with experimental work on visual aesthetics. The writer has always been interested in the psychology of art and of aesthetic problems and is glad of the opportunity to publish this book, because there is a steady increase at the present day in the scientific study of matters relating to art. From the rather restricted approaches of Fechner, the pioneer of experimental aesthetics, whose book *Vorschule der Aesthetik* was published in 1876, there has been a spread of interest out of the confines of the psychological laboratory to statistical studies, personality problems and social psychology.

The writer has viewed the book in a historical way to a certain extent throughout, although it is not strictly a history of experimental aesthetics. It is hoped that the various phases of development will be apparent, approximately as follows: at first laboratory studies, mainly on individuals; then statistically oriented studies with numbers of subjects; in the 1940s the beginnings of the mathematical analysis of aesthetic judgments; then the introduction of personality studies, including the problems of the aesthetic judgments of psychiatric patients; and in the 1950s and 1960s the development of studies based on social psychology and the cross-cultural approaches.

These changes have taken place, hand in hand with developments in psychology as a whole and of psychological techniques, as will be evident in the chapters which follow. The changes correspond to the successive developments of Fechnerian experimental work, then of Gestalt Psychology, then intelligence tests and tests of special capacities and abilities, then personality tests and the understanding of abnormal psychology, and finally the expansion of researches into what is now often called experimental social psychology. The book is therefore like a special chapter in the history of psychology since 1876—or rather, since about 1900, because little is touched upon before the present century, except the mention of Fechner's work; and one of his earliest publications on experimental aesthetics was *Zur experimentallen Aesthetik. Abhandlungen Sächischen Gesellschaft der Wissenschaft.**

It is to be hoped that the many people now occupied with the numerous problems with which the book is concerned will find it a valuable addition to the literature of the subject.

The writer is indebted to Professor George Westby for his help and encouragement, and to the inspiration provided by the establishment of the International Association of Empirical Aesthetics, largely through the influence of Professor Robert Francès, in Paris in 1965.

Glasgow   R. W. Pickford
May 1970

---

* *Math. Physical. Klasse, 9,* 536 ff., 1871.

Acknowledgements

The use of the illustrations is gratefully acknowledged to the following:
Professor William A. Sakow for the Frontispiece; Mr Donald R. Purdy, the British Psychological Society and the Editors of the *British Journal of Psychology* and the *British Journal of Aesthetics* for Colour Plate I; Mr Pratul A. Ray for Colour Plate II, 1, the Artist for Colour Plate II, 2; the British Psychological Society and the Editors of the *British Journal of Psychology* and the *British Journal of Aesthetics* for both; Mr M. Morris and the Goldsmith's Librarian of the University of London for Plates 1, 2 and 3; Messrs Routledge and Kegan Paul, Ltd for Plates 4, 5, 6, 7 and 9; Sister Jude, Director of the Notre Dame Child Guidance Clinic, Glasgow, for Plate 8; Mr Robin Gilmour, for Plate 10; the Editor of *Psychological Monographs* and the American Psychological Association for Plates 11, 12, 13, 14 and Figure 10; *Punch* for permission to use Figure 11a; Professor G. M. Wyburn and Messrs Oliver and Boyd Ltd, for Figures 1, 2, 3, 4, 12, 13, 14, 15, 16, 17, 22 and 23; the Editor of the *Psychological Review* and the American Psychological Association for Figure 5; the Editor of the *American Journal of Psychology* for Figure 6; the Editor of the *Journal of Applied Psychology* and the American Psychological Association

for Figures 7 and 8; Messrs Batsford Ltd and Messrs Baker and Taylor, for Figure 11; the Editor of the *British Journal of Psychology* and the British Psychological Society for Figures 18 and 19; Professor Roy Davis for Figure 19 and Mrs Winifred R. K. Cooper (formerly Mrs McElroy) for Figure 18; the Editor of the *Journal of Abnormal and Social Psychology,* the American Psychological Association and Dr Monica Lawlor for Figure 20; the Editor of *Behavioral Science* and Professor Charles E. Osgood for Figure 21; the Editor of the *Journal of Social Psychology* for Figure 24.

The writer would like to express his indebtedness to Miss B. J. Reid for the care and thoroughness with which she carried out the typing.

I

Introduction:
the psychological approach

Broadly, psychology can contribute to our understanding of the
problems of art and aesthetics in four ways. The first is through the
application of the results of psychological inquiry in general to
art and aesthetics where they are appropriate. The second is
through special experiments and techniques devised for the
purpose. The third is through comparative and cross-cultural
studies and the fourth is basically clinical or psychiatric. The first
three of these will be used in the present book, and the fourth only
in so far as the aesthetic judgments and preferences of psychiatric
patients will be examined.

The first psychological approach involves the application of
our knowledge of visual and other aspects of perception, for
instance, to aesthetics. The basis of this knowledge is, of course,
itself largely experimental. It is clear that the psychology of
aesthetic perception is a branch of the psychology of perception
in general, and the study of tests of artistic appreciation is a
special branch of the psychology of tests, and so on. Many
people, mainly interested and trained in art and matters relating
to it, would like to see the appropriate aspects of general psychology
explained in a way which can be understood without a specialised
study of psychology as a whole, and this will be attempted as the
various aspects of the problems we are concerned with are taken
up and examined.

The second psychological approach is through experimental techniques which were devised for the study of aesthetic judgments, such as the method of paired comparisons and the semantic differential of Osgood, by which aesthetic preferences can be brought within the scope of quantitative treatment. Many people, mostly those with a philosophical inclination and training, seriously doubt that the use of experimental techniques can be applied to art and aesthetic judgments and preferences justifiably at all. It is clear, however, that by these techniques we aim simply at controlling variables and comparing judgments so that their influences can be determined and estimated under specific conditions. It will become clear in the next chapters that many problems relating to aesthetic perception and judgment can be clarified experimentally and that others could never be settled at all without the aid of systematic experimental psychology. This approach includes studies of individual differences.

The third psychological approach, through comparative and cross-cultural studies, depends on the observation and direct comparison of art products from different cultural sources and on their history and origins. The approach followed up in this book, however, depends on the extension of experimental methods to include systematic analysis of aesthetic judgments and perception in different racial and cultural groups. The uses of experimental and statistical methods serve to control what would otherwise depend on subjective impressions and opinions.

The fourth psychological approach, the psychiatric or clinical, depends on the study and understanding of the judgments, preferences and expressive productions of persons in abnormal personality states, so that their interpretation throws light on what is recognised as true or genuine art. The study of the abnormal psychology of expressive production has not, as some people think, demeaned real art, but has enormously increased our understanding of it in many ways.

It is interesting to compare and contrast this simple fourfold scheme with the more detailed description of five principal methods in the psychology of art set forth by Müller-Freienfels, and discussed by Thomas Munro (Munro, 1948; Müller-Freienfels, 1923). According to Munro the first method of Müller-Freienfels is the *experimental method*. He says that this method was long unproductive because it was used to establish the absolute or universal pleasantness of spatial forms, colours, rhythms, and so on, but it has much wider applications to the study of individual differences and the conditions of aesthetic experience, as will be seen in later chapters.

The second method of Müller-Freienfels is that of the *question-naire*. This, he thinks, is of greater importance than that of the laboratory experiment, but has the drawback of being hard to control. He suggests that the questionnaire method affords a much greater possibility of doing justice to the field of investigation of art, and may be applied to a much greater number of individuals. However, in the accounts of experiments to be given later in the present book, it will be seen that the experimental method is not by any means confined to laboratory situations and small numbers of subjects, as it probably was at first and for a long time after the publication of Fechner's book.

The third method of Müller-Freienfels is the method of *individual psychology*. This deals with the person in his own right as an artistic creator, and also in comparison with others. It is not specially tied to psychoanalysis or other approaches by depth psychology. It is concerned not only with the personality of the individual in relation to his creative work, but also in relation to enjoying art. He calls the comparison of different individuals and groups the *differential method,* and it synthesises the results of individual psychology by classifying resemblances and differences between persons.

The fourth method is called the *pathological method,* and is a special form of the method of individual psychology. As artistic ability and sensitivity are often found among individuals of abnormal personality, they can be better appreciated if we can interpret them in terms of an understanding of pathological symptoms. He thinks, however, that it is entirely wrong to place creative talent and insanity in close proximity. This method is applicable not only to some problems of artistic creativity, but also to the appreciation of art.

Finally, the fifth method of Müller-Freienfels is the *objective-analytical* method. It involves the study of works of art of all periods and peoples, in the attempt to identify the mental states and functions which produced them. We must study, alongside the works of art, the social, cultural, political, economic and scientific aspects of life of the artists if we are to understand these works adequately. As sub-methods under this heading, we have the *ethno-psychological* method, which depends on considering works of art as expressions of the collective rather than of the individual's life and the method oriented to the exploration of the *child's* creative activities. Müller-Freienfels considers the *comparative* method, which involves the interrelating of all the others, as the most important approach of all.

It is worth pausing to consider the approach made by Fechner, who proposed the study of art from below—that is to say, the experimental investigation of judgments of preference for simple stimuli and simple combinations of stimuli in order to build up from below those stimuli and combinations which would be used in complete works of art. Although this approach is still widely applied, it will be seen in the following chapters that we are less inclined today to think that it would be possible to work on an additive system. On the contrary, every new combination creates new and unforeseen possibilities. The artistic qualities of the final product could not be successfully predicted from a knowledge of the psychological effects of the component elements taken singly.

Historical note

To follow up what was said in the Preface, a brief historical note will be given here. It is generally agreed that, as far as experimentally oriented aesthetics are concerned, G. T. Fechner laid down the basic principles in his *Vorschule der Aesthetik* (1876). His principles have been dealt with in an experimental study by Lillien J. Martin (1906). Even if we do not tie ourselves to the approaches made by Fechner, which were rather restricted in conception to laboratory experiments, it is still true that Fechner established the approach to aesthetics which made it an experimental science, a branch of experimental psychology. The other less clearly experimental approaches just mentioned in the previous paragraphs have been added since by social, individual and psychiatric psychologists, and others.

In Great Britain at the beginning of this century important work was carried out by C. S. Myers (1914a, 1914b), C. W. Valentine (1914, 1962), W. H. Winch (1909–10), Edward Bullough (1907, 1908, 1910, 1919a, 1919b, 1921), and others. Cyril Burt (1924, 1933, 1939), C. E. Spearman (1930), H. J. Eysenck (1940, 1941a, 1941b, 1942), P. E. Vernon (1930a, 1930b, 1934–5), Boris Semeonoff (1940a, 1940b), E. A. Peel (1945, 1946), G. W. Granger (1955a, b, c and d) and others, including Iliffe (1960) and the writer (Pickford, 1948, 1955), all made contributions to experimental aesthetics in various ways.

In the United States there has been a very large increase in experimental and other psychological studies of art and aesthetics. One of the earliest writers in the field was Ethel D. Puffer (1903a, 1903b). Important contributions were made to the psychology of art and of music in the *Iowa Studies in Psychology,* edited by Christian A. Ruckmick (e.g. *Studies in the Psychology of Art,* Ed. Norman C. Meier, 1933), and, in the psychology of art, from the *Cleveland Museum of Art* (Munro, Lark-Horovitz and Barnhart, 1942). In addition there have been extensive developments of experimental studies of art and aesthetics in the United States, most of which will be mentioned in the succeeding chapters of the present book.

Thomas Munro gave a very full account of the development of aesthetics as a science in America, which is very broadly based and not confined to experimental methods (1951). Another work of interest as a source of ideas and data is by Morgan (1950). In a recent work on social psychology Child has added to his many contributions to experimental aesthetics by an account of aesthetics viewed as a branch of behavioural science (1969), with a valuable bibliography. The history of colour aesthetics was dealt with very fully by Victoria K. Ball (1965).

Psychiatric and psychoanalytic studies of art and artists have developed extensively in the present century, as in the hands of Freud (1957), Jones (1923), Fairbairn (1938a and 1938b), Rickman (1940), Reitman (1950, 1954), Kris (1953), Guttmann and Maclay (1937, 1941), Pickford (1967, 1969), and many others, including especially Anton Ehrenzweig (1953, 1967).

The biographical approach has been made by Harding (1942) and by Foy (1967), and the historical approach by Pickford (1943). The study of child art was established as a major interest by Oldham (1940), Viola (1942), Phyllis Greenacre (1957) and others. The study of children's artistic judgments by Littlejohns and Needham is of great interest (1933). It is important to mention Alschuler and Hattwick's work (1947) on children's art, and the Iowa and Cleveland studies, already mentioned, were important contributions to children's artistic abilities. Other important works have also been mentioned already in this chapter (Francès, 1958, 1968; Hussain, 1967) and to these should be added the important contributions of Huisman (1954), Wellek (1963), Imberty (1969), Berlyne (1966 and 1968) and Moles (1966). These are only brief notes about the history of the subject, which is now in serious need of full treatment in a book to commemorate the centenary of Fechner's work (1876). The advancement of psychological aesthetics will be ensured by the recent establishment of the International Association for Empirical Aesthetics, with its headquarters in Paris at the Institut d'Esthétique, under the Presidency of Professor Robert Francès. Five important journals should be mentioned which serve as the vehicles for the publication of ideas and studies of the psychology of aesthetics: *The Journal of Aesthetics and Art Criticism* (USA); *The British Journal of Aesthetics* (London); *Sciences de l'Art* (Paris) and *Confinia Psychiatrica* (Basle). The first two are oriented to a great extent philosophically, the third is perhaps the central organ for empirical aesthetics, and the fourth is, as its title suggests, concerned with art among other matters related to psychiatry. In addition, there is the fifth journal, namely *Exakte Asthetik: Revue d'Esthétique Experimentale* (Frankfurt am Main).

It is unfortunate that the Fourth International Colloquium on Empirical Aesthetics, held in Glasgow University Psychology Department, August 1970, came too late for detailed treatment in this book. The Colloquium included many papers reporting new researches on visual and other aspects of experimental aesthetics, and, although these cannot be dealt with here, most of them will be published in a special number of *Sciences de l'Art*, Paris, 1972, under the editorship of Professor P. Roubertoux.

Another significant contribution to visual aesthetics, which came too late for this book, is Trevor-Roper's *The World through Blunted Sight* (Thames and Hudson, 1970). Trevor-Roper deals in an illuminating way with the effects on the artist and on his art of many aspects and abnormalities of vision, including lack of accurate focussing, defective colour vision, and blindness. The book deserves the attention of every worker interested in visual art and aesthetics.

Bibliography and References
for Chapter 1

ALSCHULER, ROSE H., and HATTWICK, LA B. W. (1947). *Painting and Personality: A Study of Young Children.* Chicago University Press. 2 vols.

BALL, VICTORIA K. (1965). The Aesthetics of Color: A Review of Fifty Years of Experimentation. *J. Aesthet. and Art Criticism, 23,* 441–52.

BERLYNE, D. E. (1966). Les Mesures de la Préférence Esthétique (1). *Sciences de l'Art. Numero Spécial,* 1966, pp. 9–22.

BERLYNE, D. E. (1968). Aesthetic Behaviour and Exploratory Behaviour. *Proc. Fifth Internat. Cong. Aesthetics,* Amsterdam, 1964. Ed. Jan Aler. Amsterdam: Mouton, 1968, pp. 865–8.

BULLOUGH, EDWARD (1907). On the Apparent Heaviness of Colours: A Contribution to the Aesthetics of Colour. *Brit. J. Psychol., 2* (1906–8), pp. 111–52.

BULLOUGH, EDWARD (1908). The 'Perceptive Problem' in the Aesthetic Appreciation of Single Colours. *Brit. J. Psychol., 2* (1906–8), pp. 406–63.

BULLOUGH, EDWARD (1910). The 'Perceptive Problem' in the Aesthetic Appreciation of Simple Colour-Combinations. *Brit. J. Psychol., 3,* pp. 406–47.

BULLOUGH, EDWARD (1919a). The Relation of Aesthetics to Psychology. *Brit. J. Psychol., 10,* pp. 43–50.

BULLOUGH, EDWARD (1919b). Mind and Medium in Art. *Brit. J. Psychol., 11,* pp. 26–46.

BULLOUGH, EDWARD (1921). Recent Work in Experimental Aesthetics. *Brit. J. Psychol., 12,* pp. 76–99.

BURT, C. (1924). Chapter I, 'Psychological Tests of Educable Capacity', in *Report of the Consultative Committee of the Board of Education.* London.

BURT, C. (1933). Chapter 15, 'The Psychology of Art', in *How the Mind Works.* Ed. C. Burt. London: Allen and Unwin.

BURT, C. (1939). Factorial Analysis of Emotional Traits. II. *Character and Personality, 7,* pp. 285–99.

CHILD, I. L. (1969). *Esthetics,* ch. 28 in *Handbook of Social Psychology.* Eds. Lindzey, G. and Aronson, E., 2nd ed., Reading, Mass.; Addison-Wesley.

EHRENZWEIG, A. (1953). *The Psycho-Analysis of Artistic Vision and Hearing: An Introduction to a Theory of Unconscious Perception.* London: Routledge and Kegan Paul.

EHRENZWEIG, A. (1957). *The Hidden Order of Art.* London: Weidenfeld and Nicolson.

EYSENCK, H. J. (1940). The General Factor in Aesthetic Judgments. *Brit. J. Psychol., 31,* 94–102.

EYSENCK, H. J. (1941a). 'Type'-Factors in Aesthetic Judgments. *Brit. J. Psychol., 31,* 262–70.

EYSENCK, H. J. (1941b). A Critical and Experimental Study of Color Preferences. *Amer. J. Psychol., 54,* 385–94.

EYSENCK, H. J. (1942). The Empirical Study of 'Good Gestalt'—A New Approach. *Psychol. Rev., 49,* 344–64.

FAIRBAIRN, W. R. D. (1938a). Prolegomena to a Psychology of Art. *Brit. J. Psychol., 28,* 288–303.

FAIRBAIRN, W. R. D. (1938b). The Ultimate Basis of Aesthetic Experience. *Brit. J. Psychol., 29,* 167–81.

FECHNER, G. T. (1876). *Vorschule der Aesthetik.* Leipzig: Breitkopf and Härtel.

FOY, James L. (1967). *Psychotic Painting and Psychotic Painters.* Fourth Lexington Conference on Phenomenology: Pure and Applied. Lexington, Kentucky.

FRANCÈS, R. (1958). *La Perception de la Musique.* Paris: Vrin.

FRANCÈS, R. (1968). *Psychologie de L'Esthétique.* Paris: P.U.F.

FREUD, S. (1957). *Leonardo da Vinci and a Memory of his Childhood* (1910). *Standard Edition of the Complete Psychological Works of Sigmund Freud.* Tr. Strachey. XI, pp. 59–137.

GRANGER, G. W. (1955a). An Experimental Study of Colour Differences. *J. Gen. Psychol., 52,* 3–20.

GRANGER, G. W. (1955b). An Experimental Study of Colour Harmony. *J. Gen. Psychol., 52,* 21–35.

GRANGER, G. W. (1955c). Aesthetic Measure Applied to Color Harmony: An Experimental Test. *J. Gen. Psychol., 52,* 205–12.

GRANGER, G. W. (1955d). The Prediction of Preference for Color Combinations. *J. Gen. Psychol., 52.* 213–22.

GREENACRE, PHYLLIS (1957). The Childhood of the Artist: Libidinal Phase Development and Giftedness. *Psychoanalytic Study of the Child, 12,* 47–72.

GUTTMANN, E., and MACLAY, W. W. (1937). Clinical Observations on Schizophrenic Drawings, *Brit. J. Med. Psychol., 16,* 184–205.

GUTTMANN, E., and MACLAY, W. W. (1941). Mescalin Hallucinations in Artists. *Arch. Neurol. Psychiat., 45,* 130.

HARDING, R. E. M. (1942). *An Anatomy of Inspiration.* Cambridge: Heffer, 2nd ed.

HUISMAN, D. (1954). L'Esthétique, Paris: P.U.F.

HUSSAIN, FAKHIR (1967). *Le Jugement Esthétique.* Paris: Minard.

ILIFFE, A. H. (1960). A Study of Preferences in Feminine Beauty. *Brit. J. Psychol., 51,* 267–73.

IMBERTY, MICHEL (1969). *L'Acquisition des Structures Tonales chez l'Enfant.* Paris: Klincksieck.

JONES, E. (1923). *Essays in Applied Psycho-Analysis.* Chapter VI. London: Internat. Psycho-Analytic Press.

KRIS, E. (1952). *Psychoanalytic Explorations in Art.* New York. Internat. Univ. Press.

LITTLEJOHNS, J., and NEEDHAM, A. (1933). *Training of Taste in the Arts and Crafts.* London: Pitman.

MARTIN, LILLIEN J. (1906). An Experimental Study of Fechner's Principles of Aesthetics. *Psychol. Rev., 13,* 142–219.

MEIER, N. C. (1933). Studies in the Psychology of Art. Ed. Norman C. Meir. *Psychol. Rev. Publications, Psychol. Monographs, Whole No. 200.* pp. i–ix and 1–188.

MOLES, ABRAHAM (1966). *Information Theory and Esthetic Perception.* Chicago: Univ. Illinois Press.

MORGAN, DOUGLAS N. (1950). Psychology and Art Today: A Summary and Critique. *J. Aesthet. and Art Criticism, 6,* 81–96.

MÜLLER-FREIENFELS, R. (1923). *The Psychology of Art,* Leipzig: Teuber.

MUNRO, THOMAS (1948). Methods in the Psychology of Art. *J. Aesthet. and Art Criticism, 6,* 225–35.

MUNRO, THOMAS (1951). Aesthetics as Science: Its Development in America. *J. Aesthet. and Art Criticism, 9,* 161–207.

MUNRO, THOMAS, LARK-HOROVITZ, BETTY, AND BARNHART, E. N. (1942) Children's Art Abilities: Studies at the Cleveland Museum of Art. *J. Exper. Educ., 11,* 97–184.

MYERS, C. S. (1914a). A Study of the Individual Differences in Attitude towards Tones. *Brit. J. Psychol., 7,* 68–111.

MYERS, C. S. (1914b). Two Cases of Synaesthesia. *Brit. J. Psychol., 7,* 112–17.

MYERS, C. S. (1925). *An Introduction to Experimental Psychology.* Cambridge: Univ. Press. (3rd ed., reprinted).

OLDHAM, HILDA W. (1940). *Child Expression in Colour and Form.* London: John Lane.

PEEL, E. A. (1945). On Identifying Aesthetic Types. *Brit. J. Psychol., 35,* 61–9.

PEEL, E. A. (1946). A New Method for Analysing Aesthetic Preferences: Some Theoretical Considerations. *Psychometrica, 11,* 129–37.

PICKFORD, R. W. (1943). The Psychology of Cultural Change in Painting. *Brit. J. Psychol. Monogr. Supp. no. 26.*

PICKFORD, R. W. (1948). 'Aesthetic' and 'Technical' Factors in Artistic Appreciation. *Brit. J. Psychol., 38,* 135–44.

PICKFORD, R. W. (1955). Factorial Studies of Aesthetic Judgments. ch. 37 in *Present-Day Psychology.* Ed. A. A. Roback. New York. Philos. Library.

PICKFORD, R. W. (1967). *Studies in Psychiatric Art.* Springfield, Ill.: Thomas.

PICKFORD, R. W. (1969). The Psychology of Ugliness. *Brit. J. Aesthet., 9,* 258–70.

PUFFER, ETHEL D. (1903a). *Studies in Symmetry. Psychol. Monogr. Suppts.,* 4, 467–539.

PUFFER, ETHEL D. (1903b). *The Psychology of Beauty.* New York: Houghton Mifflin.

REITMAN, F. (1950). *Psychotic Art.* London: Routledge and Kegan Paul.

REITMAN, F. (1954). *Insanity, Art and Culture.* London: Wright.

RICKMAN, J. (1940). On the Nature of Ugliness and the Creative Impulse. *Int. J. Psycho-Anal.,* 21, 294–313.

SEMEONOFF, B. (1940a). A New Approach to the Testing of Musical Ability. *Brit. J. Psychol.,* 30, 326–40.

SEMEONOFF, B. (1940b). Further Developments in a New Approach to the Testing of Musical Ability, with Special Reference to Groups of Secondary School Children. *Brit. J. Psychol.,* 31, 145–61.

SHUTER, ROSAMUND (1968). *The Psychology of Musical Ability.* London: Methuen.

SPEARMAN, C. (1930). *The Creative Mind.* London: Nisbet and Cambridge U.P.

VALENTINE, C. W. (1914). The Method of Comparison in Experiments with Musical Intervals and the Effect of Practice on the Appreciation of Discords. *Brit. J. Psychol.,* 7, 118–35.

VALENTINE, C. W. (1962). *The Experimental Psychology of Beauty.* London: Methuen.

VERNON, P. E. (1930a). The Phenomena of Attention and Visualisation in the Psychology of Musical Appreciation. *Brit. J. Psychol.,* 21, 50–63.

VERNON, P. E. (1930b). Synaesthesia in Music. *Psyche,* 10, 22–40.

VERNON, P. E. (1934–5). Auditory Perception. *Brit. J. Psychol.,* 25, 123–39 and 265–83.

VIOLA, W. (1942). *Child Art.* London: Univ. London Press.

WELLEK, A. (1963). *Musikpsychologie und Musikasthetik.* Frankfurt: Akademische Verlagsgesellschaft.

WINCH, W. H. (1909–10). Colour Preferences of School Children. *Brit. J. Psychol.,* 3, 42–65.

2

Form perception and art

Form perception

It may be said that form or structure is basic to art and aesthetic experiences of all kinds. While in this chapter visual form perception will be considered, it is true that auditory form perception is equally essential in music and to word music in poetry, and that kinaesthetic or flowing form experiences are essential to all the dynamic arts—music, poetry, drama, the dance and any mobile aspects of the visual arts which exist. Conceptual form experience rather than perception are also fundamental in music, drama and literature. Kai von Fieandt has given an excellent account of perception in pictorial art (1966, ch. 16).

Although many psychological theories and ideas about perception have been put forward, none has set forth the principles of form perception so clearly and in a way so significant for the visual and other arts as Gestalt psychology, associated with the names of Wertheimer (1958), Kohler (1947) and Koffka (1935). There are four essential principles of form perception or experience, according to Gestalt psychology (see Wyburn, Pickford and Hirst, 1964). The first principle is that of *'figure and ground'* by which every perceptual experience is essentially a pattern related to a background of other experiences or their absence (Fig. 1). It is clear that this applies throughout the visual arts. Even a picture made

up of a single area of colour, say red or black, would be in accordance with this principle, because the area of colour would end
somewhere, in some way, and have some kind of frame or surround.
It would therefore be a figure on a ground and its artistic interest
would depend on what kind of figure it was, and upon what ground.

Fig. 1 *Figure and Ground* (Wyburn, Pickford and Hirst, 1964). This
may be seen either as a vase or as two faces. It shows alternation of
'figure' and 'ground'.

In more complex pictures changes of hue, saturation or intensity
within the figure would themselves be subsidiary configurations,
one being ground for another, right up to the most subtle details
of expressive portraiture, landscape or abstract art.

The second principle of Gestalt psychology is that of *'differentiation'* or *'segregation'*, by which the patterns of stimulation
organise characteristic structures for perception owing to their
special properties. Thus if a ring-shaped or cross-shaped pattern
of large dots is placed among a number of small dots, or if a

group of thick lines, or of lines or dots of a certain darkness or colour, is placed among an otherwise uniform group of dots or lines, which are not distinguished by thickness, size, colour or darkness, the ring-shaped or cross-shaped dots or lines will cohere and stand out as a segregated or differentiated figure on the uniform background (Figs. 2 and 3). This is a principle of the widest application throughout the visual arts, and its effective use is part of every artist's technique. Thus, for example, a group of dark clouds is differentiated and segregated from a sunset sky which appears to be continuous behind it. The same principle applies in music (Vernon 1934–5) and sculpture.

The third Gestalt principle of perceptual organisation is that of *closure,* by which an incompletely represented outline or structure appears to be complete or tends to be completed in perception (Fig. 4). While the clouds mentioned above are segregated into a unified group, the sunset sky appears continuous and complete behind them. A face half visible behind other heads and figures in a painting appears like a whole face. A similar effect is seen frequently, as, for instance, where a part of a figure, face or any object is simply not outlined or represented in detail because it is in deep shadow, the other, illuminated, part nevertheless seems complete and to include the shadowed part as part of its full structure.

The fourth principle of Gestalt psychology is that of the *'good Gestalt'.* According to this principle a stronger or more adequate pattern in perception will tend to take precedence over weaker patterns. Very often good Gestalten are simple structures, like circular, square or rectangular patterns. While some are apparently based on simple geometrical organisations, others are based on familiarity, or the power of emotional expression. Many clever illusions of perception are based on giving two or more configurations equal weight in representation, and then alternating figures may be produced. Any influence, such as a conscious attitude or emotional response, will tend to bring out one figure rather than the other (Fig. 1).

While all these principles are fundamental to artistic technique, it is at once clear to the psychologist that not all configurations are of equal artistic or aesthetic interest or value. If we take the four Gestalt principles in turn, it is obvious to begin with that there might be many patterns strongly in accord with the 'figure

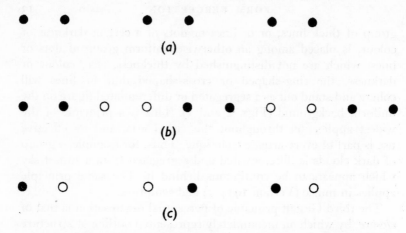

Fig. 2 *Segregation and Differentiation* (Wyburn, Pickford and Hirst, 1964). In (a) the dots group themselves in pairs because some are closer than others; in (b) because some are alike and some different; in (c) these two factors determining perceptual organisation are combined, and nearness overcomes similarity.

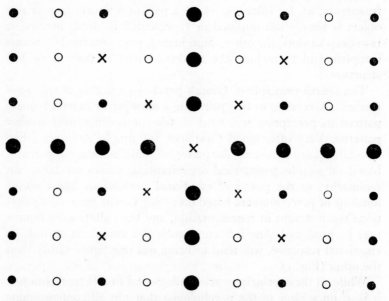

Fig. 3 *Segregation and Differentiation* (Wyburn, Pickford and Hirst, 1964). In this four kinds of stimuli are combined, and a rectangle of columns of dots and circles is perceived, which forms the 'ground' for an upright cross of large dots and a diagonal cross of small crosses.

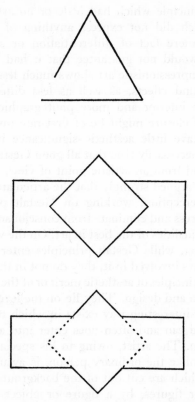

Fig. 4 *Closure and the Good Gestalt* (Wyburn, Pickford and Hirst, 1964). The top figure illustrates 'closure', by which incomplete shapes tend to be perceived as if complete. It looks like a triangle with part of one side missing.

The middle figure combines the 'figure-and-ground', 'closure' and 'good Gestalt' principles. We tend to perceive a square or diamond superimposed on a rectangle. The diamond tends to appear nearer than the rectangle, which forms a 'ground' for it.

The bottom figure shows that a simple change in the stimulus pattern makes the 10-sided outline the principal structure perceived, but 'closure' still makes the diamond and rectangle apparent. When we see the diamond the rectangle forms the 'ground' and seems behind it, but when we see the rectangle the diamond seems to form the 'ground' and to be behind.

and ground' principle which had little or no artistic interest or merit, and which did not express anything of artistic quality. Similarly, the mere fact of differentiation or segregation of a visual pattern would not guarantee that it had artistic interest. Indeed, good impressionistic art shows much less clearly marked figure and ground effects, as well as less differentiation, than much art of an inferior and more photographic kind. Thirdly, the principle of closure might be of first-rate importance in one painting, but have little aesthetic significance in another, and, lastly, it is not necessarily true that all good Gestalten are in their very nature good from an artistic point of view. Indeed Ehrenzweig (1953) has argued strongly that the articulated surface-mind of conscious perception, working on Gestalt principles, tends actually to suppress and eliminate from consciousness the dynamic and expressive qualities of the best in art. On the whole, therefore, we must say that, while Gestalt principles enter constantly into art and are always involved in it, they do not in themselves necessarily provide principles of aesthetic merit or of the most expressive qualities of form and design. They lie on the level of techniques.

One specially interesting way exists in which the phenomenon of figure-ground can and often does enter into artistic structure and organisation. The artist, owing to his special gifts, interests and training, unlike the ordinary person, is aware in perception of the shapes which are cut out of the background, or cut out of other objects or figures, by a figure or object which is given prominence in a picture. Thus the objects or persons which a picture is said to represent, and the background shape between them or against which they are seen, are something like alternative figure-ground patterns to the artist, and the design or form qualities of the cut-out shapes of the background may be just as important to him as the forms of the figures or objects represented. Indeed there is a double problem in setting up a figure or object or a group to be represented. The one aspect of it lies in the outlines and form qualities of the figures themselves, and in the balance of their relationships; the other lies in the structure, outline and form qualities of the cut-out pattern which is seen between and around them. The artist will think of the one and then the other repeatedly, and gradually make adjustments until he gets a synthesised arrangement which is exactly satisfactory and which integrates both.

In many people's view the most important Gestalt principle has been omitted. It is the principle of *'isomorphism'*, according to which the electrical dynamic processes in the brain are postulated as being congruent with the configurations perceived and with the movements made in expressive behaviour. This principle, fundamental to Kohler and the great Gestalt psychologists, has been studied in many attempts to discover the patterns of brain activity and compare them with behavioural and perceptual patterns. Although there has been some success, in general the principle of isomorphism has not been adequately substantiated. Its relationship and application to problems of art and aesthetically expressive movements, however, have been clearly set forth by Rudolph Arnheim (1966, 1967).

The relevance of the first four Gestalt principles to art in their phenomenological aspects is, however, not dependent on the establishment of the fifth principle of isomorphism. The perceptual experience and motor functions related to art are not made more or less relevant by the kind of brain process which mediates them. In addition, if the principle of isomorphism were true, its application would not differentiate good art from bad art, because it would apply equally in either case.

Preferences for simple lines and shapes

The problem arises what configurations, patterns and organisations of visual material tend to be most artistically satisfying, and why. This is where experimental psychology has been very helpful and illuminating. Appropriate psychological experiments may be carried out by presenting persons who act as subjects or judges with varied visual material in a systematic way, and asking them to report or record their preferences according to some pre-arranged plan. Such experiments almost inevitably involve some technique which enables the psychologist to make quantitative assessments of the results, either to compare one person's judgments or preferences with the average of a group, or to compare the average preferences or judgments about a given figure or work of art with those for the others in a set of similar or different works.

The subjects or judges often wonder: (a) whether comparisons and judgments of aesthetic quality can be made or represented in quantitative or numerical terms at all; (b) whether aesthetic judgments about different visual objects, patterns or designs can be compared directly, as all such objects, if they have any artistic merit, are unique; (c) whether individual persons, who vary widely in their experiences, can be compared quantitatively; and (d) whether the restrictions and formalities imposed by an experiment do not make the subject's task too artificial to have any meaning for aesthetics. The writer shares many of these doubts, but the use of quantitative and statistical techniques in psychology is justified by any insight and illumination it can give, and experimental aesthetics, like other experimental approaches in psychology, has justified itself in this way, as will be seen in this and later chapters. In this book the writer will attempt to introduce quantitative and experimental techniques and numerical comparisons and analyses in so far as they are aids to our thinking about the problems of art and not on the assumption that they offer ultimate philosophical foundations for aesthetics or are ends in themselves.

Before proceeding to accounts of other experiments on the aesthetic value of lines and figures, it will be worth while to comment briefly on the monograph of Lillien J. Martin (1906). She took from Fechner's book (1876) suitable sentences and passages to express the various aesthetic hypotheses on which he worked, although she says that nowhere does he state them in a formal way. She gives a succinct statement of his principles of psychological aesthetics. These principles, although they call for a more elaborate exemplification than we can afford space for here, if they are to be given fully comprehensive treatment, are of considerable interest. Martin says that Fechner laid down five principles: 'the principle of the aesthetic threshold; of aesthetic help or increase; of the unified combining of the manifold; of noncontradictability, of agreement or truth; and of association'. Then he added seven other or subordinate principles: 'that of contrast, sequence and reconciliation; of summation, practice, blunting, habit or custom and of satiety; of persistence, of change, and of the amount of occupation; of the expression of pleasure and displeasure; of secondary pleasurable and displeasurable ideas; of the aesthetic mean; and of the economical application of the means' (Martin, 1906, p. 143).

In her own work Martin re-formulates one hypothesis after another, using translations of Fechner's words, and reports experimental tests of hypotheses. Her experiments represented a major application of Fechner's principles in a hypothetico-deductive way to the problems of psychological aesthetics, and were a landmark in the development of research on the subject. For example, she deals with all sorts of problems of the aesthetic threshold in terms of experiments with lines and figures, to be mentioned in the next paragraph. Then she takes up the effect of looking at a picture repeatedly, or continuously, of 'semi-pseudo-chromaesthesia', of illusions and hallucinations, and of the title of a picture upon aesthetic judgment. These and many other points are dealt with by observational and experimental methods. A careful examination of Martin's monograph would be well worth while to anybody who had more than a passing interest in the experimental psychology of aesthetics, because it must have been the springboard for many subsequent workers, basing itself, as it did, on Fechner's principles.

Valentine (1962, pp. 71–6) has discussed at some length the set of experiments by Martin (1906) which were carried out with a series of straight lines, curved lines, circles and ellipses, some of the lines being longer or thicker than others, as part of her systematic study of Fechner's principles in experimental aesthetics. There were 41 lines and figures in all, and each was drawn upon a separate card. The cards were presented to eight subjects, one at a time, and the subjects were asked to say whether they disliked or liked each line or figure, or were indifferent to it. In a second experiment the cards were presented in pairs, so that every card was compared with each of the others, equally often on the right and left. The eight subjects were then asked to say which of the two figures or lines they liked better. This is the psychologist's method of paired comparisons, and by adding the preferences for each card it is possible to obtain a general order of preference showing which is most preferred and which least, with numerical estimates of the degrees of preference. Martin's 41 figures and lines are given in Fig. 5. In this experiment the average order of preference was: (1) circles, (2) straight lines, (3) waving lines, (4) ellipses and (5) arcs of circles.

Perhaps the most striking results of this experiment lay in the great variety of individual reasons and explanations given for the preferences. Only one subject found all the lines indifferent, but the others were surprised at the definiteness of their feelings of liking and disliking. In some cases the simple fact of position determined preference. This is called the 'space error' by experimental psychologists, and in this case it takes the form of a consistent tendency to give a certain response—liking or disliking, as this experiment—to the right or left of two objects presented. In other cases the pairs tended to form combined patterns which had some specially pleasing quality owing to their arrangement. There was a tendency for larger lines, arcs and circles to be preferred to smaller ones, and the thicker lines to the thinner, but not consistently. Attitudes adopted to the lines had very marked effects. For example, a circle was liked by one person because it was about the size and shape of a certain picture, a vertical line because it resembled a 'pussy-willow branch', and an oblique line because it recalled 'a road between pine trees'. Valentine himself also found that a sloping line was displeasing when regarded as a bad vertical, but pleasing when regarded as a horizontal which was raising itself to the vertical. Numerous examples of this kind are reported, and the influence of suggested movement, as in the last sample mentioned, was particularly important. This made Martin look at the results to find any effect of imitative hand and arm movements in aesthetic impressions, but nothing definite was found.

Valentine, however, himself carried out an experiment on hand and arm movements with sixteen subjects who were asked to close their eyes and draw with free and easy movements of the hand and arm simple curves and figures, such as spirals and intermingled curves, on paper. After each drawing the subject was asked to note down, without opening his eyes, whether the movement had been pleasing, very slightly pleasing, indifferent or displeasing. Each made five drawings and after the steps already described he looked at the figures and expressed a judgment about their visual appearance, whether pleasing, displeasing, etc. Marks were given to the various figures according to the judgments on a seven-point scale as follows: very pleasing, 3; pleasing, 2; slightly pleasing, 1; indifferent, 0; slightly displeasing, −1; displeasing, −2; and very displeasing, −3. For every subject but one the appearances of the lines scored much less than the movements by which they were made, the total scores being: lines as judged by movement, 172; as judged by appearance, 99. The exceptional subject made very small figures, confining himself almost to finger movements.

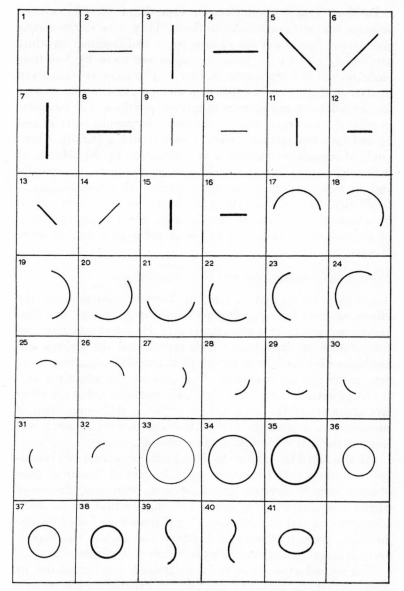

Fig. 5 *Martin's Lines and Figures* (Martin, 1906).

Barnhart (1940) conducted an experiment on fifty women subjects who were university students. They were shown simple geometrical figures cut out of blue paper and mounted on white cardboard, 3 m × 4 m. Some examples are given by Valentine (1962, p. 98) and are shown in Fig. 6. The subjects were asked to arrange the figures in order of preference, and to give reasons for the judgment and answers to further questions. The two most popular shapes were 7 and 14; the two least popular were 11 and 5; and two intermediates were 1 (sixth) and 4 (tenth). Three kinds of reasons predominated in explanation by the subjects of their choices: (1) formal criteria, such as symmetry, complexity and organisation; (2) connotative criteria such as associations of familiarity and unfamiliarity; (3) potentiality, for design, given by a small group. Formal criteria were given by 90 per cent of the subjects, and threequarters of them gave two or three criteria.

Feelings and emotions expressed by lines and shapes

Three experiments may be cited to illustrate researches into the effects of lines in expressing feelings and emotions. The first experiment was by H. Lundholm (1921). He asked four men and four women to draw lines which represented the feelings and emotions expressed by a list of 52 descriptive adjectives in 13 sets or groups of synonyms. Examples of the adjectives are: 'harsh', 'playful', 'weak' and 'dead'. He considered that the affective character of the lines had its origin in their suggestion of movement and upon the fact that this movement in some way imitates the motor expression of an emotion.

He also asked his subjects to draw lines they considered beautiful and others they considered ugly. In general 'beautiful' lines showed unity in direction and movement, continuity, absence of angles and intersections, and a periodical return of the same elements or a certain symmetry. 'Ugly' lines were full of discontinuities, irregular changes of direction, and angles. This experiment is mentioned again in the discussion of 'Ugliness' (ch. 10).

The second experiment to be mentioned was carried out by Poffenberger and Barrows (1924). In this experiment 500 subjects were asked to indicate which of a series of 18 lines, either curved or angular, best expressed one of a set of descriptive terms such as 'sad', 'quiet', 'merry' and 'furious'. Both the lines and the

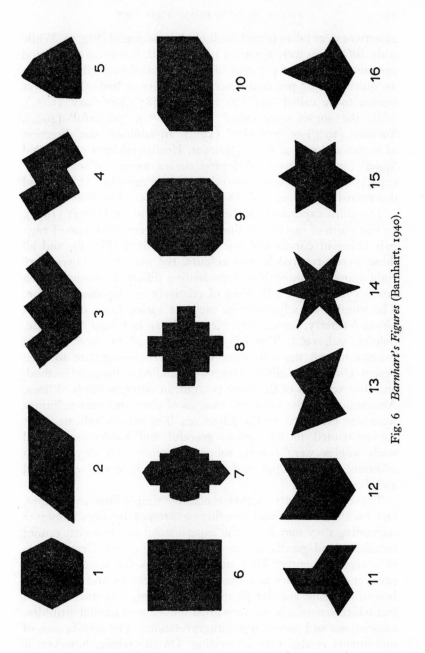

Fig. 6 *Barnhart's Figures* (Barnhart, 1940).

adjectives were taken from Lundholm's experiment (Fig. 7). While wide differences were apparent in the results, there was substantial agreement. Thus 75 per cent of the subjects described one curve as 'quiet' and 65 per cent described another as 'sad'. The curves tended to be called 'sad' (76%), 'quiet' (83%) or 'lazy' (50%), while the angles were called 'hard' (58%), 'powerful' (49%), 'furious' (39%) or 'agitating' (45%). In addition, the direction of angles and curves was significant. Horizontal lines were called 'quiet' (90%), downward-sloping curves were 'sad' or 'gentle' (74%); rising lines were 'merry' (79%) or 'agitating' (68%); and downward lines were 'sad' (85%), 'weak' (60%) or 'lazy' (51%).

The third experiment to be mentioned was by Hevner (1935). In this pairs of essentially similar designs were used, one of each pair being in curves and one in straight lines (Fig. 8), and all these were prepared in two colours, red and blue. There were eight groups of adjectives, representing different emotions, each group consisting of adjectives of relatively similar affective tone. The number of adjectives in each set varied from only six in *Group 6* (merry, joyous, gay, etc.) to eleven in *Group 2* (pathetic, doleful, sad, etc.). The subjects were asked to check from a printed list all the adjectives which were appropriate to each design. Different qualities of lines were studied by the same method, and four versions of the same portrait, in different kinds of lines. Abstractions of the lines and designs of three different paintings were also evaluated by the adjectives. The results indicated that curves tended to be serene, graceful and tender-sentimental while angles were rough, robust, vigorous and dignified. In addition, red was happy and exciting, while blue was serene, sad and dignified.

These experiments on preferences for simple lines and shapes, and on the feelings and emotions expressed by lines, however interesting they may be to the experimental psychologist, cannot be said to add greatly to our understanding of art. Certain facts of a very elementary kind emerge, such as the tendency for a preference for circles and the feeling that curves and circles are beautiful, while angular figures may be ugly. Another kind of fact which emerges is the very great influence of mental attitudes, associations and spontaneous interpretations. The significance of movements is also very interesting. On the whole, however, it seems unlikely that experimental psychology could hope to start

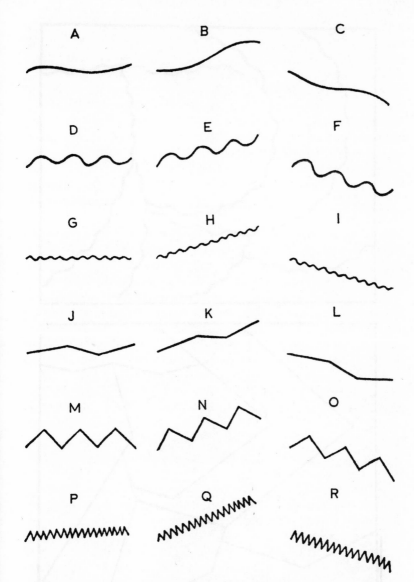

Fig. 7 *Lines from Lundholm's Experiment* (Poffenberger and Barrows, 1924).

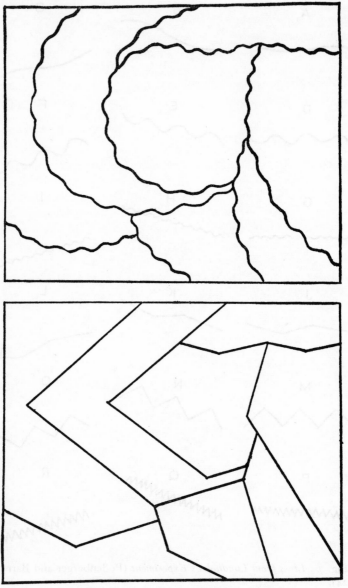

Fig. 8 *Hevner's Figures* (Hevner, 1935).

with primary facts of aesthetic valuation in relation to elementary visual lines, figures and shapes, and to proceed to show how highly developed works of art must or could be built up and organised, since the artistic value of a work of art lies in the whole and not in the summation of qualities of its parts. Similarly, it is not true that, armed with a thorough knowledge of harmony, counterpart and musical form, one could expect to proceed to the composition of good music.

The golden section, symmetry and balance

An experiment on an elementary aspect of visual organisation in relation to art, which is of classical importance and interest, is that of Fechner (1876) on the 'golden section'. He made ten rectangles of shapes varying from a square to an oblong with sides in the ratio of 5 to 2. These he presented to more than 500 men and women, who were asked to pick out the one they liked best. The most frequently chosen, for both sexes, was a rectangle which scored 33 per cent of the preferences. It is illustrated in Fig. 9 together with a square and it has the interesting property

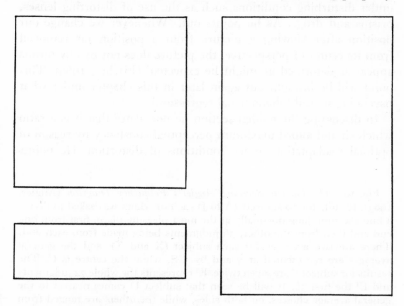

Fig. 9   *The Golden Section Rectangle, a Square and a* $\sqrt{10}$ *Rectangle* (modified from Révész, 1950).

that the perpendicular bears the same ratio to the base line which the base line bears to the sum of perpendicular and base together. This is perhaps more easily illustrated by a divided line:

A   B   C

In this AB : BC = BC : AC. The proportion in question is that BC is equal to nearly 62 per cent of AC. This is called the 'golden section', and it has a long history and considerable interest for visual aesthetics.

Experimental results for nine subjects who were asked to divide a line 160 mm long and 1·5 mm wide at the place most pleasing to them, and who made 36 judgments on either side of the centre each, are given by R. P. Angier (1903). These he arranged to show an interesting gradation from one side of the golden section to the other, in different subjects, and their distribution of choices. The results of subject E are separated to show the first 36 and the full number. Angier's diagram is shown in Fig. 10.

A discussion of the golden section has recently been included by Roland Fischer in a paper about the stability of perception under disturbing conditions such as the use of distorting lenses, prisms and drugs. As he points out, 'Whenever we change our position after viewing a picture from a position far removed from its center of perspective, the picture does not by any means appear as deformed as might be expected' (Fischer, 1969). This point will be brought out again later in this chapter under what psychologists call 'phenomenal regression'.

In discussing the golden section he postulates that it is a ratio which should afford maximum perceptual constancy by reason of optimal readaptation under conditions of distortion. He points

Fig. 10 *The Golden Section: Angier's Frequency Diagram* (Angier, 1903). Results for 10 subjects (A to J) each of whom was asked to divide a line 160 mm. long unequally at the most pleasing place, first from one end and then from the other, 36 judgments being made from each end. There are two averages for each subject (X and X), and the general averages are represented at χ and by GS, while the centre is C. The results for subject E are given twice, E² represents the whole 72 judgments and E¹ the first 36. It will be seen that subject D comes nearest to the general average choices, on both sides, while the others are ranged from subject C who nearly chooses the centre, to subject J whose choices are nearer the ends of the line.

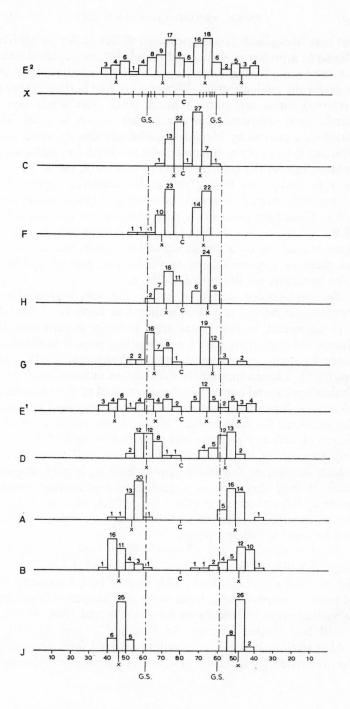

out that McCulloch (1960) measured ability to set an adjustable oblong to a preferred shape, and found that, on repeated settings for the most pleasing forms, aesthetically trained subjects came to prefer the golden section. Fischer adds, like Berlyne (1970) that preferred ratios are culture-bound, since McCulloch says the Hindu ratio comparable to our golden section is $\sqrt{10}$. These ratios were studied by McCulloch, who said that the same person who can detect only a difference of a twentieth in length, area or volume, can set the golden section to 1 to 1·618, not at 1 to 1·617 or 1 to 1·619, and that $\sqrt{10}$ can be estimated repeatedly by aesthetically trained observers, but only up to the second decimal point. These facts point to the perceptual uniqueness and stability of the golden section and its Hindu equivalent, which may have some bearing on their use in art and the preference artists have for them or approximations to them. The golden section and $\sqrt{10}$ rectangles are illustrated in Fig. 9.

Fechner's golden section, which, by the way, originated in the Pythagorean School and is constructed in Book II of Euclid, is very important in the visual arts, as many experiments have shown, although there have been variations from it in the choices made by some experimental groups (Valentine, C. W., 1962, pp. 93–6). These experiments showed that differences of average choices were found not only in the selection of preferred rectangles of various dimensions, but also in the most preferred choices for the division of a straight line. However, an examination of the shapes of ordinary pictures and their frames, and of the objects and patterns in the structure of pictures, will show that the golden section, or something approaching it, is very frequently used. It may therefore be regarded as representing a central tendency in aesthetic proportions from which there are nevertheless considerable variations and differences for some individuals and for some artistic purposes.

Another visual pattern of considerable importance in art is Hogarth's 'line of beauty', which is a balanced double curve like the curve of a woman's back. This may be built into many kinds of pictorial compositions, from those involving the human figure in various ways to landscapes with curves and hills, waves, the paired bow-shaped structure of lips, and so on. As with the golden section, it is not an absolute or fixed form according to the preferences for it and use of it, but represents a central tendency round which there may be a variety of different forms all approximating to it to some extent. It is no. 4 in the curves shown in Fig. 11.

From these points we must pass on to the well-known principles of pictorial composition, set forth, for instance, very clearly by Poore (1903), by Littlejohns and Needham (1933, ch. X, *What is a Work of Art?*) under the headings 'unity' and 'balance', 'variety', 'vitality' and 'rhythm', and by von Fieandt (1966, pp. 336–50). Many of these principles are structural and dynamic schemes of perceptual organisation, upon which the composition of a picture is based. These are mostly reducible to simple organisations of geometrical figures, and their use would fit in with the principles of the Good Gestalt and closure. Thus a composition may be triangular, circular, cross-shaped, radial, S-shaped, rectangular, elliptical, inverted triangular, and combinations of these and others. Any of them may involve depth in space, or perspective.

Other basic principles of composition depend on balance of structural parts, so that the organisation of a picture is divided, vertically or horizontally, or both together, in terms of the golden section, or otherwise. The balance may involve large objects in the foreground or near distance, against more distant objects, and whenever there is suggestion of weight balanced against weight, or resting on a support, or of movement, Lipps' principle of *einfuhlung,* usually translated as 'empathy', is involved. According to this principle we 'feel into' represented objects the movement or the pressure of weight which they must exert. A wispy and ribbon-like cloud suggests the force of the wind blowing it rapidly. A big stone resting on another suggests the pressure of the lower stone in holding it up and gives the impression of upward against downwardly acting forces. Where a depression occurs in an object resting against another, we have the impression of elasticity and so on. Some writers, such as Vernon Lee (1913), have made great use of the principle of empathy, and like the principles of form construction just mentioned, it is an important point of technique. However, it cannot be said that whenever empathy occurs we have good quality in art, any more than we can say that a circular, triangular or other compositional structure will guarantee good quality. The artist must make good artistic use of his principles of composition if his art is to be good. An excellent example of the use of empathy is given in Fig. 11a,

'That Strange Feeling', a cartoon by Dosh, reproduced by permission of *Punch*.

These principles of composition, of which there are of course many not mentioned here, are to be regarded essentially as principles of the psychology of perceptual organisation applied to art, and so is the principle of empathy, which is involved in the experiments on expressive movement suggested by lines. Thus rising lines may seem cheerful or agitating and it is because of the impression we have, owing to empathy, of the activity and energy seeming to make them rise. Downward sloping lines and curves may seem sad or lazy because of the impression, again due to empathy, of the lack of energy or activity which lets them droop.

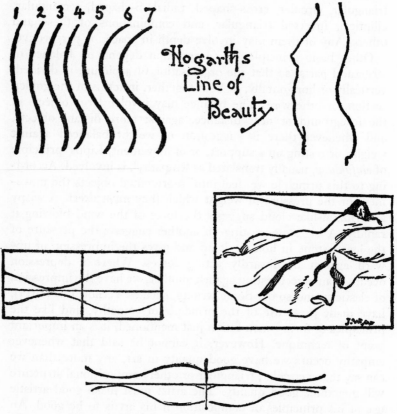

Fig. 11   *Hogarth's Line of Beauty* (Poore, 1903).

THAT STRANGE
FEELING

Fig. 11a *'That Strange Feeling'* by Dosh. An example of the use of empathy.

Further observations on the use of lines and forms will be mentioned in Chapter 10, in relation to the study of children's art and personality by Alschuler and Hattwick (1947). The aesthetic problems of symmetry in pictures and other forms of art were studied experimentally by Ethel D. Puffer, who published her work more than sixty-five years ago (Puffer, 1903).

A short mention of an unusual and original experiment related to the problems of the organisation of elements in abstract art may be included here. Discontented with the assumption of hedonism underlying much experimental study of art—the assumption that the most pleasing is the most artistic—M. Morris chose a modern work called 'Composition: Black and Red' (1954) by Kenneth Martin. It was a linocut, $25\frac{1}{4}$ in. × $19\frac{1}{4}$ in., consisting of a pattern of four black and two red rectangles on a white ground (Morris, 1957). The writer is indebted to Dr Michael Morris and to the Goldsmiths' Librarian, University of London, for permission to publish this abstract of the Thesis and the three illustrations included here as Plates 1, 2 and 3). A full-size model of the painting was made on which five of the rectangles could be moved by screw-controls to be handled by the subject of the experiment, and worked in such a way as not to interfere with the visual design.

Morris put forward the following three hypotheses to be tested:

1. If the rectangles were moved into the most pleasing positions, they would be those of the original;

2. If the original positions were not reproduced, then success would be greater the fewer rectangles manipulated;

3. If the original and variants made by the subjects were compared, the original would be conclusively preferred.

The subjects of the experiment included 50 men and 27 women altogether, and among them were 3 art students. Others were college lecturers, office workers, teachers, technicians and a group from various occupations. The scheme for the experiment in which these subjects moved the rectangles into the most pleasing positions was worked out with precise care, and exact measurements were recorded for the various positions chosen. For the comparison of variants with the original, a paired comparison experiment was conducted using eight pictures. Variants were chosen for this, corresponding to the frequencies of these types in the subject's choices, namely, 3 rectangular arrangements (of which one was the original), 2 circular, 2 diagonal arrangements and 1 unclassified.

The results of the experiment were quite clear-cut. All three hypotheses were decisively not supported. Out of 955 choices only 10 fell within 5 mm of the standard positions of the rectangles. There was no gradient of success with reduction in number of rectangles moved, and out of 8 variants the first six were equally ranked with the original, but choices of the seventh and eight differed significantly from it, and altogether it was ranked third.

Morris considers that the results throw doubt on the hedonistic assumptions of experimental aesthetics. The most pleasing positions, it appears, in comparison with the original, were not necessarily the most artistic. It appears, however, that only three of the subjects had artistic gifts or training, but the subjects were not guided solely by motives of pleasure because some idea of making a 'pattern' was nearly always present in their thoughts.

Solidity, perspective and binocular vision

In all art in which accurate representation of any except flat objects is required, the study of the psychological factors mediating the impression of solidity and perspective appearances are of vital importance. These, in normal vision, fall into two groups: (a) those which are monocular and act equally as well for a single eye as for two eyes; and (b) those which are binocular and exist only for vision with two eyes (see Wyburn, Pickford and Hirst, 1964).

The monocular factors are: (1) shadows; (2) the overlapping of more distant objects by nearer ones (Figs. 12 and 13); (3)

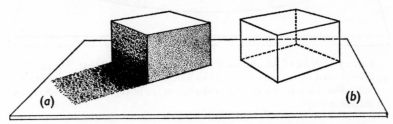

Fig. 12 *Perspective Effects, Transparency and Shadows* (Wyburn, Pickford and Hirst, 1964). (a) shows convergence of parallel lines, exclusion of the background and the effect of graduated shadows in creating an impression of solidity; (b) shows how the absence of shadows and the suggestion of visible background gives the impression of transparency.

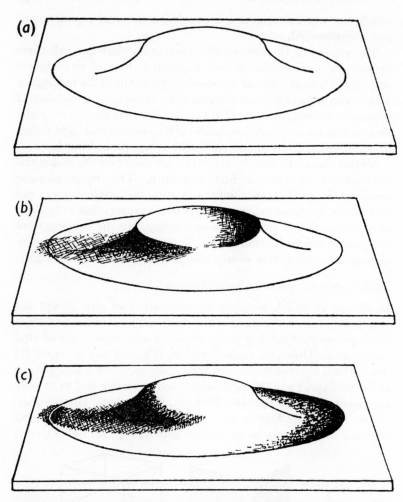

Fig. 13 *Effect of Shadows* (Wyburn, Pickford and Hirst, 1964). The outline shown in (a) may be made to look hollow like a crater, as in (b), or solid like a knob in a circular depression, as in (c) by adding shadows in different ways.

decrease in sharpness of outline and visibility of details as distance increases; (4) changes in colour with increasing distance; (5) strictly perspective effects of a purely geometrical kind; and (6) varying monocular focus.

The binocular factors are due to the distance apart of the two eyes in space, so that one retina receives a geometrical image slightly different from that received by the other, and there is varying convergence of the eye axes according to distance.

All the monocular factors have been exploited by artists to the utmost degree in their attempts to create the impression of solidity, and to fulfil the demands of the accurate representation of objects on canvas or paper. Shadows are extremely important, and it is easy to show that precise control of the expression of feeling or attitude in a portrait, for example, will depend on the most subtle management of the pattern, outline and depth of shadows cast on the skin as a result of muscular tensions beneath it. In the same way the impression of the degree of solidity of a building, hillside or any scene or object, is controlled by the shadows utilised, and these in turn depend for their effect on the viewer's impression of the direction of the source or sources of light. Indeed it is well known that solidity or hollowness may be provided as alternatives from the same pattern of shadows, by simply changing the light direction to its opposite. This depends very much on the kind and familiarity of the object in question. It is much more difficult to make a face look hollow than to make a shell-crater look solid, by changing the apparent direction of illumination.

The overlapping of objects is also very important, and is especially significant where movement is possible, but while this frequently occurs in real scenes, it is rarely or never possible in pictorial art unless some form of mobile representation is used. The effect of parallax, in which objects at various distances change their relative positions, is also very important in real vision, but not practicable in flat visual art which is also static, although it becomes important again in sculpture and architecture. Decrease in sharpness of outline is normally associated with increasing distance. This kind of distance effect is usually coupled with atmospheric haze, so that in an exceptionally clear atmosphere distant objects tend to look unexpectedly near. Coupled with decreasing sharpness of outlines, there is also a tendency for structural detail of objects to be less and less visible as they recede into the distance, and this is also affected by atmospheric haze.

Changes in colour with distance are due to the varying capacity of light of different wave lengths to penetrate haze and atmospheric dust without being absorbed or reflected out of the line of vision. For instance the blue colour of the sky is due to the fact that most of the longer light waves (red, orange and yellow) have disappeared into space, and only the short waves have been reflected back from the sun into our eyes by the dust in the earth's atmosphere. There is a tendency for very distant objects to look bluish in hue, but the exact changes of colour owing to distance will depend very much on the peculiar physical properties of a certain kind of dust or haze, and the direction of the light source. Thus, if the light is coming fairly directly towards the eyes the effect of dust may be to make objects more reddish because the red rays have more directly penetrating power, and the shorter rays are reflected out of the line of vision.

Strictly geometrical perspective effects are very important and have been studied by artists in the greatest possible detail. It is not necessary to give a full analysis of visual perspective here, but it is sufficient to say that it depends on the geometrically exact diminution in size of the retinal images of objects of the same real size as they increase in distance from the eye. Thus exact vanishing points may be worked out for all parallel lines in every object to be represented on canvas or paper, in such a way that the picture casts on the retina an optical image exactly imitating the image which would be produced by the real object or scene. This depends on choosing an arbitrary point of vision from which all calculations are made. In practice the eye, and visual system, are very tolerant, because a viewer generally does not know where the true point of vision for looking at a given perspective picture would be, and rarely adopts it. Instead his eye adjusts itself surprisingly to view the picture from all sorts of other points, so that the picture itself will be seen in perspective, as if a transparent prism were placed at an angle between the viewer and the real scene, the surface of the prism corresponding to the canvas of the picture. In effect it may be true that pictures which are less elaborately studied in geometrical perspective look more real from all sorts of viewing positions, since they depend less on the viewer taking up a precisely predetermined viewing point.

Lastly among monocular factors, the tension of muscles of accommodation of the crystalline lens of the eye, in accordance with focussing on near or more distant objects in a scene, has a considerable effect. This is of course defeated in looking at flat pictures, except that we do almost certainly change our accommodation when directing our gaze at representations of distant objects, and near objects, quite without knowing it, even in looking at a flat picture.

The problem of binocular vision like geometrical perspective is a very complex subject and can be dealt with only very briefly here. It is usually true that one eye is dominant over the other and is directed straight at the object viewed, while the other eye is directed towards it at an angle. This is the angle of convergence, which is greater for nearer than for more distant objects and provides a binocular cue for distance, although we are not aware of the actual process or degree of convergence itself. Most often the right eye is dominant, but the left may be, and in some cases the eyes tend to be used equally and both are directed at the same angle towards the object. The image on the retina of the dominant eye is usually the image of which we are conscious in perception, whereas the image on the retina of the non-dominant eye tends to be suppressed. However, the two images are necessarily not

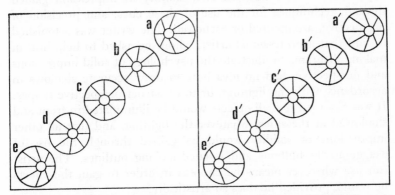

Fig. 14 *Influence of Binocular Disparity* (Wyburn, Pickford and Hirst, 1964). If the two halves of the figure are super-imposed binocularly in a stereoscope, varying degrees of solidity or hollowness are perceived in the football-like objects according to their varying degrees and directions of binocular disparity: a + a′ will look bulbous, but e + e′ will look hollow, while c + c′, which are identical, will look flat.

exactly alike, for all objects, at least for objects up to near distance, and the suppressed image, although not experienced consciously unless we close the other eye, contributes to vision by giving rise to an impression of solidity in the dominant image. Where both images are fused and we see an object of intermediate shape, then the impression of solidity is also gained (Fig. 14).

In all flat representations in pictorial art these binocular functions are defeated. The convergence of the eyes is the same for representations of near and for distant objects and the retinal images for the two eyes are so slightly different, if different at all, that they do not give rise to an impression of solidity. There is no way of overcoming this except by combining monocular and appropriately different views of a scene or object in a stereoscope, when the impression of solidity becomes very marked again. An interesting effect of the defeat of binocular stereoscopic vision in viewing flat pictures of perspective shapes is that these pictures usually look more solid when viewed with one eye than with two. Any persons not familiar with this fact should try the experiment of looking at such pictures with one eye.

It is well known and quite obvious that art does not necessarily depend on the exploitation of cues for solidity and detailed perspective. In much or most of Eastern Art, Primitive Art, Child Art, Psychotic Art and Modern Art, solidity of impression gained through techniques for the use of these cues, and precision of perspective, are ignored or eschewed. The writer was astonished to find that a professional artist, whom he asked to help him in making diagrams to illustrate the psychology of solid impressions and perspective, had no idea how to draw accurate shadows in accordance with the lighting, or to construct perspective shapes. It was assumed that all objects would be illuminated in front and shadowed at the sides, whatever the lighting, and that all other impressions of solidity would be gained through the use of exaggeratedly bulbous and inflated-looking outlines. The artist can use whatever means he chooses in order to gain the effects he wants, provided he does so artistically.

In connection with the supposed importance of accurate representations of perspective in the works of many artists, it is interesting that recent studies of a picture by Vermeer, *L'Atelier*, have thrown doubt on the correctness of perspective in it, although the perspective would appear to be handled with the greatest precision. Careful calculations were made by G. Ferdière and Madeleine Moquot (1969) of the dimensions of the black and white tiles on the floor of the studio, the relative positions of the artist, his easel and other objects, and of the size and shape of the studio. These calculations showed, among other things, that:

1. The line of the horizon is placed too low;
2. The vanishing point is not in the middle of the picture, where it would be expected to be;
3. The lines of the floor and ceiling are not in true perspective relationship;
4. The artist's stool is not in the axis of the easel.

In fact the apparent precision of the perspective is an optical illusion, because it could not exist in that particular form but nevertheless seems correct. The picture is a conjunction of objects observed separately. The representation of perspective on a flat surface is not strictly an illusion if it is correct, because it appears to be what it is, but in this picture it is an illusion because it appears to be what it is not. This does not, of course, detract from the aesthetic merit of the picture in the least degree.

The latter point is well brought out by Osborne (1969). He says that in artistic naturalism it is not the aim of the artist to deceive an observer into falsely believing that he is seeing not an image itself, but the reality of which the work of art is an image. Here the use of the concept of illusion is inappropriate, although in strictly *trompe l'œil* art it is in order, because then it may well be the artist's aim to make the observer feel he is looking at the object which the picture represents. He might move towards a picture to remove a fly, and then find it was part of the picture.

Osborne concludes that in regard to the special phenomenon of 'presence' or the convincingness of the pictorial image itself, the language of illusion is out of place. It is the phenomenal image which becomes real to us, he says, making its impact for what it is in itself and not as a veridical representation of something other than itself (Osborne, 1969, p. 126).

Shape and Size constancy

In the previous section it was pointed out that in viewing a flat picture in which perspective is important, the eye or visual system is so adaptable that the viewer is able to take up any one of many positions none of which is the true viewing position for the perspective the artist has used, and still see the picture relatively unaffected by the distortions which the student of geometry would be inclined to predict. The fact that such a picture looks much the same and very little distorted over a wide range of viewing positions is an example of an important principle which has been one of the most interesting contributions to the psychology of perception this century.

Thouless (1931a, 1931b, 1932) called it the principle of the phenomenal regression to the real object. Others have called it size or shape constancy according to which of these it affected. In his original experiments Thouless showed that a cardboard circular disc the size of a tea plate, seen in perspective at about two metres distance, did not appear to be as narrow an ellipse as the geometrician would predict. He was able to show this by psychological experiments of a simple kind. He made his subjects view the disc placed flat on a table, when they were sitting on a stool about two metres away, with the chin placed on a chin rest in a suitable position. He was able readily to calculate the predicted short diameter of the ellipse subtended at the viewer's eye. He could measure the diameter of the real disc. The shape of ellipse seen by the subject was measured by offering him one by one a series of ellipses, some much wider and others narrower than the predicted ellipse, only one being exactly like it. The subject was asked to choose which of these ellipses were the same shape as the one he saw.

By this means it was established that each subject tended to be consistent in choosing a size which fell at some point between the predicted ellipse and the circle actually lying on the table (Fig. 15). The predicted ellipse was the perspective size; the actual circle was the real object; the chosen ellipse measured what the subject saw. In this way it was possible to calculate a reasonably consistent index of phenomenal regression for each subject, and Thouless was able to show many interesting facts about phenomenal regression which are set forth in his publications.

Similar experiments were also performed which showed that the apparent size of a disc, circular or square, seen at a distance, under similar conditions, did not diminish in proportion to the diminution of the retinal image calculated according to the laws of perspective. It remained much nearer the real size of the actual object viewed (Fig. 16). Again an index of phenomenal regression for size could be calculated from data for each subject who carried out the experiment.

Thouless showed that under these conditions phenomenal regression was dependent on the subject receiving distance cues from the general setting of the experiment. These were essentially the cues of monocular perspective and binocular vision mentioned in the previous section. It was not true that the subject made a conscious judgment that the disc was at a certain distance and/or seen at a certain angle, but that his visual system utilised these cues automatically in a perceptual process which gave rise to the conscious experience which he had. If any steps were taken to

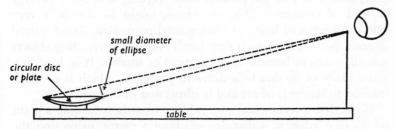

Fig. 15 *Shape Constancy* (Wyburn, Pickford and Hirst, 1964). This shows the view of a plate seen in perspective by a person sitting at a distance from it.

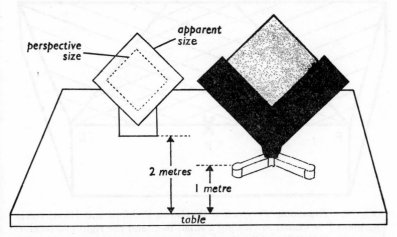

Fig. 16 *Size Constancy* (Wyburn, Pickford and Hirst, 1964). The 'perspective' and 'phenomenal' sizes of a diamond seen at a distance of two metres and the variable or comparison diamond at one metre.

cut out or increase the size or distance cues, then phenomenal regression was altered accordingly. For instance, it was reduced in monocular vision as compared with binocular vision, or it was increased if exaggerated converging lines of perspective were drawn on the table, while the actual margins of the table were observed by black cloth (Pickford and Martin, 1938).

While we are dealing with this subject it is interesting that Thouless (1932) pointed out that often in Eastern and Primitive Art, boxes and rectangular objects may be drawn, not merely with a strong phenomenal regression to the real shape, so that perspective effects are partly diminished, but with reversed perspective, so that the parallel lines receding into space diverge instead of converge. This, of course, might be due to a very much exaggerated index of phenomenal regression, found indeed in some persons, although very rarely, for whom receding objects actually seem to become larger instead of smaller. It is, however, more likely to be due to a different principle, which is of some interest to students of art and is illustrated in Fig. 17.

If we view a rectangular object like a cigar box, fixating a point on its near edge, at a distance of about a metre, using first the

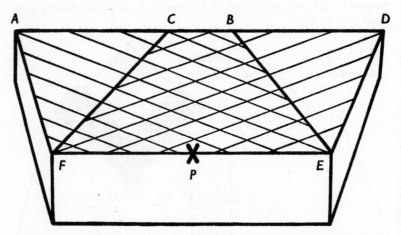

Fig. 17 *Expanding Perspective* (Wyburn, Pickford and Hirst, 1964). The point P is fixated in viewing a small box, and the right eye receives the image C D E F, while the left eye receives the image A B E F. The binocular combination of these may be A D E F, which shows 'expanding' perspective.

right and then the left eye only, we shall find that we see quite different views of it with each eye. The right eye view diminishes in perspective towards the right. The left eye view diminishes towards the left. But when we look with both eyes together, the difference between the views is too great for that of the non-dominant eye to be altogether suppressed, and we see a combined image which diverges to the left and right together, and which is in effect wider at the back than in front (Fig. 17). This has been argued by Zajac (1961) to be the basis of at least some examples of divergent perspective.

Phenomenal regression, or size and shape constancy, have become a central part of the experimental psychology of vision and good accounts of them can be found in all textbooks on perception (Wyburn, Pickford and Hirst, 1964). From the point of view of the psychology of aesthetics, however, it is necessary to ask what parts, if any, they may play in art. It is quite clear that there are two divergent principles operating in different kinds of art. In all classical art which is highly dependent on the exact use of perspective, phenomenal regression is at the same time annulled and eliminated. This, in some people's opinion, is one principle which makes highly photographic art look almost unnatural. It is exactly and precisely true to something which we never experience. On the other hand, in much Primitive, Eastern and Modern Art which is not dependent on perspective representations, phenomenal regression plays a considerable part. Objects are drawn as they appear and not as the geometrician says they ought to appear. A good example of this is van Gogh's famous 'Yellow Chair', and many other examples will be found by the reader who takes the trouble to look, especially in modern art, which has put aside rigid perspective to a great extent.

Bibliography and References
for Chapter 2

ALSCHULER, ROSE H., and HATTWICK, LA B. W. (1947). *Painting and Personality : A Study of Young Children.* Chicago University Press, 2 vols.

ANGIER, R. P. (1903). The Aesthetics of Unequal Division. *Psychol. Review, Monogr. Supplements, 4,* 541–61.

ARNHEIM, R. (1966). *Towards a Psychology of Art: Collected Essays.* London: Faber. pp. 51–73.

ARNHEIM, R. (1967). *Art and Visual Perception.* London: Faber (1954). p. 51 and chs. II and III.

BARNHART, E. N. (1940). The Criteria Used in Preferential Judgments of Geometric Forms. *Amer. J. Psychol., 53,* 354–70.

BERLYNE, D. E. (1970). *Sciences de l'Art, 7,* 1–6.

EHRENZWEIG, A. (1953). *The Psycho-Analysis of Artistic Vision and Hearing, An Introduction to a Theory of Unconscious Perception.* London: Routledge and Kegan Paul.

FECHNER, G. T. (1876). *Vorschule der Aesthetik.* Leipzig: Breitkopf and Härtel.

FERDIÈRE, G., and MOQUOT, MADELEINE (1969). Les Portraits de Vermeer. *Art and Psychopathology: Proc. V. International Colloquium of the International Society of Art and Psychopathology,* 1967, pp. 255–65. Eds. R. Volmat and C. Wiart. Paris and Amsterdam: Excerpta Medica.

FIEANDT, KAI VON (1966). *The World of Perception.* Homewood, Ill.: Dorsey Press, ch. 16.

FISCHER, R. (1969). Out on a (Phantom) Limb. Variations on the Theme: Stability of Body Image and the Golden Section. *Perspectives in Biology and Medicine, vol. 12,* pp. 259–73.

HEVNER, K. (1935). Experimental Studies of the Affective Value of Colors and Lines. *J. Appl. Psychol., 19,* 385–98.

KOFFKA, K. (1935). *Principles of Gestalt Psychology.* New York: Harcourt Brace.

KÖHLER, W. (1947). *Gestalt Psychology.* New York: Liveright.

LEE, VERNON (1913). *The Beautiful: An Introduction to Psychological Aesthetics.* Cambridge University Press.

LIPPS, T. (1897). *Raumaesthetik und Geometrisch-Optische Tauschungen.* Leipzig.

LITTLEJOHNS, J., and NEEDHAM, A. (1933). *Training of Taste in the Arts and Crafts.* London: Pitman.

LUNDHOLM, H. (1921). The Affective Tone of Lines. *Psychol. Review, 28,* 43–60.

MCCULLOCH, W. S. (1960). *Embodiments of Mind.* Cambridge, Mass.: M.I.T. Press.

MARTIN, LILLIEN J. (1906). An Experimental Study of Fechner's Principles in Aesthetics. *Psychol. Rev., 13,* 112–219.

MORRIS, M. (1957). *A Study of Some Hypotheses in Experimental Aesthetics.* Ph.D. Thesis: University of London (unpublished).

OSBORNE, H. (1969). On Artistic Illusion. *Brit. J. Aesthet., 9,* 109–27.

PICKFORD, R. W., and MARTIN, T. M. (1938). The Effect of Veiling Glare on Apparent Size Relations. *Brit. J. Psychol., 29,* 91–103.

POFFENBERGER, A. T., and BARROWS, B. F. (1924). The Feeling Value of Lines. *J. Appl. Psychol., 8,* 187–205.

POORE, H. R. (1903). *Pictorial Composition and the Critical Judgment of Pictures.* New York: Baker and Taylor; London: Batsford.

PUFFER, ETHEL D. (1903). Studies in Symmetry. *Psychol. Rev. Monograph Suppts., 4,* 467–539.

REVÉSZ, G. (1950). *Psychology and Art of the Blind.* London: Longmans.

THOULESS, R. H. (1931a). Phenomenal Regression to the Real Object. *Brit. J. Psychol., 21,* 339–59.

THOULESS, R. H. (1931b). Phenomenal Regression to the 'Real' Object, II. *Brit. J. Psychol., 22,* 1–30.

THOULESS, R. H. (1932). Individual Differences in Phenomenal Regression. *Brit. J. Psychol., 22,* 216–41.

VALENTINE, C. W. (1962). *The Experimental Psychology of Beauty.* London: Methuen.

VERNON, P. E. (1934–5). Auditory Perception. *Brit. J. Psychol., 25,* 123–39 and 265–83.

WERTHEIMER, MAX (1958). Principles of Perceptual Organisation. *Readings in Perception,* Eds. Beardslee, D. C. and Wertheimer, Michael, *Selection 8,* 115–35. From: *Psychol. Forsch.* 1923, *4,* 301–50.

WYBURN, G. M., PICKFORD, R. W., and HIRST, R. J. (1964). *Human Senses and Perception.* Edinburgh: Oliver and Boyd; Toronto: Univ. Press.

ZAJAC, J. L. (1961). Studies in Perspective. *Brit. J. Psychol., 52,* 333–40.

3

Haptic perception and the art of the blind

There has been an interesting difference of opinion about the art of the blind. Viktor Lowenfeld advocated the idea that there were two creative types, the haptic and the visual, and that the art of the blind was essentially an expression of the haptic creative type—that is to say, dependent on perception by experiences of touch, vibration and movement rather than by vision, and that this kind of art was found also among some artists who could see, and was in certain ways especially expressive. Revész objected that the art of the blind was of no aesthetic value except in so far as it depended on visual experience. K. von Fieandt has made some valuable comments on the problem. In this chapter an attempt will be made to explain the problems and assess the relationship between Lowenfeld's claims and the objections of Revész.

Haptic and visual perception

According to Viktor Lowenfeld (1951, 1952, Lowenfeld and Brittain, 1964) there is a marked distinction between the two kinds of perception which are called haptic and visual. Haptic perception arises from within and is subjective. It is in a sense an externalisation of the inner feelings and experiences of the individual, especially with respect to bodily sensations of muscular movement, all the aspects of touch and responses to vibration. These experiences result from what is happening to the individual and especially what is due to his own impulses and muscular efforts. Certainly they are indications of environmental events, but they are always charged with subjectivity and often with an emotional quality which makes Lowenfeld say that haptic perception brings the individual's experiences out into the environment. Visual perception, on the other hand, is a system of experiences which depends primarily and directly on the structure and organisation of the environment. It is like a reflection of the details of the outside world in the individual's experience. Lowenfeld therefore says that visual perception is objective and brings the outside world up to the individual, and into his mind and consciousness. It is a map-like scheme of the external world, representing its three dimensions in a flat visual pattern.

In consequence, in haptic perception the objects of the outer world which are apprehended do not take their shapes, sizes and relative positions from the map-like system of vision, but from the exploratory activities made by the individual in his tactile and motor contacts with them. These activities, of course, give rise to sensations of muscular activity, tensions and relaxation, and to experiences of touch in all its complex qualities—hardness, softness, elasticity, roughness, smoothness, protuberance, indentation, and so on, not to mention sensations of warmth and coldness. These experiences are integrated, if anything, successively, whereas visual perception is to a much greater extent unitary, or simultaneous for large groups of objects related in space, except in so far as we explore successively by eye-movements. Then, of course, there are again experiences of movement, and the successively inspected parts of the environment are integrated. They are, however, integrated in the sense that they fit together continuously whereas in haptic exploration the isolated tactile and movement aspects are very much more independent and the parts of the environment explored successively in perception may not readily unite into a whole.

Viktor Lowenfeld's view is that perception in infancy is at first haptic, and that visual perception becomes superimposed on it, gradually taking a dominant position for most people. He feels no doubt that there can be said to be 'haptic space' experiences, but this haptically perceived space differs considerably from 'visual space', and the two may be difficult to integrate, as found by many congenitally blind subjects who have gained their sight, but do not even recognise visually perceived objects as the same as those previously known only haptically. The perception of space and shape by congenitally blind subjects, before and after operation to restore sight, has been very fully dealt with by von Senden (1960).

It can be understood readily from what has been said that haptic space differs from visual space mainly in the following ways: (1) The relative sizes and proportions of objects in haptic space depend more on the amounts and kinds of exploration which contributed to their perception than on their objectively measured dimensions; (2) This exploration is often emotionally toned and the amount of feeling or interest excited may be reflected in the apparent sizes and shapes of the haptically perceived objects; (3) Haptic perception tends to be successive, with the result that objects and parts of objects are perceived one by one, and the whole grouped pattern must be appreciated as a result of secondary and additive functions; (4) The individual tends to form schemata or symbols of objects and when thinking about them or representing them he uses these symbols instead of perceiving each scene or situation in its entirety with all its special attributes, differences from other scenes and unique dimensions, relationships and qualities. It is clear that visual perception does not share these characteristics to any great extent. This is the main reason why it has superseded haptic perception in evolution, and does so over again in each normal individual's development towards maturity in most cases. It enables the seeing organism to deal with the environment in a precise and objective way which would never be possible through haptic perception alone.

The case for haptic perception and the existence of a haptically perceived space is not really in doubt. Revész has analysed all the psychological problems involved with convincing thoroughness (Revész, G., 1950). In the first part of his book he discusses the psychology of spatial perception in general and of haptic spatial perception in particular. He stresses the need to think of two kinds of haptic persons—those totally without sight and those whose sight does contribute to some extent to their perception of space, even if only in a very small degree. He also analyses very fully the important functions of the hand as an instrument in the spatial perception of haptic persons. It is not in respect of the existence of haptic perception, or of its main characteristics and differences from visual perception, that Revész differs from Lowenfeld, but in respect of the contribution haptic experience makes to art, and this will be dealt with later.

Haptic and visual types

Viktor Lowenfeld claims that visual perception does not develop in such a way as to dominate and to exclude haptic perception in all children. Excluding the totally and partly blind, haptic perception is predominant in the early years of childhood, and visual perception certainly displaces it in most children, at least before the age of puberty when reality demands and interests displace and exclude the fantasy interests of childhood. These children become completely normal in their perception and visually controlled in their behaviour. However, with a series of tests (V. Lowenfeld, 1945, with Brittain, 1964) he studied 1,128 American children for visual or haptic aptitude. He found that 47 per cent were clearly visual, 23 per cent were clearly haptic and 30 per cent were not clearly identifiable in type. Thus about half the children tested were of the visual type and one quarter haptic, while the other quarter were intermediate or indeterminate. He was prepared to agree that many people fell between the extreme types, and are mixed visual and haptic perceivers.

His tests included the following:

(1) *A test of integration of successive impressions.* For this test ten sets of five curved and five angular symbols each are used. The card on which each symbol is drawn is placed behind a horizontal slot through which it is seen part at a time. The subject has to recognise the correct symbol out of each set of five. This is most successfully done by visual perception.

(2) *A test of subjective impressions.* For this test the subject is asked to think of an object, such as a table or a building, and draw it. The haptic tends to draw a table in profile without depth or perspective, whereas the visual person tends to draw it in perspective.

(3) *A test of visual versus haptic word association.* In this test the subject is given a series of stimulus words and is instructed to write down his immediate reaction word. A visual reaction to 'climbing' might be 'mountain'; a haptic association might be 'hard'.

(4) *Visualisation of kinaesthetic experience.* In this test the subject is blindfolded and asked to pass his finger round the edge of a cut-out cardboard figure or pattern. Afterwards, with the blindfold removed, he has to identify this pattern among five similar figures all somewhat different from it.

(5) *A test of tactile impressions.* For this test the subject has to look at a board with cut-out shapes in it (like a 'form-board' test) and must select the correct piece from several others to fit each of the cut-out shapes, by means of feeling it with his hand inside a bag and invisible to him.

Lowenfeld also refers to an unpublished study by Henry W. Drewes (Cornell University, 1958), who used a variety of techniques, among which was the Rorschach Ink-Blot Technique. In this the subject is shown a series of ten ink-blots, one by one, and asked to describe or say what they seem like to him or make him think of when he looks at them. The visualisers tended to give responses in which the whole ink-blots seemed like concrete objects or like three-dimensional forms. The non-visualisers tended to give more kinaesthetic or movement responses and responses involving the use of shading or chiaroscuro. No difference in intelligence was found between these types.

The implication of Lowenfeld's studies is that visual and haptic modes of perception or aptitudes tend to exist side by side even after the visual functions become important, and that often they continue to interact so that many people remain of mixed haptic-visual type to varying degrees, some more visual and some more haptic. At the extreme end of the scale, however, we still find, in a minority, those who remain predominantly haptic, although, of course, they can use visual functions quite normally, while those who become chiefly visual are more frequent.

According to Lowenfeld, this accounts to some extent at least for the difficulty which some children have in continuing their studies of art successfully after the adolescence age at which vision takes over for the majority and visual modes of perception are assumed to be dominant by the teacher and visual methods are relied upon in art teaching. Much of Lowenfeld's work was aimed at giving insight to art teachers and inculcating a new attitude to haptic pupils which would enable them to continue with their predominantly tactile mode of creative activity. Thus

Lowenfeld came to speak and write of the two creative types, and it was for this reason that his book was called *The Nature of Creative Activity*, and not because it sought to analyse and expound the essence of creativity, although he certainly thought its deeper sources were haptic.

It seems that Revész had great difficulty in understanding and appreciating the ways in which haptic functions could continue to operate, interact with visual functions and sometimes even to dominate them after their normal development. He tended to think of all the perception of sighted persons as visually dominated and all its valuable artistic qualities as those contributed by vision. Viktor Lowenfeld's work, however, has had a tremendous influence, and it has given a very wide public an understanding of kinds of art and especially of artistic creation in children which could never be appreciated on the purely visual basis. In spite of this, his difficulty in fully appreciating Lowenfeld's contribution, however, Revész contributed a tremendously gifted analysis of the visual and haptic functions of perception.

Haptic and visual art

The emphasis placed by Viktor Lowenfeld upon haptic perception, upon the haptic type of person and upon the interfusion of haptic with visual modes of experience, has coincided and accords with our great increase in understanding child art, ancient art and the art of so-called primitive peoples. In all these the haptic aspects of perception and experience are present, either to a limited extent or in a very prominent way. All art which involves expressive distortion of realistic or photographic shapes and relationships of objects is to some extent haptic. Consequently expressionistic art is haptic, in contrast to impressionism and realistic or photographic and classical nineteenth-century art, which are visual. Also psychiatric art, or the art of mental and neurotic patients, which has excited much interest recently, partakes considerably of haptic qualities. This probably accords with its tendency to be dominated by emotions and experiences derived from early childhood.

It is worth recalling that Bernhard Berenson (1930, pp. 62–74) has stressed the importance of tactile values in giving us a true appreciation of depth and of the third dimension, both for solid objects and in representations of space, especially when helped by muscular sensations of movement. 'It follows that the essential in the art of painting . . . is somehow to stimulate our consciousness of tactile values, so that the picture shall have at least as much power as the object represented, to appeal to our tactile imagination.' He analyses the art of Giotto to show how he fulfils this, 'the first condition of painting as an art'.

Viktor Lowenfeld has given numerous examples of the importance and functions of tactile and kinaesthetic impressions in visual art. At this point we are not concerned with the problem of a blind artist or the problem whether we should appreciate his art by touch without viewing it, but the point is that the tactile and kinaesthetic impressions contribute to our appreciation by re-enforcing our visual impressions, so that we see the objects as though we were feeling them. Nothing, again, could make this clearer than Berenson's observations about Giotto, first published in 1896. He says we turn to a painting by Giotto, from one by Cimabue, hanging side by side with it in the Uffizi at Florence, with a sense of relief, of rapidly rising vitality. 'Our eyes scarcely have had time to light on it before we realise it completely—the throne occupying a real space, the virgin satisfactorily seated upon it, the angels grouped in rows about it. Our tactile imagination is put to play immediately. Our palms and fingers accompany our eyes much more quickly than in the presence of real objects, the sensations varying constantly with the various projections represented, as of face, torso, knees, confirming in every way our feeling of capacity for coping with things—for life, in short. I care little that the picture endowed with the gift of evoking such feelings has faults, that the types represented do not correspond to my ideal of beauty, that the figures are too massive, and almost unarticulated; I forgive them all, because I have much better to do than to dwell on faults' (pp. 69–70).

One of the interesting features of haptic art lies in its use of expressive distortions of visual and geometrical perspective shapes. The arm which stretches out to reach something is elongated and the other arm, which perhaps does nothing, is either diminished in size or not even shown. The sizes of objects distributed in space are not in strict proportion to their relative distances, but may all be the same, as if all the objects could be touched equally easily. It may be found that the more important of two objects is larger. Events which occur successively may be shown together. Temporal events, like the heart beating or lips trembling, are expressed by showing rhythmical ridges between the ribs or giving the lips an undulating pattern. All through haptic art, however, there may be the tendency to fit together items of experience perceived separately instead of starting with the whole and differentiating it into interrelated parts. This, ultimately, is given by Revész as the greatest weakness of the art of the blind, as will be seen in the next section. The haptic use of colour is interesting. According to Lowenfeld colour is used by haptically oriented artists in 'symbolic' or 'arbitrary' ways, but he does not make a clear distinction between them. If colour is assigned to objects according to some set of rules—all women's faces are pink, but all men's brownish; all hair is black, all grass is green, all sky is blue, and so on—we can speak of colour symbolism. In a boy's drawings of ships, the writer noticed that to indicate sea he simply made several sweeping brush strokes of blue-green; to indicate sky, patches or irregular dabs of pale blue were made, and so on, without any attempt to colour all the areas or to be realistic in graduations of tone and hue. When colour is used in an apparently arbitrary way it corresponds to emotional ideas or associations of the artists and expresses them. A face is green to show jealousy or anger as he feels it, or yellow to show fear or terror. Milk in a pail is black to show how hateful the artist feels it to be.

It is clear, therefore, that in the history of the development of nineteenth-century photographic art there has been a long evolution in which the primitive and early rise of haptic qualities integrated with visual aspects of art has been gradually overpowered and displaced by geometrical and perspective accuracy of dimensions and relationships. In this evolution a strong tendency has been present for the more direct and powerful expressiveness of haptic qualities to be lost, and for art to become formal and inexpressive. Ehrenzweig has emphasised this very strongly in his books (1953 and 1967), by his discussion of the conflict between unconscious influences and the surface Gestalt of conscious or photographic art which controls them.

The art of the blind

Quite apart from the ingression of haptic perceptual and creative functions into visual art among artistically gifted people with normal vision, Lowenfeld has stressed the interest of the art of those people who are weak sighted, for whom haptic perception plays a larger part than it usually does for those with normal sight. New and somewhat different problems are raised by the art of the blind. In connection with these problems Revész has pointed out that there are two kinds of haptic persons, namely, (a) those who are haptics of an essentially optical character, and (b) those who are pure or autonomous haptics. Even in the study of the perception of the blind we have to distinguish those who were born blind, or lost their sight at a very early age, and are non-visual or pure haptics, from those who became blind at a later stage. All these are, of course, different from the subjects who have always had weak sight, and those sighted persons who, for psychological reasons, have become more than normally dependent on haptic perception.

However, in one of his chapters which is important for his conceptions, *Haptics and Aesthetics* (1950, pp. 201–13), Revész says that from the point of view of the problem of the aesthetic experiences of the blind, 'it does not make any difference whether we are dealing with sighted subjects trained in haptic methods, or with subjects born blind, or with those who have lost their sight early or late in life, or with the degree of education among observers'. Admittedly, he says, there are differences of type, but there is a complete similarity in respect of haptic perception, recognition and interpretation. 'In view of the fact that a total image of haptically observed objects, representing the complete morphological and phenomenological significance of the data, cannot be obtained, it seems justifiable to assume that in the field of haptics one can hardly speak of an aesthetic appreciation in the stricter sense' (1950, p. 201).

After this Revész discusses the views of Riegl, that the experience and recognition of form originally developed out of the tactile function, and of Wölfflin, that in the apprehension of objects through their tangible character an emphasis is laid on boundaries, while in the visual apprehension, which renounces the palpable, emphasis is laid on appearance, which transcends the boundaries. He feels one might misunderstand Riegl, for his haptically oriented art presupposes seeing, and has developed through the controlling and supplementary activity of the visual perception of form (1950, pp. 206–13). In the end Revész concedes the importance for art of the interplay of haptic and optical functions. Thus to him purely haptic processes could not lead to convincing aesthetic creation or appreciation, but purely visual processes could, and so could haptic processes if they interfuse with visual processes and are integrated and organised visually. This is the essential basis of his approach to the art of the blind, in the second part of his book.

Revész gives numerous examples of the art of the blind, comparing them in many cases with corresponding works of sighted subjects. In his opinion the outcome of these comparisons is that the work of the blind, whether they are trained or not, is always artistically inferior to that of the sighted. The essential difference is that the work of blind subjects is, in comparison, less accurate and represents the human figure and other objects with incorrect proportions or in a way which results from the piecemeal fitting together of parts or items each first apprehended separately, without the unity of perception given by sight.

Examples of normal art, visual and haptic, and of the art of the blind, are given in Plates 4-7 and 9. Plates 4 and 5 show illustrations of the theme, Moses striking the rock, by normal sighted subjects, the one of visual and the other of haptic type. Plate 6 shows a sculpture, 'Being Throttled', by a congenitally blind subject, aged 23 years, visual type. Plate 7 shows a sculpture, 'Longing for Sight', by a congenitally blind subject, 18 years of age, visual type. Plate 9 shows a sculpture, 'Inner Decay', by a congenitally blind subject, haptic type.*

One of the most interesting parts of Revész's book is the discussion of the works of blind sculptors (1950, pp. 246-315). He sums up the whole problem in his final chapter (pp. 216-330).

Revész discusses eight blind sculptors. The first is the Tyrolese sculptor of crucifixes, Kleinhans (1774-1853), who lost his sight at the age of four years as a result of smallpox. At the age of seven he was apprenticed to a cabinet-maker who taught him wood-carving. Later he had other teachers, became a famous carver of crucifixes, and is supposed to have produced over 300 of them, but Revész has attempted to trace them and believes that this number is grossly exaggerated. However, there is no doubt that he was an extremely talented artist, and many of his works are

* The writer is indebted to Messrs Routledge and Kegan Paul for permission to use these illustrations (Lowenfeld, 1939).

so good that Revész puts forward three possible approaches to it. (1) If we assume that he was completely blind throughout his life except for early childhood, then Revész feels that we cannot attribute the majority of his supposed works definitely to him. (2) If he lost his vision only in youth and learned sculpture while he could see, then it is still difficult to ascribe to him all the works supposedly his. (3) If he did not ever become fully blind, but retained vision to some extent, then it would be possible to ascribe to him all the sculptures which are supposed to be his work. Revész favours the third supposition.

The second sculptor discussed is Louis Vidal, who was born at Nîmes in 1831, and went to Paris to study under Barye. At the age of twenty-two he lost his sight as a result of an illness, although an improvement occurred and he regained some vision so that he was able to continue working at sculpture. He learned to model on purely haptic lines, without using vision. Later he lost his sight altogether. It seems that during the period of partial sight he was able to train himself to carry out good work by a combination of haptic and visual perception, but that later, when his visual memories faded and he lost his sight completely, his work declined in aesthetic value.

The third sculptor dealt with is Jacob Schmitt (1891) of Mainz. Trained as a silversmith, he joined the German Army in 1914, and lost both eyes through a gunshot wound. In 1915 he entered a sculpture class. He had to copy figures after handling them, but he used a tape-measure and a yardstick, and always worked from ideal proportions—the head must be one-eighth, the face one-tenth, the hand one-tenth of the length of the body, and so on. He was visited by Revész, and told him that details of a sculpture meant something concrete to him, but the whole was the product of fantasy, and that he would be completely helpless without a synthetic construction. He built up his objects out of separate perceptions, and it seems very doubtful whether he was guided by true aesthetic values in the sense in which Revész views them— as available only in the visual world.

The fourth sculptor considered is Ernesto Masuelli, born at Nice in 1899. During the war of 1914–18 he lost his sight through a shell splinter. In 1932 he began to work in plastic modelling, and was soon very successful without the help of any teacher. Revész considered that nobody is likely to deny the artistic value of his works and that few people would attribute them to a blind artist. Even the errors are not the errors typical of haptic perception. A very careful study of Masuelli's methods and his works, carried out partly on a visit to see him in Rome, suggests to Revész that these works reflect the visual and not the haptic world and it is to their success in the visual qualities that he attributes their aesthetic value.

Four other blind sculptors are considered. Giovanni Gonnelli (1603–64) had eye trouble which led to blindness in 1632. He worked in Florence and Rome. Hubert Moudry (1865–1920) developed a cataract in 1900. He was born in Moravia, was at school in Olmutz and joined the Institute for the Blind in Prague for about a year. Georges Scapini (1893) lost both eyes in the war in 1915. Filippo Bausola (1893) also lost his sight through a gunshot wound during the war in 1917. Gonnelli was a legendary personality about whom there is little accurate information. Moudry was a talented sculptor who gave up his artistic work when he became blind. Scapini, according to Revész, worked on a level of handicraft rather than artistic ability, and the same applies to Bausola.

The final judgment, in the view of Revész, may be summed up by saying that complete blindness is a bar to true aesthetic experience and expression, which, if they are to succeed, in a late blind or partially blind person, must depend on vision or visual memory and impressions derived from visual perception. True aesthetic experience and expression cannot exist at all in those born totally blind and never able to see.

Some experiments on haptic perception and art

A study of the relation between haptic perception and literary creative work with children was made by Peddie (1952). He studied one hundred secondary school pupils varying from first to sixth year, who submitted drawings and paintings which were graded as haptic or visual on the basis of careful consideration of their qualities. In each year-group haptic types were balanced with visual types for age, sex, intelligence and educational attainment. Those who could not be balanced successfully were eliminated and this left two groups of 25 pupils, one group nearest the haptic and the other nearest the visual end of the continuum between haptic and visual types. Only about 30–50 per cent of the pupils in the whole group had haptic tendencies, and extreme haptics were quiet, rather introverted children.

A poetry completion test by P. Gordon Smith was used and consisted of 19 unfinished poems. The completions by the pupils were graded by three qualified judges for fitness of completion to given mood, while rhythm, poetic feeling and self-projection in the verse were noted. Mood corresponded to the Gestalt aspect of haptic art, rhythm to colour and movement, poetic feeling to feeling qualities, and self projection to inner experience. Each piece of poetry was rated a 5-point scale for these qualities.

The results showed that the correlation of haptic tendency and poetic ability was high (0·852); but the correlation between visual tendency and poetic ability was also high (0·748), and the correlation of poetic ability scores between haptic and visual groups was 0·719. Thus there was evidence that poetic ability was not dependent upon haptic rather than upon visual ability, but accorded with either or both. At the same time the mean poetic ability of the haptic group was 7·5 points higher than that of the visual group in a range of 40 points, and this was a statistically significant difference. Peddie concludes that, while one sense modality may dominate poetic creative work more than another, whether tactile or visual, nevertheless haptic perception is slightly more related to literary creative work than is visual perception.

Some experiments with the art of the blind are mentioned by K. von Fieandt (1966, pp. 304–9). He says that Revész showed 14 clay sculptures, produced by patients of the Institute for the Blind in Vienna, to about 80 university students, asking them to write down for each sculpture what they thought it might represent. Interpretations 'adequate to', or 'in agreement with', the original meaning were rare. In some cases there were more 'opposite' or inconsistent interpretations than within the 'same general motif' as that intended by the sculptor.

Von Fieandt carried out a further check on Revész's claims. Some of the same works by the blind, together with some modern artistic productions, were shown as photographs projected on a screen to 285 university students. The subjects were asked to judge whether they obtained an impression of a certain sentiment, emotional reaction or mood, and to name it. Adequate interpretations of the artist's works were given in 30·9 per cent of the responses, but for the works of the blind only in 14·3 per cent.

He considers the result is not overwhelmingly in favour of the works of normal artists, but adds that some of the works of the blind were judged to be more expressive, which is not surprising. He reports (1966, p. 309) an experiment carried out by a Finnish weekly magazine, *Viikkosanomat,* in 1958. Its readers were asked to judge the aesthetic value of works including three by normal painters and three from Revész's book, by blind artists. The result was that, for 1,409 readers who responded to the request, the first place was given to Herzog's 'Enjoyment' (47·4%), the second place to Gwen Lux's 'Eve' (30·7%), while the next two places were taken by works of blind sculptors, 'Rejected' and 'Old Man'; the fifth place was taken by Picasso's 'Face', and the sixth by a blind artist's work, 'Loving Couple'. These results confirm what von Fieandt says of the outcome of his own experiment, mentioned above. However, it must be remembered that the judges were not chosen for aesthetic appreciation or ability.

It is interesting that Revész has shown that haptic persons, and blindfolded seeing persons acting haptically, tend to prefer the shape of a square to the shape of a rectangle based on Fechner's golden section, which is preferred by sighted persons acting visually (Revész, 1950, p. 199). The golden section rectangle and a square are shown in Fig. 9.

The reader who takes the trouble and compares Viktor Lowenfeld's and Revész's writings may consider that Revész has been unduly influenced by his own predominantly visual conceptions of art and what he thinks is to be considered of the greatest aesthetic value. Revész would not be likely to agree with the views of Berenson, mentioned above in his discussion of Giotto, and to allow considerable errors of shape, structure or dimension because the tactile values of the work were exceptionally good, or, even less, to accept as significant contributions to art the works showing expressive 'distortions', so fascinating aesthetically and shown in many of the illustrations in Lowenfeld's books, and in much modern art. Revész, however, may be right in thinking that purely haptic artists, born blind or very early blind, will not be at all likely to be successful in producing works of art to be appreciated by normally sighted persons. Whether he is right in thinking they have no aesthetic perception or appreciation of their own may still be an open question.

This question has met with an experimental test in the research reported by Stewart (1968). He took 10 congenitally blind subjects in a Lighthouse for the Blind School, considered by their teacher to be normal children otherwise. There were also 3 groups of 10 sighted Junior High School students between 11 and 15 years of age, of IQ range 101 to 150. They included 10 for visual experience; 10 for visual tactile; 10 for tactile experience (blindfold).

A set of 52 non-objective three-dimensional sculptural forms were made from plaster and vermiculite, and the four groups of subjects rated these objects on a 5-point scale for 'overall aesthetic quality'. One of the sighted groups rated the objects under three conditions, visually only, visually and tactually, and tactually only. The other two sighted groups rated the objects visually and tactually or tactually only. The objects were also divided into those with holes and those without holes, and 12 of the non-hole objects were removed, making two groups of 20 objects in each.

Analysis of variance showed no statistically significant differences between the four groups, and the reliability for hole and non-hole objects was almost the same. However, it was shown that the visual subjects rated all the objects lower than the blindfold and these lower again than the visual-tactile subjects. In contrast the blind rated the non-hole objects higher, and the hole objects lower than any of the other groups.

Stewart draws the conclusion that 'there are no significant differences in overall aesthetic judgment among blind and sighted subjects'. He says that this leads to the conclusion that the aesthetic perception of the blind can be of educational importance for them and that a truly creative arts programme would be possible in schools for the blind.

An attempt to use Lowenfeld's test of visual and haptic types was made by Jane M. Palmer (1970). Five of Lowenfeld's six tests were used, namely: (1) the test of successive impressions, (2) the test of subjective impressions, (3) the test of visual *versus* haptic word associations, (4) the test of visualisation of kinaesthetic experience and (5) the test of tactile impressions.

The necessary material for the tests was made up as far as possible in accordance with Lowenfeld's rather inadequate instructions (1954). The following groups of subjects were then tested: (1) twenty 8–9-year-old children, (2) twenty 14–15-year-old children, and (3) twenty adults. Ten of each were in each group. The results for these groups are given in Table 3.1, which shows 'scores' based on the classification of each individual as 'visual', 'indefinite' or 'haptic' on each of the five tests.

TABLE 3.1

Scores on the visual/haptic tests according to age and classification of each subject on each test

	8–9 years	14–15 years	adult
Haptic	27	24	28
Indefinite	43	31	25
Visual	30	45	47

Although it will be seen that about as many young and adolescent children were haptic as adults, and more adults were visual than young children, there is not a statistically significant difference by the Chi-squared test for this frequency table.

Miss Palmer considered that the tests did bear out Lowenfeld's contention that there are both children and adults with a predominantly haptic rather than visual talent, but the tests have several weaknesses which would have to be eliminated before they could be used efficiently. She probably did not have a young enough group of children to bring out a marked age change.

Bibliography and References
for Chapter 3

BERENSON, BERNHARD (1930). *The Italian Painters of the Renaissance* (revised ed.). Oxford: Clarendon Press.

DREWES, HENRY W. (1958). Unpublished Thesis. Cornell University.

EHRENZWEIG, A. (1953). *The Psycho-Analysis of Artistic Vision and Hearing: An Introduction to a Theory of Unconscious Perception.* London: Routledge and Kegan Paul.

EHRENZWEIG, A. (1967). *The Hidden Order of Art.* London: Weidenfeld and Nicolson.

FIEANDT, K. VON (1966). *The World of Perception.* Homewood, Ill.: The Dorsey Press.

LOWENFELD, VIKTOR. (1945). Tests for Visual and Haptical Aptitude. *Amer. J. Psychol. 58,* 100–11.

LOWENFELD, VIKTOR (1951). Psycho-Aesthetic Implications of the Art of the Blind. *J. Aesthetics and Art Criticism. 10,* 1–9.

LOWENFELD, VIKTOR (1952). *The Nature of Creative Activity* (2nd ed.). London: Routledge and Kegan Paul.

LOWENFELD, VIKTOR, and BRITTAIN, W. LAMBERT (1964). *Creative and Mental Growth* (4th ed.). London: Collier-Macmillan.

PALMER, JANE M. (1970). *An Adaptation of Viktor Lowenfeld's Test of Visual and Haptical Aptitudes.* M.A. Thesis. Psychology Department, University of Glasgow (unpublished).

PEDDIE, R. L. (1952). The Relation of Haptic Perception to Literary Creative Work. *Brit. Psychol. Soc. Quart. Bulletin, 3, 15,* 19–21.

RÉVÉSZ, G. (1950). *Psychology and Art of the Blind.* Tr. H. A. Wolff. London: Longmans.

SENDEN, M. VON (1960). *Space and Sight.* Tr. P. Heath. London: Methuen.

STEWART, R. L. (1968). Tactile Aesthetic Perception among the Blind: A Comparison of Blind and Sighted Subjects. *Psychiatry and Art. Proc. 4th Int. Coll. Psychopathology of Expression,* 1966. Washington, D.C. Ed. Irene Jakab, pp. 180–7. Basel and New York: Karger.

4

Colour perception and colour preferences

In this chapter in the first place an attempt will be made to explain very briefly the present-day position with regard to colour vision theories, and then to consider individual differences in normal colour vision. Problems concerning defective colour vision in relation to art will be reserved for the next chapter. The second part of the present chapter will deal with experimental studies of preferences for colours and colour combinations in adults, and allied matters. For general accounts of colour aesthetics see Burnham (Committee on Colorimetry, 1953, chs. 4 and 5) and Burnham, Hanes and Bartleson (1963, ch. 12). Cross-cultural studies will be reserved for Chapter 7 and children's colour preference studies for Chapter 9, while personality influences will be dealt with in Chapter 10.

Colour vision theories today

We live in an age when the long-drawn-out controversy between the supporters of the four great theories of colour vision appears to be dying down, or perhaps it is resolved. These theories are: (1) The Young-Helmholtz or Trichromatic Theory, which claims that all differences in hue, saturation and brightness of colours can be explained on the basis of only three primary sensations—red, green and blue; (2) The Hering or Four-Colour Theory, which claims that it is necessary to postulate two pairs of sensations acting as opponents, namely, yellow/blue and red/green, while black/white differences were also explained as due to a comparable pair which had no hue or saturation but only brightness variations; (3) The Edridge-Green Theory of seven types of colour sensitivity difference, namely, monochromacy (black/white discrimination), dichromacy (yellow/blue); trichromacy (yellow/green/blue), tetrachromacy (red/yellow/green/blue), pentachromacy (red/yellow/green/blue/violet), hexachromacy (red/orange/yellow/green/blue/violet), and heptachromacy (red/orange/yellow/green/blue/indigo/violet); and (4) the Ladd-Franklin or Evolutionary Theory, according to which colour vision has evolved owing to the splitting of the light sensitive molecules, which at first gave the colourless response (black/white), then dividing into two components (black/white and yellow/blue), and then the yellow part splitting again and giving black/white, yellow/blue and red/green.

Very exact and detailed colour vision researches exemplified by those of Rushton, Wald and others have led more and more definitely to the conclusion that there are only three photochemical substances in the retina, namely red-sensitive (erythrolabe), green-sensitive (chlorolabe) and blue-sensitive (cyanolabe). These would correspond to the primary sensation mechanisms of the trichromatic theory. Their sensitivity regions in the spectrum would overlap widely, so that only hues seen at the red and blue limits of the spectrum could be 'pure' or single sensations and, indeed, the reddishness of violet would be due to the blue-sensitive substance giving rise slightly to red sensations as well as to blue. Then all differences of hue would be due to differential excitation of more than one response, all saturation differences to variations in the degree to which complementary sensations giving rise to whiteness or greyness were excited together and all differences of brightness to the intensities of the total sensation responses excited. Cobb suggests a fourth cone pigment (Cobb, 1972).

Other experiments, as those by the writer (Pickford, 1967), have strongly suggested that at the perception level rather than the sensation level there are two pairs of opponent colour experiences, yellow/blue and red/green, which correspond to the Hering Theory. An integration of the trichromatic sensation theory and the bipolar or four-colour theory would seem to be possible on the assumption that there are only three primary sensations (or pro-sensations, as Walls liked to call them), but that at a higher level of nervous response the red and green sensations are integrated to give rise to yellow, and contributions from all three are integrated to give a general experience of brightness.

The other two theories do not appear likely to contribute much to present-day concepts, in spite of their great historical interest. For instance, it seems almost certain that all the variations of individual colour vision which Edridge-Green described under his theory can be accounted for fully on the combined trichromatic and opponent colours theories. Also, it is apparently not true that colour vision has evolved in the steps suggested by either Edridge-Green or Ladd-Franklin. Many animals, such as insects, fish, reptiles, birds and the higher apes have colour vision not unlike that of Man. In Man himself, however, the best average red/green vision is found in the most 'primitive' groups, such as Australian aborigines, and the best yellow/blue vision in Western whites, among whom there is, on the average, much more red/green defective colour vision. Racial differences will be discussed more fully in the next chapter, but they do not appear to give any support to Ladd-Franklin's theory.

In a book dealing with problems of art it is perhaps wise to comment on the artist's method of making green by mixing blue and yellow pigments, because to the artist red, yellow and blue, rather than red, green and blue are the accepted 'primaries'. This is because among pigments used by artists the yellows and blues, especially those which are valuable for making greens, both reflect into the eye a large amount of green light rays. These green rays are, however, combined with other rays, also reflected, to form yellow for the one pigment and blue for the other. Yellow pigments, however, reflect little or no blue light rays, and blue pigments little or no yellow rays, and when the blue and yellow pigments are put together they tend in combination to exclude yellows and blues respectively, but to reflect greens, and in consequence the combination looks green. The more green rays reflected by the yellow and blue pigments, and the less the yellow pigment reflects blue and the blue pigment yellow rays, the better will be the green produced by mixing them. On the trichromatic theory, however, the red and green retinal responses combine in the visual system to give rise to a yellow sensation, and this is quite another matter. In the mixing of pigments it is the question which light rays are reflected into the eye by the pigments or combinations of pigments used. In colour vision theory the questions concern which retinal responses are excited and what sensation they give rise to in combination.

Individual differences in normal colour vision

A distinction must be drawn between small or minor variations among individuals who have normal colour vision, and major or large differences between them and people whose colour vision is properly called defective. Valentine (1962) mentions the writer's work on individual differences in colour vision (Pickford, 1951, pp. 47–9) and suggests that small differences in colour sensitivity must affect aesthetic appreciation, especially in impressionistic art which depends on subtle variations of colouring more than upon clearly defined outlines. The major variations certainly affect art, where colour is concerned, but it is an interesting question whether small variations in normal colour vision affect colour preferences and art to a noticeable extent. Major colour vision defects will be dealt with in the next chapter.

These minor differences of colour sensitivity among normal people are most easily understood in terms of the four colour or bipolar hypothesis mentioned in the previous section. In order to discover and measure such differences the writer used an instrument called an anomaloscope (Pickford and Lakowski, 1960: and Pickford, 1967), by means of which a mixture of red and green lights can be compared with a standard yellow, or a mixture of blue and green compared with a standard blue/green, or a mixture of yellow and blue with a standard colour almost grey in hue. It must be remembered that in mixing coloured lights additively instead of mixing pigments, which, as described in the previous section, is subtractive, the result of the additive mixing yellow and blue complementaries is a grey and not a green. If individuals are asked to make the colour matches mentioned above, it is found that about 92 per cent of males and over 99½ per cent of females in our population choose very nearly the same mixture of red and green to match the standard yellow. The other 8 per cent of males and ½ per cent of females have major defective colour vision and will be considered in the next chapter. In red/green vision there is a very marked separation between them and the normal group. Broadly the same applies for the green/blue and the yellow/blue tests, but for these pairs of colours there is not a sharp division between the 'normal' group and the 'abnormal' because variation is continuous from those who have very good colour vision to those who have red difficulty or inability to distinguish these colours. This means that the really abnormal green/blue and yellow/blue major defectives are much less frequent than red/green major defectives, while those who are affected by small differences in sensitivity to green/blue and yellow/blue differences are more frequent.

There are two kinds of differences among normal people found with the anomaloscope. The first is that the person tested will consistently choose a mixture of red and green which looks to the ordinary person with absolutely average colour vision either too reddish or too greenish to match the yellow. The same holds for the green/blue and yellow/blue tests. If these individuals choose colour matches sufficiently different from the average to be noticeable in daily life even to a small extent, they are called 'deviants' in the colour affected. Thus there may be red, green, yellow or blue deviants, and it may probably be assumed that deviants on the green/blue test are not basically different groups. About 15 per cent of men are yellow and 9 per cent blue deviants, whereas for women the figures are about 6 per cent and 7 per cent for blue. Similar figures are found for red and green.

The second kind of variation is that the person tested will have an ability to discriminate the hues in each pair noticeably less than the average, and in consequence tends to make a wide range of matches called an enlarged matching range for the pair in question. This form of variation may be combined with the deviations just mentioned and is called 'colour weakness' in a given pair if it is sufficient to cause slight difficulties in daily life. Minor variations, including colour weaknesses as well as deviations, affect about 20 per cent of the population. That is to say, about 20 per cent of the population in our part of the world have either deviations or colour weaknesses sufficient to be noticeable in daily life, and it is found that among dark-skinned people yellow/blue minor variations are more frequent than among Western whites. Also, as Lakowski (1958) and others have shown, yellow/blue minor variations affect persons over middle age more than younger persons, because, as age increases, there is an increase in pigmentation of the transparent parts of the optical system, which alters the proportions of light rays affecting the retina.

While the study of minor variations of colour vision is very important for science and industry and is very interesting in many ways, the writer does not know of any systematic researches on the extent to which they may affect colour preferences or aesthetic judgments about works of art. One could imagine two kinds of experiments in which this problem could be studied. In the first we might select a suitable group of persons who showed certain colour deviations and weaknesses and compare their colour and aesthetic judgments with those for persons with no such minor differences of colour vision. Obviously it would be very difficult to equalise the two groups for other factors, such as the effects of artistic training and experience, personal preferences owing emotional associations and personality differences, and for intelligence.

In the second kind of experiment we might arrange for carefully selected pictures or colour chips to be viewed by a group of persons previously tested with the anomaloscope and found to have perfectly average colour vision. Then the colour of the lighting for the pictures and other test items might be changed in a systematic way by means of very slightly coloured pieces of glass or gelatine which would act as 'colour filters' to exclude certain colours in proportions about the same as the known deviations of normal colour vision. If the experiment were adequately planned comparisons might be made between preferences under the various conditions of changed lighting. On the basis of this experiment, however, it would not be possible to imitate the effects of colour weakness, because it does not result from changed balance in the proportion of the light rays reaching the eye, but from a slight inability to discriminate certain hues from each other, although the appropriate light rays still reach and affect the retina.

The effects of artificial lighting and colour constancy

While considering how the effects of small variations in colour vision might be imitated for experimental purposes by the use of colour filters made of coloured glass or gelatine, it is worth while to consider the effects of artificial lighting, which is in principle much the same.

The most familiar type of artificial lighting for many years has been half-watt or tungsten lighting from electric lamps with an incandescent filament. This kind of lighting differs from north daylight chiefly in being considerably less blue. To make it equivalent to daylight a blue glass is necessary to reduce its yellowness and this is seen in the so-called daylight-blue light bulbs, but these do not really make it blue enough. The effect of this lighting is to make all coloured objects, including paintings, of course, considerably weaker in blue and stronger in yellow than the artist intended, but no experiments or tests known to the writer have been carried out to see how far the effect is aesthetically disturbing.

At the present day many public buildings, including art galleries, are lighted with fluorescent tube- or strip-lighting which is much more disturbing because it looks much more white in appearance than tungsten lighting, which is manifestly rather orange or yellow-looking. Unless care has been taken to use the tube- or strip-lighting which is truly balanced for equivalence to north daylight, this kind of lighting is the usually opposite in effect from tungsten lighting, because it is much too blue or violet. However, since its peculiar composition gives a white or daylight appearance, it is very deceptive. Pictures illuminated by it are abnormally strong in violet and blue, and this would be quite sufficient to upset their colour harmony considerably. However, as before, there are no experiments known to the writer which measure the effect, and, since strip-lighting is itself considerably variable, it would not be easy to measure. The effect of tungsten lighting is, presumably, something like the effect of a marked blue deficiency in colour vision, whereas that of strip-lighting is like a deficiency of red or orange sensitivity.

Other types of lighting, not used in art galleries, because their colour effects are quite noticeably too disturbing, are sodium and mercury lighting. These both have the special peculiarity that they are limited to very narrow bands of spectral light rays. Sodium lighting is restricted to a very narrow band of yellow rays, but since it is manifestly very yellow in appearance, one easily perceives it to be abnormal. Objects not reflecting yellow light tend to look black by it, unless there is some subsidiary illumination as well. For instance, a blue bus going along a road which has sodium lighting will look black except in so far as it may also be illuminated by tungsten or other lighting from shop fronts and windows. Mercury lighting is restricted to narrow bands of yellow, green and violet-blue rays, but has a more approximately whitish appearance than sodium lighting. However, it makes all objects which reflect mainly red, orange and yellow rays look peculiarly drab or colourless.

As in the case of objects whose shape or size is distorted by perspective or distance, the visual system has great powers of adjustment to abnormalities due to the seen colour of lighting. This is called colour constancy. It may be easily demonstrated by experiment that an object, such as a blue book, seen to be illuminated on one half by white light and on the other half by red light, will not seem to change colour in perception in accordance with the changes in colour of the lighting. If the difference in the lighting is apparent because the lamps or sources of light are themselves seen, or because of other visual cues, the book will tend to look blue, even in the red light, or at least much more blue than the red light by itself would suggest. Even if it is known to be a blue book the effect of seeing it only in red light will be less than predicted on the basis of the colour of the illuminating light alone. This general principle of colour constancy applies to any differences in lighting provided the colour of the illuminating light is in some way apparent.

Since tungsten lighting is manifestly too yellow or orange for daylight, colour constancy to a considerable extent corrects our perception of the colours of objects seen by it. One can even do painting in colour by tungsten lighting without finding it surprisingly abnormal on seeing it later by north daylight. True artificial daylight might itself be disturbing, because we are so much accustomed to see all objects illuminated by tungsten light when rooms are artificially lighted.

Strip-lighting is very much more disturbing because, as already mentioned, its appearance is much more like that of white light, and therefore the colour constancy functions of the eye and visual system do not give our colour perception the necessary degree of correction. Its effects on aesthetic perception may be considerable. As for sodium and mercury lighting, however, they are too manifestly abnormal in colour to be used for art galleries and similar purposes.

Constancy affects not only the hue, but also the brightness and saturation of objects which are seen in the illumination of more than one source of light, as described above, and this often occurs when an object is shadowed in part, because the illumination of the shadowed part can be different in hue or saturation and is, of course, always different in brightness from that of the other part. Thus experimental psychology can help much in the study of the appearance of shadowed objects, and shadows are extremely important in pictorial art. Katz (1935) has discussed many aspects of colour and brightness constancy very fully. Thouless (1932) gave accounts of experimental studies, and the subject is mentioned by Wyburn, Pickford and Hirst (1964). More exact experimental measurements of colour and brightness constancy effects have been made (Burnham, Evans and Newhall, 1957; and Newhall, Burnham and Evans, 1958 and 1959). Further experiments on the effects of different kinds of illumination on apparent colour have been reported by von Fieandt and others (1964). These experiments by Burnham, Evans and Newhall, and by von Fieandt and others, are too technical to be dealt with in detail here, but the reader who wishes to follow up such researches for himself will find the references valuable.

Colour preferences of adults

One of the most extensive experiments on colour preferences of adults was carried out by Walton, Guilford and Guilford (1933). In this 1,279 students in the University of Nebraska were tested for colour preferences, some between 1910 and 1921 and others between 1928 and 1931. Coloured papers were used and the technique was that of paired comparisons. This technique, which has been one of the most widely used, is carried out by presenting each coloured paper patch with every other patch in pairs, systematically holding one constant and changing the other. The subject reports whether he likes the one which is changed better than, equally with or less than the constant patch. After all colours have been used in the constant position, if it was on the right-hand side, then the whole series is repeated with the constant on the left. In the end it is possible to add up the numbers of preferences for each colour over each of the others. This certainly has its disadvantages as an experimental technique, because it imposes somewhat rigid restrictions on the subject, and it is doubtful how far the free choices of an aesthetic attitude can be said to exist with such a method. However, if satisfactory numerical results are to be obtained it is difficult to see how to proceed in a better way, except by asking the subject to give a rating for each colour patch, taking them in irregular order, on a 5-point or 7-point scale. Such scales usually have an indifference point, thus: +2, +1, 0, −1, −2, for the 5-point scale. Again there is artificiality, and many people find such experiments radically unsatisfactory. Another useful technique for determining preferences is to present the subject with all the items, coloured chips or papers in this case, and ask him to arrange them in order from the most liked to the least liked. Then the order is converted into a numerical scale of quantitative units by using positions as quantitative steps.

Walton and the Guilfords found some interesting results. Altogether there were 815 women students, and red was the most preferred colour on the average for them, while for the men blue was most preferred, red second and violet blue just below it. Orange was more popular with men than yellow, but yellow was more popular than orange with women. Women varied more over the whole period of years than men, who changed little. Red declined in its strength of preference for both men and women between 1910 and 1917, but recovered to an even stronger position after 1928.

It is interesting that Margaret W. St George (1938) obtained a result on 500 college students which was almost the same for men and women, the order of preference being: blue, green, red, yellow, orange, violet, white. Half the students were undergoing art training involving colour, and for them the only difference was that orange was more preferred than yellow. As with the Walton and Guilford study, women preferred yellow to orange, but men preferred orange to yellow.

Winch (1909–10) reported studies of colour preferences on 24 men, 20–39 years of age, and 41 women, 18–46 years of age, by the technique of asking them to write down the names of the colours: white, black, red, green, yellow and blue, in the order in which they preferred them. He found that men gave the order: green, blue, red, white, yellow, black; and the women: blue, green, white, red, yellow, black. The men were in the solicitor's department of the National Telephone Company (London Offices) and the women were teachers in five municipal schools.

A research was carried out by Eysenck (1941) on a group of 12 students, some of each sex, and groups of 15 men and 15 women, mostly students, who were tested with colours from the Ostwald series of coloured papers. For saturated colours the following orders of preference were found: (1) 12 students—blue, red, green, orange, violet, yellow; (2) 15 men—blue, red, green, violet, orange, yellow; (3) 15 women—blue, red, green, violet, yellow, orange. Again blue was the most preferred colour for all groups, and women preferred yellow to orange while men preferred orange to yellow, as in the research of St George.

In order to control any differences arising from saturation or chroma and brightness, lightness or value as well as colour or hue on colour preferences G. W. Granger (1955a) carried out a thoroughly planned research on 50 subjects, aged 19–36 years, who included university and technical college students, members of university tutorial classes and civil servants, equal numbers being men and women. He made up sixty sets of Munsell colour chips, including about seven in each set, selected to represent the entire colour solid in respect of hue or colour, chroma or saturation and value (lightness) or brightness on the Munsell and CIE systems. The technical details and information about these systems of colour measurement and specification cannot be given here, but may be found in the following: Wright (1958); Burnham, Hanes and Bartleson (1963); Newhall, Nickerson and Judd (1943); Committee on Colorimetry (1953).

The subjects were tested with the Ishihara, Rabkin and Farnsworth 100 Hue tests, to exclude colour vision defectives. The three tests together would exclude major defectives, and the Farnsworth test would probably also exclude those with minor colour vision defects. The fifty subjects had good colour vision.

A special booth was used to control the lighting, and the subjects were asked to rank the colour chips in each set in order of preference. Adequate statistical methods were used to analyse the results, and Granger mentions the following points as general conclusions: (a) that there is a general order of preference for each attribute of colour at all levels of the colour solid; (b) that the order of preferences for any one attribute of colour is the same while the other two attributes change in level; and (c) that there are no marked sex differences in colour preferences.

The subjects also carried out the Maitland-Graves Test of Design Judgment, and there was a reasonably high correlation, namely, 0·588, between this test and the combined hue, saturation and brightness results. This suggests that the investigation of preferences for simple colour stimuli has significance for aesthetic appreciation in other ways, as measured by the design-judgment test.

In a second and equally efficient experiment Granger (1955b) carried out four tests of colour harmony on twenty subjects of normal colour vision, three tests concerned with hue, saturation and brightness, and the fourth only with saturated hues. The subjects were also tested with the Maitland-Graves Design Judgment test. A general order of preference for intervals along each dimension of colour was found. This order of preference was such that preference tends to increase with increasing size of hue interval; to decrease with increase of brightness interval; and to decrease with increasing size of saturation interval. Preferences for intervals of hue, saturation and brightness were independent of particular colours chosen for standards, and a score on one test of colour harmony had considerable predictive value for other similar tests and also for preference tests for single hues and for the test of design judgment.

In a further experiment Granger (1955c and 1955d) gave six sets of binary colour combinations and one set of triadic colour combinations to twenty subjects, 20–35 years of age, all of whom had been tested with colour vision tests mentioned above to exclude colour vision defectives. Illumination and other conditions were fully controlled. The subject's rankings for preference were for each set and the amount of agreement was determined. The coefficients thus obtained were then correlated with the order predicted by Moon and Spencer's formula for an aesthetic measure applied to colour. Granger found that Moon and Spencer's formula (to be mentioned in the next paragraph) was of little use for the prediction of preferences, but put forward an empirical formula for binary combinations of hues. This depended on, (a) preferences for the component colours making up the combination, and (b) a relational term depending on the combination as such. It will be remembered that there was a general tendency for preference of colour pairs to increase with increasing hue interval, to decrease as the brightness interval increased and to decrease as the interval in saturation increased. Eysenck (1957) has concluded that the liking for a colour combination depends mainly on liking for the individual colours concerned and on the degree of their separation on the colour circle, complementary pairs being liked most.

The formula of Birkhoff (1933) was $M = O/C$, where M is the measure of aesthetic experience, O is the order and C the complexity of the stimulus. It states that the degree of aesthetic experience depends directly on the order but inversely on the complexity of the stimulus. This formula was applied to colour by Moon and Spencer (1944). Order related to area, balance or relative sizes of areas. Complexity was the number of colours added to the number of colour pairs having hue, saturation and brightness differences. Eysenck (1942) found that the formula $M = O/C$ was more successful in predicting aesthetic judgments for his experimental results on polygons, which means that the aesthetic pleasure would be determined by the product of the complexity and the ordered similarity. In this paper Eysenck explained the problems of the good Gestalt very fully, especially in relation to aesthetics. He considered the relation between perception and aesthetic appreciation to be very close, and, in fact, that the fundamental law of the good Gestalt must be identified with the fundamental law of aesthetics, in the sense that the 'good' quality of organisation of the good Gestalt in perception is the same quality which gives rise to aesthetic pleasure. This is not by any means agreed to by all students of the psychology of aesthetics.

The difficulties of finding a qualitative formula or measure for the aesthetic pleasure to be obtained from a given colour stimulus pattern were reviewed very fully by Victoria K. Ball (1955). She pointed out that Eysenck (1941), after summarising the results of many experimenters, in which the total number of subjects concerned was 21,060, showed that there was a total average preference for blue, while yellow was the least preferred colour. He said at the start that there has been little agreement about a general order of preference for colours, or that saturated colours were generally preferred, or that there were sex differences in preferences for colours. However, he concluded his research by saying: (a) that there is a certain amount of agreement between the colour preferences of people as high as that between intelligence tests and not restricted to people of European origin; (b) that a second and bipolar factor divides those who prefer saturated from those who prefer unsaturated colours; and (c) that there is high agreement between the sexes in their colour preferences. A further reference to this work will be made in Chapter 7.

Granger considered that the empirical formulation which he put forward, depending on preferences for single colours, together with the effect of the colour combinations as such, did not support a 'wholistic' or Gestalt approach strongly, but rather an atomistic approach to art. A picture might be liked because it had colour combinations of a high order of aesthetic value although individual colours in it were little liked. The Gestalt approach, however, does not demand that we should be unable to say what component factors or influences are integrated in the 'whole'. It says that the essential quality and character of the whole cannot be arrived at by a mere addition of separate elements. This would be more true of aesthetic experience than of any other experience. No laws of colour harmony could show an artist how to make a work of value as art, or what an artist would create, any more than a knowledge of the laws of musical harmony and counterpart could show anybody how to compose a work of musical value, although such a work might conform to these laws, and they would have guided the musician in its composition.

A very thorough review of the work up to 1952 on the affective or feeling value of colours was given by Norman and Scott (1952). This includes 93 references to previous work.

In 1959 Guilford and Smith published a report of an experiment using 316 samples of Munsell colours differing systematically in hue, saturation and brightness, including 21 which had zero saturation, which were rated for pleasantness on a 10-point scale by 20 men and 20 women students on two different occasions. The subjects were tested for colour vision before being accepted. The lighting conditions were adequately controlled.

The analysis of the results showed that there was a positive relationship between increasing brightness and increasing affective value (pleasantness) of the colours. With regard to hue, blues and greens were given the highest ratings for pleasantness and yellows the lowest. For saturation the most general relationship was that the greater the saturation the higher the hedonic level (pleasantness).

Three very efficiently controlled experiments on preferences for colour combinations were reported by Beglan Togrol (1966). Her first experiment was intended to determine what interval differences would be used in hue, chroma and value (colour, saturation and brightness) when the subjects were free to make three binary colour combinations which were pleasant and three which were unpleasant. They were also asked to indicate their five most preferred colours in rank order. This was carried out with 20 men students at Cambridge, England, all tested with the Ishihara test. The second experiment was planned to verify the findings of the first experiment on 10 men of Istanbul University who had normal colour vision. The third experiment investigated the conditions contributing to discrimination of colour pairs at very brief exposure intervals, and was carried out on 10 women students of Istanbul University, whose colour visual was normal. A tachistoscope was used to obtain $\frac{1}{100}$ second and $\frac{1}{50}$ second exposure intervals. Lighting was adequately controlled in all the experiments. Togrol drew the most general conclusion that differences of brightness between members of colour pairs were the most significant influences both for pleasantness and for unpleasantness and that this was also true for short durations of exposure. In summarising her results Togrol says that any two colours with interval differences of zero or nearly so on the value (brightness) and chroma (saturation) dimensions on the Munsell system are generally judged unpleasant. For pairs judged pleasant the interval difference of three Munsell units was consistently a modal or most frequent choice for brightness, with smaller hue and chroma differences. Hence it could be said that a typically pleasant pair would possibly have hue differences of two units, three units of brightness difference and no chroma or saturation difference.

Although this research was carried out on some European whites and some Turkish students, it was not a cross-cultural study and therefore it is included in this chapter.

In recently published researches James Hogg (1969a and b) studied a principal components analysis of semantic differential judgments of single colours and of colour pairs and the prediction of semantic differential ratings of colour pairs from the observed ratings of single colours.

There were 30 single colours, systematically distributed in hue, brightness and saturation, and 40 colour pairs generated from them, in the first research; all colours were defined on the Munsell system. Fifty subjects took part. The analysis of the resulting data showed four factors for the single colour judgments, namely: (1) 'impact', 'obtrusiveness' or 'blatant-muted'; (2) 'usual-unusual'; (3) 'pleasant-unpleasant'; and (4) 'hot-cold', 'lush-austere' or 'exciting-calming'. Similarly four factors emerged for the colour combinations, namely; (1) 'blatant-muted' or 'active-passive'; (2) 'pleasant-unpleasant'; (3) 'warmth and lushness', and to a lesser degree 'excitingness'; (4) 'usual-unusual'.

In the second research there were 50 single colours and 20 subjects took part. Four sets of colour pairs were then produced, one set for each of the four semantic differential scales: pleasant-unpleasant, hot-cold, strong-weak and usual-unusual. The combinations selected were based on a study of the semantic differential ratings for the single colours, in order to give a suitable number of pairs for experiment, the ratings for which could be predicted, (a) by simple average and (b) by congruity-formula from ratings obtained for the colours taken singly.

The predicted and observed ratings were then correlated for each of the semantic differential scales. These correlations were greater than 0·9 for the 'warm-cold' and 'strong-weak' scales, but lower than 0·7 for the other two scales except where ratings predicted by average and observed ratings were correlated. This means that, with certain exceptions which Hogg considers, when the average ratings for the individual colours of a pair are high, the predicted ratings and observed ratings will also be high, and where the average ratings for single colours are low, then the predicted and observed ratings will also be low, and so on, especially for the 'warm-cold' and 'strong-weak' scales.

These experiments are interesting to record here, although they were not essentially experiments on aesthetics. However, the results could perhaps be summarised for aesthetics by the following statements: (1) Single colours have their influence mainly through 'impact'; 'usualness-unusualness'; hedonic effect; and 'excitingness–calmingness'; in that order, the first being most important. (2) Pairs of colours have mainly the same kinds of influence, but in a different order, namely, 'impact'; hedonic effect; 'warmth-coldness' and/or 'excitingness'; and 'usualness'. (3) Additive predictions of the ratings for pairs of colours based on the ratings of the colours taken singly were well borne out by experimental observations for the 'strong-weak' and 'warm-cold' scales, but less well for the hedonic and the 'usual-unusual' scales. Further experiments of a similar kind definitely aimed at aesthetic problems would be interesting.

In Ian Scott's English version (1970) of the *Lüscher Colour Test,* a personality test based on order of preference for eight colours, percentage frequencies for first and last choices of single colours are given, calculated from 36,892 tests on male students ranging in age from 20 to 30 years. First choice frequencies are red (28·9%); green (18·1%); blue (15·9%); violet (15·3%); yellow (12·5%); brown (4·7%); grey (2·7%); and black (0·3%). Similarly, last choices for single colours are: black (35·1%); grey (23·1%); brown (11·4%); violet (11·0%); yellow (8·6%); blue (4·7%); red (3·4%); and green (2·8%).

The two orders are nearly but not quite in reverse. Red and green are the most frequent first choices, with blue next, and grey and black the least frequent, while green and red are the least frequent last choices, and blue next again, and black and grey are the most frequent last choices. Percentage frequencies for choices of pairs of colours are also given and may be considered by any readers who care to look them up in the book.

It is interesting to compare the Lüscher Test frequencies alongside other data for colour choices. It will be remembered for instance that Eysenck showed that the order of choices for six saturated colours, pooled for 26 experiments, was blue, red, green, violet, yellow and orange, for white people, and almost the same for non-whites. In the Lüscher Test, of course, the red is an orange-red and the blue is a greenish blue, while it includes brown, grey and black.

The correspondence between musical sounds and colours

Various aspects of the possible correspondence between musical sounds and colours have been discussed by Jean Dauven (1970). Perhaps the most interesting of these is the possible relationship between the musical tones in an octave and the sequence of colours from violet to red. This relationship is best seen, according to Dauven, if we take two octaves of sounds from middle C (264 vibrations per second) to the C two octaves above (1,056 vps), and parallel the middle range of the two octaves from G to F by colours from violet to red, showing their wave lengths in Angstrom units. This is seen in Table 4.1, giving the Pythagorean frequency ratios.

TABLE 4.1

Relationship of colours to musical tones

Tone	Frequency ratio	vps	Colour	Angstrom units
C	1	264	—	—
D	9/8	297	—	—
E	5/4	330	—	—
F	4/3	352	—	—
G	3/2	396	Violet	405
A	5/3	440	Violet-blue	438
B	15/8	495	Blue	473
C	2	528	Green	527
D	9/8	594	Yellow	580
E	5/4	660	Orange	597
F	4/3	704	Red	700
G	3/2	792	—	—
A	5/3	880	—	—
B	15/8	990	—	—
C	3	1,056	—	—

This table obviously raises some interesting problems. One could use it to make several colour combinations which correspond according to it to musical chords. The most obvious of these could be G B D, the tonic chord of G major, the colours corresponding to which would be violet, blue and yellow, and A C E, the tonic chord of A minor, with the corresponding colours violet-blue, green and orange. Others chord might be G B E and A D F, the one a first and the other a second inversion, to which the corresponding colours would be violet, blue and orange, and violet–blue, yellow and red. A four-note chord would be G B D F, dominant seventh of G major, the corresponding colours for which would be violet, blue, yellow and red.

Various familiar two-tone combinations would be imitated, but the octave itself is not available. Others, in order of corresponding tonal fusion, might be fifth, violet to yellow; fourth, violet to green; sixth, violet to orange; major third, violet to blue; minor third, violet to violet-blue; diminished seventh, violet to red, and so on. Whether purple might be regarded as the major seventh above G, namely F sharp, is an interesting question, since purple, although distinctive in quality, is not a spectral colour.

These possibilities suggest interesting experiments on harmonies of colours, to see whether certain combinations of two, three or more colours would tend to be matched with their theoretically corresponding musical chords.

When it is suggested that there might be a parallel between musical harmony and colour harmony, the difficulty is immediately apparent that the ear is an analyser of sounds in a way that the eye is not an analyser of colours. Thus two or more tones heard together remain distinguishable, at least to the trained ear, in spite of their integration to form a distinctive chord, whereas two or more beams of light rays will fuse to form an intermediate colour indistinguishable in any way from a single beam of light of that colour. Consequently colour harmony always presumes positional relationships in space, although succession may be obtained by changes in temporal sequence as in music.

Another difficulty is that the degree of assonance or dissonance of musical tones in combination, although much affected by the context in which they are heard, depends basically on beats and the clashes of overtones, whereas this is not the basis of colour harmony.

A further difficulty is that while two of the fundamental qualities of tones and colours are comparable, namely, pitch with hue and loudness with intensity, timbre for sounds and saturation for colours are not comparable in physical basis.

A fourth difficulty remains, namely, that at least in traditional Western music only the precisely defined and tuned notes of the scales have been employed, without any variations to intermediate pitches. In colour harmonies the fullest range of variations of hue are possible. Continuous variations of loudness are possible for sounds, and of intensity for colours. For the timbre of sounds variation has been possible in the sense of differences between instruments and voices, although saturation has been continuously variable for colours. Certainly in some present-day Western music continuously graded variations of pitch have been employed, and in some Eastern music variation of pitch has been accepted traditionally. On the whole one might say that the continuous variation of hues in visual art has been compensated for in music by having more than seven octaves of usable tones.

The possibilities in speculations about colour and tonal harmonies do not seem to be absolutely absurd, however, because it may be recalled that Granger showed that the order of preference of colour pairs tended to increase with increasing size of hue interval, the most preferred being complementaries, and Beglan Togrol showed that a typically pleasant colour pair would possibly have two Munsell units difference of hue, three of brightness and none of saturation. Whether pleasantness necessarily goes with fusion or harmoniousness is an open question, but it is not unlikely that interesting experiments might be devised on the basis of what has been suggested as a parallel between colours and musical tones.

In connection with the correspondence of musical sounds to colours synaesthesia should also be mentioned. This is an intimate fusion or association of one sensory excitation with another, in such a way that the second is not merely thought of as appropriate to the first, but is experienced with it. The commonest form is auditory-visual synaesthesia, in which sounds seem coloured. Many other forms exist. (Myers, 1911; Riggs and Karwoski, 1934; Karwoski and Odbert, 1938; Odbert, Karwoski and Eckerson, 1942; Karwoski, Odbert and Osgood, 1942; Wyburn, Pickford and Hirst, 1964; Trevor-Roper, 1970). There are two possible explanations. The first is that there may be some fusion or crossing of nerve pathways so that the consciousness of a colour is excited at the same time as that of a sound by an auditory stimulus. The other is that there must have been some personal and individual experience of a very intense kind in infancy causing an intimate association of certain colours and sounds.

Synaesthesia is very individual and is not frequent enough to be important in aesthetics, although some interesting cases have been reported, generally in connection with musical rather than visual art. The Russian composer Scriabine, for instance, had well-attested auditory-visual synaesthesia, and composed music on this basis. His 'Prometheus, a Poem of Fire' is an example. Other people, however, do not follow, appreciate or gain from his colour harmonies because they do not share his particular form of synaesthesia.

Not only notes of certain pitch may be experienced as if coloured in characteristic ways, but the timbre of different instruments may seem coloured. Thus the timbre of the flute might be white, of the oboe scarlet, of the clarinet crimson, of the violin sky blue, of the viola green, of the 'cello purple or violet,

Brass instrument tones are usually thought of as gold, yellow, orange or brown. These 'synaesthetic tendencies', however, are not usually true synaesthesias.

Associations and attitudes to colour

Valentine (1962, pp. 29–33) quite rightly gives emphasis to purely personal and individual associations to colours. These are suppressed or avoided as far as possible by the instructions given to subjects taking part in the experiments just mentioned on colour and on colour combination preferences. The subjects are usually asked to judge the colours as objectively as possible and to think of their preference, liking or otherwise for the colour or colours presented without taking their own associated ideas or memories into account. Individual variations of judgment or impression of pleasantness are also eliminated in statistical analyses, which are aimed at the determination of the most general or average results. Throughout his discussions of colour preferences Valentine (1962, chs. II and III) has pointed out important individual variations from the most general results, as do many of the research workers and writers on the subject.

In many cases the subject is entirely unaware of the associations with colours which influence him. They are lost with forgotten memories of childhood and infancy. While many researches have shown that yellow or orange may be the least preferred colour, this is only an average result. The writer's father, for example, had a special and intense liking for yellow and was delighted by clumps of yellow flowers. The explanation of this was never discovered. Former owners of the writer's house had a special liking for pink. The house was pink and nearly all the flowering plants in the garden had pink flowers. The writer introduced red, yellow, orange and blue flowers as soon as possible, because an excess of pink is not pleasing to him, although he has nothing against pink flowers.

In some cases the events relating to colour preferences or changes in them can be remembered. A man well known to the writer remembered clearly that when he was at school and as a university student he always preferred blue and yellow/blue colour schemes. Later his personal taste changed imperceptibly to a preference for reds and red/green schemes of colour. It is, however, usually very difficult to recall and analyse in detail the special influences at work. In the change just mentioned the blue and yellow colours were linked or associated with a puritanical upbringing and the strictness of school and student life. Later there was a great change in outlook of an emotional kind and the preferred colours changed completely. This is not to say that puritanical attitudes are always associated with yellow and blue, but these colour associations and the subsequent changes must have been determined by other personal influences which are difficult or impossible to trace.

An interesting example is that in our culture girls are conventionally given pink clothes and boys blue. The extent to which a girl or boy will accept these and like them will depend on his acceptance or rejection of his sexual role in society, and this in turn will be the outcome of a complicated sequence of emotional events in his or her life since infancy.

Personal likings and dislikings for colours and combinations of colour will always affect artists very strongly. The characteristic yellow ochres with pinks and greens found in Cézanne's paintings must have been very important to him. Since artists are concerned with emotional expression through design and colour, artists will always tend to work on the basis of personal likings rather than generalised orders and degrees of public preference. Nevertheless a knowledge or understanding of any laws or general rules of colour harmony which he can have will help the artist in appreciating how he can best produce his effects. While he may expect to work within general schemes accepted by his public, at the same time, if he is capable, he may create new schemes and educate his public to accept them.

One of the earliest and most influential and interesting studies of attitudes to colour, which has since become a classic of the psychology of aesthetics, was that carried out by Edward Bullough (1907, 1908, 1910, 1921). In his experiments there were 35 subjects, three being women, and they were shown 70 different shades of colours. The subject looked through a circular hole at the illuminated coloured paper, in a dark room, and was asked whether he liked or disliked it and to give his reasons. The reasons given showed that colours had different aspects for different people which determined their liking or disliking of the colours. There were found by Bullough to be four of these aspects, and they were as follows:

(1) *The objective aspect.* In this the colours were found to be pleasing because they were saturated, pure or bright; or displeasing because they were thin, mixed, dull or foggy. The essence of this aspect or attitude was that consciousness is fixed upon the qualities of the colour itself.

(2) *The physiological aspect.* In this the colour was found pleasing because it was stimulating, soothing, warming; or displeasing because it was dazzling, depressing or otherwise emotionally disturbing in a physiological way. Consciousness is fixed upon the subject himself with special reference to his bodily functions and activities.

(3) *The associative aspect.* Here the colour is pleasing because it reminds the person of some object or situation which he liked, or a person in whose company he was happy or experience he enjoyed. Colours were disliked because they reminded the person of unpleasant objects, situations, persons or experiences.

(4) *The character aspect.* In this the colour was liked because it seemed jovial, fearless, energetic, truthful, sympathetic; or disliked because it seemed stubborn, treacherous, over-aggressive or otherwise objectionable. Here the colour was treated as if it were a person and had a certain character.

According to Bullough a subject in his experiment might give more than one of the types of explanation of his liking or disliking, but the majority tended to be mainly influenced by one aspect rather than the others. Thus one comes to think of types of subjects, and an aspect or attitude is characteristic of a subject of a corresponding type.

We may say that persons of the objective type tend to take up an intellectual and critical rather an emotional or personal attitude. The physiological type tended to respond and to be aware of responding in a bodily way and to think of the colour less in terms of its own objective characteristics than in terms of its effect on their emotions or feelings with physiological accompaniments. They were more appreciative of colours than people of the objective type. Those of the associative type were less frequent and mostly women. Their attitudes to colour depended less on critical, objective analysis or on emotional effects of the colours on their physiological systems and more on circumstances and accidents of experiences related to colours. Lastly, subjects of the character type, the least frequent, were the least truly objective and analytic of all, because they thought of the colour as having the character qualities they appreciated it by, and did not judge it by its own qualities or by their emotional experiences or by the experiences they associated with it.

These types were subsequently found by Myers (1914) to be applicable in the appreciation of music, and can be applied to the appreciation of forms, lines and shapes. In fact they are widely applicable in aesthetic appreciation.

It is interesting to consider briefly the aesthetic standing or value of the four types. Bullough himself put the physiological type lowest; the associative type, in which the colour impression and associated content are not 'fused' but held separate, he placed next; the objective type, which was too aloof to reach the highest aesthetic experience, was next; the 'fused' associative type he put next and the character type at the top. This is a problem about which one might have long discussions. Many people, especially intellectuals, think of the objective type as highest. Whether the physiological or associative type is considered lowest might depend on what kind of art we are concerned with, and how it is best appreciated. Some people would agree that the character type is highest, especially in so far as the qualities felt to belong to the colour or to works of art themselves are generally accepted and agreed to by others, and apparently this was quite marked in Bullough's experiment. To the writer it seems that a blending and combination of types is best, or that a person should be able to adopt an attitude appropriate to a particular work of art.

In a later paper (1921, p. 89) Bullough drew a comparison between his four types and the four types set out by Binet, as follows:

Bullough		Binet
objective	—	descripteur ; érudit
physiological	—	observateur plus émotionel
associative	—	observateur plus émotionel plus érudit
character	—	émotionel plus observateur

Apparently he did not think there was a very good correspondence, because the objective type of Bullough corresponded both to Binet's descripteur and érudit, whereas the physiological type corresponded to observateur coupled with émotionel, the associative corresponded with observateur, émotionel and érudit together, and the character type to *émotionel* coupled with *observateur*. This comparison brings to mind Jung's four personality types, and the possibility of a comparison with them. While the objective and physiological might correspond to Jung's thinking and feeling types, it is less easy to see which of Bullough's types would correspond to the sensing and intuiting types of Jung.

In an experiment on Bullough's perceptive types in colour appreciation, Bradford (1913) used as subjects 26 university students, 18 of them graduates, 13 from each of the arts and science faculties. He used as material rectangular pieces of paper 30 square inches in area, in 15 different colours. The subjects were asked to write down the numbers of the colours in order of preference, and then to note against each the reasons for liking or disliking that colour.

Out of the 15 possible positionings for each colour, dark blue was highest, with a rating between 1 and 3, while pale pinkish brown, bluish green, pink and yellowish green were lowest, with ratings between 9 and 12. Bradford does not give the exact ratings for each colour, but he says that no colour had a median position below 10·2, which confirmed the general impression of the subjects, that hardly any colour was really disagreeable when taken by itself.

The proportions of responses to the colours which fell into the four perceptive types were as shown in Table 4.2. This is interesting because Bradford did not find wide variations in frequency, except between arts and science students for the physiological type.

TABLE 4.2

Numbers of responses to single colours falling within each of the four perceptive types (Bradford, 1913, p. 547)

Type	Physiological	Objective	Associative	Character
Arts	59	34	35	35
Science	40	48	40	32

After an interesting discussion, Bradford suggests that there are two associative types, the sensational and the emotional and he thinks the character type alone has claim to the title 'aesthetic'. It is the most highly developed. The objective and emotional-associative, he thinks, are partly developed, while the physiological represents the crude undeveloped content of experience, and the sensational-associative can hardly claim to be called appreciative at all. The order of aesthetic value of these types of response, therefore, would be as follows, the top being the highest:

1. Character;
2. { Objective;
     Emotional-associative;
3. Physiological;
4. Sensational-associative.

This may be compared with Bulloughs' own ordering of the types, mentioned on p. 88, which was as follows:

1. Character;
2. 'Fused' associative;
3. Objective;
4. Associative 'not fused';
5. Physiological.

If we assume that the 'fused' associative type of Bullough can be roughly equated with the emotional associative type of Bradford, and the 'not fused' associative of Bullough with Bradford's sensational-associative, then the main difference of aesthetic ordering is that Bullough puts the physiological type lowest, but Bradford puts the sensational-associative type in this position.

Bullough's earliest work on the aesthetics of colour is much less generally known. In it (1907) he shows that there is a very general tendency for darker colours to appear heavier than lighter colours. When he asked the subjects of his experiment why this should be so, they often answered, either that they had never considered the question, or that the effect was due to association. In nature it is most usual for more brightly illuminated objects and parts of objects to be above, where the light fell on them, and for the darker objects to be below. Hence the darkness of colours was associated with the impression of weight. Bullough was discontented with this explanation and considered that the light-dark relationship was far too infrequently associated with the up-down relationship for it to be convincing. He pointed out that if a pink and a red are put side by side, the red looks heavier than the pink, and in order to change the pink into the red we have to add more of the pigment. If this is true of differences of saturation, more saturated colours are also less luminous, and with differences of brightness and darkness, it is also true that a less luminous looks heavier than a more luminous colour, and to make a pale colour into the dark colour we have to add more, not of the hue but of black. Thus he concludes that the association which makes more saturated and darker colours look heavier is the association with 'more-ness', either of colour or of darkness. In the end, however, it is essentially the 'more-ness' of black which is significant, and luminosity, not saturation, which is the true index of the weight of a colour.

On reconsidering Bullough's argument, however, it seems that for colours of equal lightness but different saturations, the more saturated will tend to look heavier, and, in addition, for colours of equal saturation but different brightness, the darker will be the heavier-looking. Thus both principles probably apply. Moreover, it is very generally true, in spite of what Bullough says, that darker colours are more often seen in nature below lighter colours; after all, this principle of association may operate too, and the impression of heaviness in darker and more saturated colours may result from all three influences often acting together.

Bullough's findings with respect to the apparent heaviness of colours were confirmed by Marion Monroe (1925), who asked three questions: (1) Upon what factor or factors, brightness, chroma (hue), saturation, relation to the background, does the apparent heaviness of a colour depend?; (2) To what extent do these factors influence judgments of aesthetic proportions?; (3) Do these factors also influence the judgment in bisecting a line?

She showed that the apparent weight of a colour varied inversely with its brightness, and that blue appeared heavier than red, red than green and green than yellow, which might be a function of hue or brightness. An increase in brightness of the background decreased the apparent heaviness of dark red, but increased that of dark yellow. There was a close correspondence between the direction of the judgments of the apparent weight of a colour and judgments of aesthetic proportion, greatest between colour pairs of the same hue but differing in brightness and saturation, but least between colour pairs of different hue. In bisecting a line joining two coloured circles judgments of the mid point of the line were biassed towards the heavier colour.

In 1938 Margaret W. St George (1938) recorded the frequencies of different kinds of associations to six colours and white in an experiment mentioned on p. 74 on colour preferences of 500 college students, half of whom were undergoing art training. These associations are shown in Table 4.3. Her research showed that associative responses were recorded more frequently by non-art than by art students, and this difference also applied to emotional responses and to colour symbolism. It appeared, therefore, that art students had a tendency to look on colours in a more 'objective' way than non-art students, in the sense that they looked on

TABLE 4.3

Frequencies of various kinds of association for 500 college students to seven colours (from St George, 1938)

| *Association* | Frequency | | |
	ART	NON–ART	TOTAL
Nature	75 (40%)	34 (17%)	109 (28%)
Objects	68 (36%)	86 (42%)	152 (39%)
Locations	30 (16%)	36 (18%)	66 (17%)
People	20 (10%)	61 (30%)	81 (20%)
Other sensory	6 (3%)	15 (8%)	21 (5%)
Imaginative	6 (3%)	12 (6%)	18 (4%)
Literature, drama	4 (2%)	4 (2%)	8 (3%)
Folklore, superstition	0 (0%)	4 (2%)	4 (1%)
Miscellaneous	9 (5%)	11 (6%)	20 (4%)

colours as objects in themselves rather than as the vehicles or stimuli for associations or emotions, or as expressing something other than themselves. Another point demonstrated was that pleasant emotions were recorded approximately two and a half times as frequently as unpleasant emotions, although both kinds of emotion were more often recorded by non-art than by art students.

Several researches have dealt with emotional associations of colours other than their pleasantness or unpleasantness, and suggest some interesting consistencies and uniformities. In one of these, Odbert, Karwoski and Eckerson (1942), 243 student subjects reported the moods of ten musical selections and upon hearing them again they stated what colours they associated with each. The musical implications of this study are of considerable interest, but for the present it is significant that the moods were associated with colours in the following way: red (exciting), orange (gay), yellow (playful), green (leisurely), blue (tender), purple (solemn) and black (sad).

Later Wexner (1954) carried out an experiment in which eleven names of mood tones were used together with eight colours. The subjects were 46 males and 48 female students, and they were asked to fit each mood-tone with a colour. The colours were exhibited as pieces of paper $8\frac{1}{2} \times 11$ in., in random order, each mounted on a grey card 30×40 in. in size. The predominent associations obtained were as follows: exciting—red, yellow or orange; secure—blue, brown or green; distressed—orange or black; tender—blue or green; protective—red or brown; despondent—black or brown; calm—blue or green; dignified—purple or black; cheerful—yellow or red; defiant—red, orange or black; powerful—black or red.

Another experiment with the same selections of colours and moods was carried out by Murray and Deabler (1957). These workers used 18 male and 7 female students of Louisiana University, 69 male nursing assistants, 108 unselected, newly admitted, male neuropsychiatric patients and 47 male and 47 female students of Purdue University. The following predominant colour-mood associations were reported: exciting—red; secure—blue or green; distressed—black or orange; tender—blue or green; protective—red, green or blue; despondent—black or blue; calm—blue or green; dignified—purple or brown; cheerful—yellow, red or green; defiant—red; powerful—red or black.

The results bear a close correspondence to those of Wexner. In Murray and Deabler's study a very interesting conclusion, other than the associations of colours with moods, was that socio-economic differences between subjects appeared to be more important in causing different choices of colours to go with given mood-tones than either mental health differences or differences of geographical region in USA.

It is interesting that Bullough (1907, pp. 439–40) gave the character aspects of 35 colours by those of his subjects who fell into the character type, and these were not unlike the mood-tones found half a century later by Wexner and by Murray and Deabler although there were considerable differences. For example, in Bullough's list one or other of his yellows is given as gay, cheerful, restless or jovial, and orange as aggressive, oppressive. Reds are given variously as expansive, self-confident, plenty of life, or as fiery temperament; red-orange as cheerful. Bright green is given as pleasant, serene life; green-blue as mild, calm, placid. Blue is given as expansive, grand, distant, insipid, restful. Red-blue is given as sullen, mournful, dismal; purple as undecided, soft, reposing, slightly mystic. These are only a few examples to illustrate possible correspondences; there were many differences from what Wexner found. Bullough also showed that darker colours appear heavier than lighter colours (1907).

Another research by Wright and Rainwater was carried out with the help of the Osgood Semantic Differential. (Osgood, Suci and Tannenbaum, 1957). This method required the subject to circle one of seven positions between a pair of polar adjectives, such as:

Cold ... . warm

The subjects were men and women in Western Germany, and each was given three-inch squares of colour one at a time, in daylight, on a door-to-door basis within the structure of an area probability sampling plan. The number of subjects was 955 men and 2,705 women, ranging in age from 16 to 65 years. Fifty colours covering the Munsell ranges of hue, lightness and saturation were judged by each subject. Six principal dimensions were deduced by statistical analysis, which can be characterised as: 'happiness', 'showiness', 'forcefulness', 'warmth', 'elegance', 'calmness'. 'Happiness' depended on lightness and saturation to a lesser extent, but hardly at all on hue. 'Showiness' depended on saturation and to a lesser extent on lightness. 'Forcefulness' depended mainly on colour darkness. 'Warmth' depended on hue, greater redness corresponding to greater warmth. 'Elegance' depended on saturation and on hue, greater blueness corresponding to greater elegance. 'Calmness' depended on darkness or blueness. Apart from these points, greater lightness and greater saturation corresponded with greater colour preferences, but only in the sense of greater 'happiness' and 'showiness'.

Further problems about the preferences of colours in relation to personality differences and abnormalities of personality and their relationships to certain moods and emotional attitudes will be dealt with in Chapter 9.

In all the many experiments which have been carried out on colour preferences, both for single colours and colour combinations, some workers have taken much trouble to control and standardise backgrounds and others have not. In a recent paper to the *British Association for the Advancement of Science, Section J,*

Psychology, G. W. Granger (1970) stressed the importance of control of backgrounds, and the tremendous effect due to simultaneous contrast of colour backgrounds on colour samples being judged. He also emphasised the importance of the fact that almost all, or perhaps all, experiments on colour preferences have been carried out with 'surface' colours, that is, coloured papers or paints used for colouring. Surface colours have 'object' quality or character in contrast to 'film' colours, such as the colours seen on a spectrometer or rainbow, and 'volume' colours, like the colour of a transparent or translucent liquid. The 'object' quality of surface colours increases the likelihood that subjects of an experiment will think of them as colours for wallpaper, a hat, or some other object, and that this will affect their judgments of preference even with the best of intentions otherwise. If film or volume colours could be used the subject would be less inclined to think of objects of a certain colour rather than of colours in themselves.

Bibliography and References
for Chapter 4

BALL, VICTORIA K. (1955). The Aesthetics of Colour: A Review of Fifty Years of Experimentation. *J. Aesthet. and Art Criticism, 23,* 441–52.

BIRKHOFF, G. D. (1933). *Aesthetic Measure.* Cambridge, Mass., USA.

BRADFORD, E. J. G. (1913). A Note on the Relation and Aesthetic Value of the Perceptive Types in Color Appreciation. *Amer. J. Psychol., 24,* 546–54.

BULLOUGH, EDWARD (1907). On the Apparent Heaviness of Colours: A Contribution to the Aesthetics of Colour. *Brit. J. Psychol., 2* (1906–8), 111–52.

BULLOUGH, EDWARD (1908). The 'Perceptive Problem' in the Aesthetic Appreciation of Single Colours. *Brit. J. Psychol., 2* (1906–8), 406–63.

BULLOUGH, EDWARD (1910). The 'Perceptive Problem' in the Aesthetic Appreciation of Simple Colour-Combinations. *Brit. J. Psychol., 3,* 406–47.

BULLOUGH, EDWARD (1921). Recent Work in Experimental Aesthetics. *Brit. J. Psychol., 12,* 76–99.

BURNHAM, R. W., EVANS, R. M., and NEWHALL, S. M. (1957). Prediction of Color Appearance with Differing Adaptation Illuminations. *J. Obt. Soc. Amer., 47,* 35–42.

BURNHAM, R. W., HANES, R. M., and BARTLESON, C. JAMES (1963). *Color : A Guide to Basic Facts and Concepts.* London and New York: Wiley.

COBB, S. R. (1972). Ph.D. thesis. Glasgow University (unpublished).

COMMITTEE ON COLORIMETRY, OPTICAL SOCIETY OF AMERICA (1953). *The Science of Colour.* New York: Crowell (3rd printing 1963).

DAUVEN, JEAN (1970). *'Sur la Correspondance entre les sons musicaux et les couleurs'. Couleurs* (Paris), *no. 77,* September 1970, pp. 9–13.

EYSENCK, H. J. (1941). A Critical and Experimental Study of Colour Preferences. *Amer. J. Psychol., 54,* 385–94.

EYSENCK, H. J. (1942). The Experimental Study of the 'Good Gestalt'— A New Approach. *Psychol. Rev., 49,* 344–64.

EYSENCK, H. J. (1957). *Sense and Nonsense in Psychology.* Penguin Books.

FIEANDT, K. VON, AHONEN, LEA, JARVINEN, J., and LIAN, ARILD (1964). Colour Experiments with Modern Sources of Illumination. *Annales Acad. Sci. Fennicae, B. 134, 2,* 1–89.

GRANGER, G. W. (1955a). An Experimental Study of Colour Preferences. *J. Gen. Psychol., 52,* 3–20.

GRANGER, G. W. (1955b). An Experimental Study of Colour Harmony. *J. Gen. Psychol.*, *52*, 21–35.

GRANGER, G. W. (1955c). Aesthetic Measure Applied to Color Harmony: An Experimental Test. *J. Gen. Psychol.*, *52*, 205–12.

GRANGER, G. W. (1955d). The Prediction of Preference for Color Combinations. *J. Gen. Psychol.*, *52*, 213–22.

GUILFORD, J. P., and SMITH, PATRICA C. (1959). A System of Color-Preferences. *J. Psychol.*, *72*, 487–502.

HOGG, JAMES (1969 a and b). *J. Gen. Psychol.*, *80*, 129–40 and 141–52.

KARWOSKI, T. F., and ODBERT, H. S. (1938). Color-Music. *Psychol. Monogr.*, *50*, *2*; 1–60.

KARWOSKI, T. F., ODBERT H. S., and OSGOOD, C. E. (1942). Studies in Synaesthetic Thinking: II The Role of Form on Visual Responses to Music. *J. Gen. Psychol.*, *26*, 199–222.

KATZ, D. (1935). *The World of Colour*. London: Kegan Paul.

LAKOWSKI, R. (1958). Age and Colour Vision. *Advancement of Science*, *59*, 231–6.

MONROE, MARION (1925). The Apparent Weight of Color and Correlated Phenomena. *Amer. J. Psychol.*, *36*, 192–206.

MOON, P., and SPENCER, D. E. (1944). Aesthetic Measure Applied to Color Harmony. *J. Opt. Soc. Amer.*, *34*, 234–42.

MURRAY, D. C., and DEABLER, H. L. (1957). Colors and Mood-Tones. *J. Appl. Psychol.*, *41*, 279–83.

MYERS, C. S. (1911). A Case of Synaesthesia. *Brit. J. Psychol.*, *4*, 228–38.

MYERS, C. S. (1914). A Study of the Individual Differences in Attitudes towards Tones. *Brit. J. Psychol.*, *7*, 68–111 (with contributions by C. W. Valentine).

NEWHALL, S. M., BURNHAM, R. W., and EVANS, R. M. (1958). Color Constancy in Shadows. *J. Opt. Soc. Amer.*, *48*, 976–84.

NEWHALL, S. M., BURNHAM, R. W., and EVANS, R. M. (1959). Influence of Shadow Quality on Color Appearance. *J. Opt. Soc. Amer.*, *49*, 909–17.

NEWHALL, S. M., NICKERSON, D., and JUDD, D. B. (1943). Final Report of the OSA Sub-Committee on the Spacing of the Munsell Colors. *J. Opt. Soc. Amer.*, *33*, 385–422.

NORMAN, R. D., and SCOTT, W. A. (1952). Color and Affect: A Review and Semantic Evaluation. *J. Gen. Psychol.*, *46*, 185–223.

ODBERT, H. S., KARWOSKI, T. F., and ECKERSON (1942). Studies in Synaesthetic Thinking: I. Musical and Verbal Associations of Color and Mood. *J. Gen. Psychol.*, *26*, 153–73.

OSGOOD, C., SUCI, G., and TANNENBAUM, P. (1957). *The Measurement of Meaning*. Urbana: Univ. Illinois Press.

PICKFORD, R. W. (1951). *Individual Differences in Colour Vision*. London: Routledge and Kegan Paul.

PICKFORD, R. W. (1967). Colour Blindness: Anomaloscope Tests and Physiological Problems. *Internat. J. Neurology*, *6*, 210–21.

PICKFORD, R. W., and LAKOWSKI, R. (1960). The Pickford–Nicolson Anomaloscope for Testing and Measuring Colour Sensitivity and

Colour Blindness and other Tests and Experiments. *Brit. J. Physiol. Optics, 17,* 131–50.

RIGGS, L. A., and KARWOSKI, T. F. (1934). Synaesthesia. *Brit. J. Psychol., 25,* 29–41.

SCOTT, IAN (1970). *The Lüscher Test.* London: Cape.

ST GEORGE, M. W. (1938). Color Preferences of College Students with Reference to Chromatic Pull, Learning and Association. *Amer. J. Psychol., 51,* 714–16.

THOULESS, R. H. (1932). Individual Differences in Phenomenal Regression. *Brit. J. Psychol., 22,* 216–41.

TOGROL, BEGLAN (1966). An Experimental Study of Colour Combinations. *Internat. Farbtagung,* Luzern, *vol. 2,* 895–906. Göttingen: Musterschmidt.

TREVOR-ROPER, P. D. (1970). *The World Through Blunted Sight.* London: Thames and Hudson.

VALENTINE, C. W. (1962). *The Experimental Psychology of Beauty.* London: Methuen.

WALTON, W. E., GUILFORD, R. B., and GUILFORD, J. P. (1933). Color Preferences of 1279 University Students. *Amer. J. Psychol., 43,* 322–8.

WEXNER, L. B. (1954). The Degree to Which Colors (Hues) are Associated with Mood Tones. *J. Appl. Psychol., 6,* 432–5.

WINCH, W. H. (1909–10). Colour Preferences of School Children. *Brit. J. Psychol., 3,* 42–65.

WRIGHT, B., and RAINWATER, L. (1962). The Meanings of Color. *J. Gen. Psychol., 67,* 89–99.

WRIGHT, W. D. (1958). *The Measurement of Colour* (2nd ed.). London: Hilger and Watts.

WYBURN, G. M., PICKFORD, R. W., and HIRST, R. J. (1964). *Human Senses and Perception.* Edinburgh: Oliver and Boyd; Toronto: Univ. Press.

5

Colour vision defects and
pictorial art

The problem of individual differences in colour vision was mentioned in Chapter 4, where minor differences or variations were discussed in relation to their possible bearing on aesthetic experiences and judgments. It was left for the present chapter to discuss the effects of major differences or defects, commonly called forms of colour blindness. While there may be some doubt about the effects of minor colour vision variations on aesthetic creation and appreciation, there is no doubt that major defects have a marked influence, which varies with the nature and degree of the defect.

These defects have long been recognised, and their possible influences on pictorial art were first discussed by Goethe. Subsequently a number of workers have dealt with them, and the writer has made a number of observations on colour vision defects in relation to pictorial art.

The first point to consider in this chapter is the special interest for art of defective colour vision today. Then the historical aspects of the problem may be considered, followed by questions of the nature and definition of the defects themselves and then some observations will be made on the work of colour vision defective artists and art students.

Present-day interest in colour vision defects in relation to art

Four reasons may be given why there is a greater interest in the relation of colour vision defects to pictorial art than previously (Pickford, 1972). The first is the unprecedented freedom of colouring in much modern art. Why, for instance, should milk be black or a horse blue? Is it possible that such examples of extraordinary colouring might be explained in terms of defective colour vision in the artists? It will be seen that the answer is that a small number of peculiarities of colouring might be due to such causes but that this is extremely unlikely for the majority of extravagant peculiarities.

The second reason is that our greatly improved knowledge of colour vision and its abnormalities gives us a much greater capacity to explain the effects of defective colour vision and to understand them. Not only do we know more than ever before about the physiology of colour vision, but we also know more about the frequencies of various defects. We can estimate how many children in a school are likely to have such defects, observe what proportion of them go into art schools and find out how their art is affected. Round the world we can try to answer the difficult questions whether in ancient societies, and in present-day groups of non-white peoples, colours have been used and are used in ways which seem strange to us.

The third reason is that there is a greater interest in the application of experimental science to aesthetics than ever before, owing to the importance of the scientific study of individuals and individual differences of all kinds. The study of colour vision defects in relation to art is an aspect of these developments.

The fourth reason is the growing interest in the problems of the selection of individuals for training in professions, trades and occupations. This raises the questions whether possible pupils for schools of art should be selected for colour vision, and if so, by what means and on what standards; if not, then how they should be guided and advised by their teachers if they have some difficulty with colours.

The nature of major colour vision defects

Major red/green defects are to be understood in their effects on the individual's colour perception as extensions to extreme degrees of the minor defects which were described in Chapter 4 (Pickford, 1967b and 1969). Thus if the subject is asked to match a yellow standard colour with a mixture of red and green, he may choose a match which has much too much green or red in it for the person with normal vision. This difference is great enough to make ordinary colours different for him. For the person who requires abnormally much green, all desaturated greens must be markedly less green than for the normal, and similarly with desaturated reds for the person who requires much more than the normal amount of red. Such subjects are called 'anomalous trichromats', because they can match all the colours in the spectrum with three primaries, but in abnormal proportions. They are red anomalous (protanomalous) and green anomalous (deuteranomalous).

Two other groups of subjects have very much diminished capacity to distinguish red from green, and they are called 'extreme anomalous' subjects. Their defect is often or usually combined with the great deviation of matches just described, and therefore we can have extreme red anomalous (or protanomalous) and extreme green anomalous (or deuteranomalous) types of defectives.

If the incapacity to discriminate red from green is carried to its limits, the person sees no difference between these colours. Then he is called a dichromat, because he can match all the colours of the spectrum with two primaries, yellow and blue. There are two forms of dichromats, those whose defect is due to complete loss of the red sensation, who called are protanopes, and those who simply confuse red and green, called deuteranopes. Protanopes see black where normal people see red, and the rest of the spectrum must be made up out of green and blue. Deuteranopes see yellow from the red end right through orange, to yellow and green, and then blue to the violet end. The loss of red sensation found in protanopes is also found in the protanomalous subjects, who all have the red end of the spectrum darkened or shortened in some degree. The term protan defect is used for protanopia and both kinds of protanomaly, and the term deutan for deuteranopia and both kinds of deuteranomaly.

Yellow/blue major defectives are very rare. They appear to suffer from loss of blue sensation, comparable with that in protanopia for red, and hence are called tritanopes, or from a confusion of yellow and blue without loss of sensation, comparable with that in deuteranopia for red and green. There is, however, the pseudo-tritanopia found in subjects with marked yellowing of the transparent parts of the optical system, described for Mulready by Liebreich (1872), and for the cataract patient mentioned by Trevor-Roper (1959).

Another very rare form of colour defect is total colour blindness, or achromatopsia. There are two forms of this, but the difference between them is not important for the present book. The writer has not seen a totally colour-blind artist, but he has met and studied the colour vision of several totally colour blind persons. They usually have weak vision and have to wear dark glasses because normal lighting is too bright for them. They know colour names, but have no way of telling to which colours to apply them because all colours look like various shades of lightness and darkness of grey to them.

The frequencies of these defects are very important and interesting. In the Caucasian white stock there are about 7 to 8 per cent of red/green major defective men, and this number will be made up of about 1·3 per cent of deuteranopes, 1·4 per cent of protanopes, 0·6 per cent of protanomalous, 4·0 per cent of deuteranomalous, 0·5 per cent of extreme deuteranomalous, and 0·2 per cent of extreme protanomalous (Pickford, 1951, p. 334). Women defectives are much less frequent, namely less than 0·5 per cent for Caucasian whites. These frequencies vary considerably, however, even within the British Isles, and even more round the world, because there are markedly fewer red/green defectives among Indians, Pakistanis, Japanese, Chinese and American Indians, fewer still among Negroes and fewest of all among Australian aborigines (Kherumian and Pickford, 1959).

The frequency of yellow/blue blindness may be as low as one in 60,000, and total colour blindness may be about equally rare. In these subjects, however, it is probable that men and women defectives are equally often found. The reasons why red/green major defects are much less often found in women than in men is that they are sex-linked in heredity, and have to be on both sides of her family if they are to be manifest in a woman. This is fully explained in articles dealing with the inheritance of defective colour vision (Pickford, 1965c).

An historical approach to the problems

The problems of defective colour vision in relation to art were first raised by Goethe, who, in his *Farbenlehre* (1810; Goethe, 1894), describes two men, not over twenty years of age, who compared pink with the colour of the sky, called a rose 'blue', and confused green with dark orange and red with brown. Goethe thought they must lack the sensation of blue, but with our present-day knowledge we feel sure that they lacked the red sensation and were protanopes—a term explained in the previous section.

Goethe speculated about the ways in which such defects would influence art, and illustrated the effects with a landscape painting of his own, the sky rose-coloured and most of the other colours in it of an autumnal kind. He must have been the first to illustrate the possible effects of colour vision defect in art. He also discussed the painter Paolo Uccello, who, he says, made coloured landscapes for colourless figures, but it is far from clear that Uccello's colour vision was abnormal. He may have had quite other reasons for not colouring the figures.

There was an interval of more than fifty years before the ophthalmologist, Liebreich, in a lecture to the Royal Institution (1872), gave an account of the changes in Turner's paintings after 1830. He suggests that, 'After he had reached the age of fifty-five, the crystalline lenses of Turner's eyes became rather dim, and dispersed the light more strongly, and in consequence threw a bluish mist over illuminated objects'.

After discussing Turner, Liebreich also mentions the painter Mulready, whose paintings showed a marked change after he was about fifty years of age. The same scene for instance, painted in 1836 and again in 1857, showed a marked increase in blueness. This Liebreich attributed to the yellowing of the optical lens of the eye owing to increasing age which made it necessary for the painter to compensate by using more blue.

One of the most interesting suggestions made by Liebreich was that persons with congenital red/green colour vision of a moderately severe kind, who have diminished red discrimination, might see saturated reds quite well, while less intense or desaturated reds could appear as green to them. He instanced a picture by a painter whose work he saw in an exhibition. The painting represented a cattle market and the roofs of the surrounding houses were all painted red on the sunny side, but green in the shadow, while oxen were also red in the sun but green in shadow. This tendency to paint reds of low intensity as green and of high intensity as red was called Liebreich's Sign by another ophthalmologist, Angelucci (1908), who described it and also discussed in more detail the effects of abnormal colour vision in the work of artists known to be defective.

Angelucci had in his collection paintings by six artists who had red/green blindness and who showed Liebreich's Sign in varying degrees. He also mentions that these artists, after long experience, may discover how to compensate for their faulty perception of red, but he thinks they have more difficulty with green, tending to use it in flesh-tints. According to him they also make excessive use of violet in shadows. He thinks red/green defectives should confine themselves to white, black, yellow and blue. In connection with this it is worth mentioning that Patry (1918) discussed the case of Carrière, considering whether he might have been totally colour blind.

Several other writers, one of whom was Edridge-Green (1920), had the opportunity of studying the paintings of known colour defectives. He examined a Royal Academician who proved to be a red/green defective, but there was no abnormality in his art because his wife used to give him the correct colours to use. An art student he examined had a major red/green defect, but passed through his training without anyone suspecting it. Raehlmann studied the influence of colour vision defects in copying paintings (1901).

One of the most interesting writers on the subject was Strebel (1933), an ophthalmologist of Lucerne, who mentions a certain German-Polish painter he tested for colour vision in 1916 who was a red/green defective. He painted largely in loam-grey, sulphur-yellow and dark blue. Strebel mentions the case of El Greco, who was not only suspected of perpendicular astigmatism, but also of a form of yellow/blue colour vision defect arising from pigmentation of the transparent parts of the optical system due to age. According to Strebel, as he grew older El Greco favoured yellow and blue/violet colours. The possible defect in El Greco cannot be established, because we have no means of testing El Greco's colour vision. Podestá (1949), however, gives an account of the art of Wilhelm von Kugelgen (1802–1867), a self-acknowledged colour vision defective painter.

In one of the most instructive of all the publications about defective colour vision in relation to art, with many illustrations in colour, Trevor-Roper (1959) suggests that Constable may have had a defect of red vision, because, in spite of the predominant brown colour of his paintings, he said that he never did admire autumnal tints, even in nature, but loved the exhilarating freshness of spring. At the same time, it must be agreed that brown paintings were conventional at the time. Constable was also challenged by Sir George Beaumont, who asked, 'Do you not consider it very difficult to determine where to place your brown tree?' To which Constable replied, 'Not in the least, for I never put such a thing into a picture.'

Trevor-Roper also gives a report on a patient of another ophthalmologist, who had cataracts extracted from both eyes. Before the operation he painted a picture of the scene from his bedroom window, which he made overall reddish brown. A year later, after the operation, he painted the same scene again, making it largely greenish blue. Presumably in these pictures he did not compensate for the yellowing effect of the cataract, as Liebreich suggested of Mulready, but painted the pictures more exactly as he saw the scene. Wirth (1968) has given a very clear account of the whole subject of defective colour vision in relation to art, in a monograph with many coloured illustrations.

This section may be concluded with a note about the Canadian artist, Thoreau MacDonald, about whom the writer was informed by the late Professor George Humphrey, who knew him and who had a painting of his entitled 'Winter Evening with Jesus and Mary', which he allowed the writer to photograph in colour (Pickford, 1964). It shows the child Jesus in a brown overcoat, and having a pale golden halo, walking in a snowy scene hand in hand with Mary, who is in a dark blue overcoat. There is a pale yellow sunset sky fading into pale blue above, a white new moon, and a dark brown hare runs across the snow. Three conical cypress trees are very dark brown. Humphrey said that those who have not seen such a scene in Canada can hardly believe how true to life it is, and that the artist told him he had no red or green vision. His father, who was also a painter, had to put in these colours for him when necessary. In this way he was able to avoid the down-right confusions of colour, such as making the flames of a fire green, which have been noticed in the work of people with colour vision defects who have copied paintings without taking any precautions to identify the colours by the names on the tubes or asked help from normal people.

Racial differences of colour vision in relation to colour names and art

Rivers (1901a, 1901b, 1905) showed as a result of tests he carried out that many non-white people, and in particular the modern Egyptians he tested, have diminished sensitivity to blue, and also to some extent to yellow, as compared with white races. These differences were, of course, differences of averages and do not imply that all the members of a group tested were weaker in blue or yellow than all white people. There would be some as good and some as weak in the one group as in the other, but in the non-white groups there were more who were weaker than in the white groups.

Myers (1925, ch. 1) presented the data of Rivers and discussed the possible relationship of the weakness of blue vision with the absence of a definite word for blue among many non-white peoples and also, incidentally, in some European languages. The question is a very difficult one. What evidence do the numbers and kinds of colour names in various languages provide concerning the colour vision peculiarities of the people concerned? A people who used the same general name for green and blue, as many do, might be just as good as white peoples in discriminating these hues in a critical test. No definite word for blue or brown occurs in the *Iliad,* and this and other peculiarities of the use of colour names in Homer also occur in other ancient writings such as the *Zendavesta* and the *Norse Edda.* The Uralis and Sholagas of Madras have a word for green, which may also be used for brown and grey, but they have no special words for brown, violet, or light blue. The Todas of Madras and the Murray Islanders of the Torres Straits have no word of their own for blue, but are beginning to use the English word. The Welsh may use 'glas', which means green, for blue. In Scottish Gaelic the word 'gorm', which means blue, may be used for the green of grass or for dark grey such as the colour of a grey horse. 'Glas', which means grey, may be used for the green of trees and hills. 'Gormghlas' is sea-green. The discovery of Rivers that more among non-white peoples were slightly weak in blue and yellow than in our own population was confirmed on small numbers by the writer (Pickford, 1951, pp. 200–2; Wyburn, Pickford and Hirst, 1964, p. 207). Such small differences, however, would not be sufficient to account for the complete absence of a name for blue or for other differences in a whole language on colour names.

Robertson (1967) has claimed again like many others that the differences in colour naming in various ancient and modern languages reflect differences in colour vision of the people in question. The writer agrees with Myers, however, that the non-existence of colour names in a language and apparent abnormalities in colour naming, like using the same word for green and blue, are not adequate evidence of colour vision differences. Myers thought that these peculiarities of language were due to interest and linguistic conventions, just as we can speak of red brick or a red cow without meaning that it is fully red, as distinct from orange, yellow or brown, and without any suspicion that we, as a people, are defective in red vision. This view would accord with the view taken recently by Osborne in an article about the colour naming of the Greeks (1968).

The lack of blue sensitivity shown by Rivers in modern Egyptians would not be great enough to account for the lack of a name for blue, and indeed these people now appear to have evolved such a word. As Myers points out, the ancient Egyptians 'frequently used blue pigment in their pottery, on their stone figures, and—eccentrically it is true—in colouring the surface of their reliefs and their sculptures'. Myers added: 'We have yet to discover the origin of the extraordinary schemes of colouration which were employed among ancient civilisations and resulted in blue bulls, green men and the like. . . . Consequently, there seems no direct connexion between apparent insensitivity to blue and a want of interest in the colour.' The ancient artists to whom he refers must have been like some modern artists, and made objects in the colours which satisfied their aesthetic judgment, often very highly developed, irrespectively of the real colours of the objects.

As far as red/green colour vision defects are concerned, we now know that they are less frequent in non-whites than in our own people. Therefore it is less likely that an Indian, Chinese, Egyptian, Negro or Australasian artist's colouring would have been influenced by colour vision defect than the colouring used by a Caucasian white artist, although red/green defects would, in themselves, be sufficient to account for some abnormalities of pictorial colouring, as will be seen in the next section.

In connection with some of the colour-naming difficulties of Homer, which have led to speculation whether the ancient Greeks may have had different colour vision from ours, a colleague of the writer, Mr Robin Gilmour, recently visited Greece and considers that the sea may sometimes well merit Homer's expression which is usually translated 'the wine-dark sea'. Some Ilford colour transparencies which he took in Samos looking towards Pythagorion show the purplish colour of the sea very clearly. It would be instructive if it were found that all the disputes which have taken place about the colour vision of the ancient Greeks were settled by finding that their descriptions were quite normal and correct.

Colour defective artists studied by the writer

In spite of the difficulties of persuading serious artists to come forward for colour vision tests when they might be suspected of defective colour vision, the writer has been able to test four artists, two of whom were amateurs and two were professionals.

One of the professional artists was Mr Donald R. Purdy, of New Haven, Conn., USA. He came to the writer's notice through an article in a local newspaper, *The New Haven Register,* 25 August 1963 (Pickford, 1964 and 1965a). The writer got in touch with Mr Purdy and he was kind enough to discuss his colour vision very fully and to try to explain how it influenced his work as a painter. He also visited the Medical Research Laboratory, US Submarine Base, New London, where by kind permission of Dr Jo-Ann S. Kinney, he was tested by Dr Kevin Laxar, with the standard tests used in the laboratory, and, in addition, the Nagel anomaloscope.

Mr Purdy was sophisticated in matters relating to colour vision, because he had studied psychology and knew of his defect owing to tests at Ohio State University where he was sent by the USA Air Force for training as an engineer.

In the tests at New London he proved to be a case of simple deuteranomaly. His paintings were mainly woodland scenes, sometimes with deer or human figures in them. In the earliest phase of his art he had used dull colours. Later he became most attracted to 'Barbizon' colouring, with a predominance of browns

Plate I

Paintings by a Deuteranomalous Artist

No. 1 shows the kind of colouring the artist prefers.

No. 2 shows an unusual introduction of red against blue, white and yellow.

No. 3 shows the artist's most usual way of construction, using blues, yellows and browns or black.

No. 4 shows an unusual introduction of green against yellow, brown, blue and black.

Red and green are almost never used as important colours in contrast, but yellow and blue are frequently used in this way.

No. 1 (*above*)   No. 2 (*below*)

Plate II

Paintings by Two Protan Artists

No. 1 *An Indian Gentleman*, by P. A. Ray, is the work of a protanomalous artist, and shows his use of red, blue, yellow and black, with more green than is usual in his work.

No. 2 *Puerto de Soller, Majorca*, by a protanope, illustrates his characteristic range of colours, and, in this scene, it is relatively true to nature. Blues are used for sea, sky and mountains; brown, grey and fawn for near hillsides. There is almost no red, but reddish-brown is present, and there is a suggestion of grey–green for the olive and cork trees, but no true green at all.

and greys. Then, because of the interest of the public in bright colours, he developed a colourful art. Few of his paintings, however, contain both red and green and if one or other of these colours is used there is a 'framework' based on yellows and blues. The 'Barbizon' type of colouring remained his own favourite. He thought that his colour vision defect had led him to study values of light and shade in order to be able to distinguish colour better, and he complained of a dazzling effect of red and green when they were present together, like many red/green defectives.

Colour Plate I shows four paintings by Mr Purdy.* The first shows the kind of colouring he preferred. The second shows an unusual use of red; the third shows his most usual colouring and the fourth shows an unusual use of green.

The writer studied two protan artists, both of whom were amateurs (Pickford, 1965b, 1966). The first was an Indian artist, Mr Pratul A. Ray, who was a simple protanomalous defective, and the second was a pupil of his, who was extreme protanomalous. Mr Ray made many pictures of an expressionistic kind. He used saturated reds, blue, golden yellow and black very freely. He also used green to some extent, and said he was fond of this colour. He was tested with the Ishihara Test, the Farnsworth Dichotomous Test and the Pickford–Nicolson Anomaloscope. As he had been a student of psychology he was able to accept the results of the tests, but doubted that his colour vision defect had much influence on his art. However, it did result in his avoidance of greens to a great extent and certainly of red/green contrasts. An example of Mr Ray's painting is shown in Colour Plate II, no. 1 for which the writer makes the same acknowledgments as for Colour Plate I.

Mr Ray's pupil also used blue, yellows and browns freely, with little red or green. He was tested with the Ishihara Test and the Nagel and Pickford–Nicolson Anomaloscopes. He had very poor red/green discrimination, and had learned to avoid these colours in his painting which was generally of an expressionistic kind.

Another protan artist was a professional painter. He was tested

* For permission to use this colour plate the writer is indebted to the Editors of the *British Journal of Psychology* and the *British Journal of Aesthetics,* and they were produced in the first place with financial aid from the Carnegie Trust for the Universities of Scotland.

with the Ishihara Test, Farnsworth Dichotomous Test and the Pickford–Nicolson Anomaloscope. He was a complete protanope. He had passed through his art training without his defect being suspected. At a later stage he found that small dots and narrow strips of colour confused him. He gave up colour work altogether for fifteen years, but not because of his defect. It was because black and white work was more paying. Later he took up painting in colour again, and exhibited a number of works. He used yellows, ochres, oranges, blues and black, with a very little red and green. However, he could use red for special purposes. He is a most skilful artist and never made a mistake in the use of colours. He knows that reds have a scale of values different for him from what they have for most people. He accepted the results of the tests, but did not believe that his defect had much effect on his painting. This was certainly because of his great skill is using colours in such a way as to avoid the difficulties, and produced excellent works of art within the limits imposed by his own colour vision.

An example of this artist's work is shown in Colour Plate II, no. 2, for which the writer makes the same acknowledgments as for Colour Plate I.

Colour defective art students and colour workers

There are interesting questions about the colour vision of normal art students and artists in comparison with persons who are not art students, and of colour workers and people who do not work with colour. Also there are the questions how many art students are colour defective, whether they have the same frequency as in the population of other students and whether the proportions of the various types of colour defectives among art students are the same as in the population in general. Some of the questions so raised can be at least partly answered.

Heine and Lenz (1907) compared 18 normal artists with normal people other than artists and showed that their performance on colour vision tests was better on the average, like that of people who are accustomed to work with colours. Pierce (1934) found that, among 54 members of the staff and students in a school of art, the best colour workers were better at his tests than average colour workers of equal experience. The groups with most experience usually did better at the tests. The writer (1951) showed that 16 art students with normal colour vision, 13 of whom were women, were a little more sensitive to red and green than the general population in the same district.

A number of colour vision defective students were found for the writer in four art schools, by the help of friends who were teachers and used the Ishihara Test (Pickford, 1967a). The writer then saw them individually and tested them with the anomaloscope. The art schools in question were at Croydon, Nottingham, Aberdeen and Glasgow. Nine men students had red/green defects, namely three from Croydon, two from Nottingham, two from Aberdeen, and two from Glasgow, where one woman art student was also found. The frequency distribution of types of defect did not differ in statistical significance from that for the population at large and there seemed to be no self-selection according to type of defect. Since the schools of art were widely separated, there was apparently no tendency for the defectives to be found in one school of art or area more than in another.

Two of the men students first found their defects by taking part in the investigation, five had been tested before going to the art schools and one knew of his defect owing to errors made in daily life. The woman student did not know of her defect until she did the writer's tests. One reported that his art teacher had tried to help him by advising a very restricted palette, but the student wanted to experiment with and enjoy many colours. Another said he was rejected by one art school because of his defect.

In a further research (Pickford, 1969) the writer had the help of Mr Donald I. A. Macleod, who tested almost the whole intake of students in a school of art in two years, namely, 112 men and 111 women, with the Ishihara Test. Six men and one woman defectives were found. These were then retested with the anomaloscope by Mr Macleod and the writer, who also interviewed them. The overall frequencies of men and women defectives in these samples of art students do not differ in a statistically significant degree from the frequencies in the whole population in the same area. The distribution of types was also the same as that for the general population. The influences were that as many men and women students who are colour vision defectives were found in a school of art as in the general population, and that, as before, there was no self-selection according to degree and type of defect.

One defective out of the seven did not know of his defect previously, four were tested by a school doctor before coming to the school of art and two found their defects as a result of tests by friends after going to the art school.

Table 5.1 shows the frequencies of types of colour defective men in the four art schools and in the second research in which the whole intake of two years was studied, compared with the writer's results showing the frequencies of the same types in the population of the Glasgow area as a whole.

TABLE 5.1

Frequencies of types of red/green defectives in schools of art and in the population as a whole

Type of defect	In four art schools	In one art school	Pickford (1958)
DA-simple deuteranomaly	2	2	54
EDA-extreme deuteranomaly	4	3	71
D-deuteranopia	0	1	12
PA-simple protanomaly	0	0	15
EPA-extreme protanomaly	2	0	31
P-protanopia	1	0	21
Totals	9	6	204

General observations about art students with colour vision defects

If an art student has simple deuteranomaly or protanomaly it may have little effect on his colour work, because he will have good hue discrimination, although on a scale of hues different from that of normal people.

If he has extreme deuteranomaly or extreme protanomaly he will have poor hue discrimination for reds, oranges, yellows and greens, and for blues, violets, magentas and purples. In protanomaly, however, reds will be much darkened and may be confused with dark brown or black, while pale blue will be confused with rose pink. The protan subject will have an advantage because, other things being equal, colours dark for him are likely to be red, which gives some guidance.

For deuteranopes and protanopes, who are dichromats, colour confusion will be complete for reds, oranges, yellows and greens on the one hand, and for blues, violets and purples on the other.

Such art students or artists will have to learn, either consciously or unconsciously, how to avoid downright errors, and how to satisfy the colour harmony expectations of normal people, if their art is to be appreciated as realistic. If it is not to be regarded as realistic, then it will still be necessary that the artist should not make confusions and mistakes within his own intended schemes of colour. For example, he might unrealistically intend to paint a giraffe blue with black spots, for aesthetic reasons of his own. It would, however, be desirable that he should not paint it violet with red spots by mistake—although this might look the same to him. It is clear also that the colour defective artist has a double problem. He has to use colours he can use correctly to produce a colour scheme satisfactory for him, and also to satisfy the possibly different colour vision requirements of his clients, who are normal.

The factors of temperament and personality are important. The artist or art student who is bold and insensitive to his defect may be able to use colours in a striking and often original way, but if an artist is sensitive he may become involved in self-criticism and doubts in the effort to overcome his defects. This will lead to anxiety and worry about his work, and about his examinations if he is a student, and may make it difficult for him to complete his course of training. The greater the defect the more may it excite anxiety if he is sensitive in personality, and the more will it tend to make him bold and perhaps apparently original if he is not sensitive.

It would be a mistake to think that all colour vision defective students must be excluded from schools of art. In general, artistic ability is not correlated with the absence of colour vision defects. Many colour defective students could become very good artists. Also, it is not always desirable that they should confine themselves to black, grey and white, or dull colours. They should be consulted by persons who understand their problem and can deal with them adequately from the point of view of a psychological adviser. It would then be possible to help those who are likely to have difficulties owing to their anxiety about colour vision defects. Practical advice could be given about the colours likely to give rise to difficulties and errors. Art teachers themselves may not be the best people to deal adequately with these matters, and they would need a more than ordinary understanding and knowledge of colour vision and its defects, and of methods of testing. The most popular tests of colour vision in general use are not adequate. They are 'all-or-nothing' tests, and in spite of what may be said in the instructions which go with them about how to interpret the results, something more valid and reliable is required for discrimination of degrees and types of defect.

Influence of colour vision defects in viewing paintings

Since there are about 8 per cent of men and boys and rather less than ½ per cent of women and girls in the white population of European countries and America who have major red/green colour vision defects, it seems that the appreciation of coloured pictures by these defectives must be considerably affected. In the previous chapter suggestions were made about experiments to study the possible effects of minor colour vision variations on art appreciation. Such studies would be even more important where major defects of colour vision were concerned. Experiments with pictures, to be described in the next chapter, would provide opportunities for this kind of work, if we were able to collect a sufficient number of defectives in each of the major classes, and to compare their appreciation of a suitable set of colour pictures, in standard lighting, with that of an otherwise comparable group of normal people.

The appearance of pictures to the protanopic dichromat, for whom red is the same as black, while green, yellow and brown of the same lightness are alike, blue and violet are the same, and rose pink looks like sky blue, may be imitated for the ordinary normal person by looking through a blue-green glass of suitable type. The colour perception of the deuteranopic dichromat cannot possibly be imitated in a similar way because his defect is one of confusion rather than of subtraction. Also the colour perception of the various types of anomalous trichromats is not easy to imitate. The appearance of pictures to a tritanope, or a person with pseudo-tritanopia due to yellowing of the optical system, might be imitated by looking through a yellow colour filter. However, on the whole, experiments with colour filters on picture preferences would not be very satisfactory, and the most useful experiments would certainly have to be carried out with actual colour vision defectives.

Bibliography and References
for Chapter 5

ANGELUCCI, A. (1908). 'Les Peintres Daltoniens.' Rec. d'Ophthal., 30, 1–18. Trans. O. Valli and Beauvois.

EDRIDGE-GREEN, F. W. (1920). The Physiology of Vision, with Special Reference to Colour Blindness. London: Bell.

GOETHE, J. W. (1894). Goethes Naturwissen-schaftliche Schriften. 4 Band, Zür Farbenlehre. Historischer Thiel II. Weimar: Herman Böhlen.

HEINE, L., and LENZ, G. (1907). Über die Farbsehen besonders der Kunstmaler. Jena: Fischer.

KHERUMIAN, R., and PICKFORD, R. W. (1959). Hérédité et Fréquence des Dyschromatopsies. Paris: Vigot Frères.

LIEBREICH, R. (1872). Turner and Mulready. On the Effect of Certain Faults of Vision on Painting, with Special Reference to their Works. Not. Proc. Roy. Inst., 6, 450–64.

MYERS, C. S. (1925). An Introduction to Experimental Psychology (3rd ed. reprinted). Camb. Univ. Press.

OSBORNE, H. (1968). Colour Concepts of the Ancient Greeks. Brit. J. Aesthet., 8, 269–83.

PATRY, A. (1918). Annales d'Occulistique, 155, 60–2.

PICKFORD, R. W. (1951). Individual Differences in Colour Vision. London: Routledge and Kegan Paul.

PICKFORD, R. W. (1958). A Review of Some Problems of Colour Vision and Colour Blindness. Advancement of Science, 25, 104–17.

PICKFORD, R. W. (1964). A Deuteranomalous Artist. Brit. J. Psychol., 55, 469–74.

PICKFORD, R. W. (1965a). The Influence of Colour Vision Defects on Painting. Brit. J. Aesthet., 5, 211–26.

PICKFORD, R. W. (1965b). Two Artists with Protan Colour Vision Defects. Brit. J. Psychol., 56, 421–30.

PICKFORD, R. W. (1965c). The Genetics of Colour Blindness. In Colour Vision, Physiology and Experimental Psychology. Eds. A. V. S. de Reuck and Julie Knight. A Ciba Foundation Symposium. London, Churchill, (pp. 228–48).

PICKFORD, R. W. (1966). 'Brève Étude sur Quarte Artistes présentant des Troubles de la Vision Colorés'. Sciences de l'Art, Paris, 1966. Special Number, 110–18.

PICKFORD, R. W. (1967a). Colour Defective Students in Colleges of Art. *Brit. J. Aesthet., 7*, 132–6.

PICKFORD, R. W. (1967b). Colour Blindness: Anomaloscope Tests and Physiological Problems. *Internat. J. Neurol., 6*, 210–21.

PICKFORD, R. W. (1969). The Frequency of Colour Vision Defective Students in a School of Art and the Influence of their Defects. *J. Biosocial Sciences, 1*, 3–13.

PICKFORD, R. W. (1972, Unpublished M.S.). *Defective Colour Vision and Its Relation to Pictorial Art and Art Education*, ch. 1.

PIERCE, W. O'D. (1934). *The Selection of Colour Workers*. London: Pitman.

PODESTÀ, H. (1949). '*Zur Seh- und Malweise farbenblinder Maler. Selbstzengnisse des Malers Wilhelm von Kügelgen.*' *Klin. Mbl. Augenheilkunde, 114*, 401–12.

RAEHLMANN, E. (1901). *Über Farbsehen und Malerie*. Munich: Reinhart.

RIVERS, W. H. R. (1901a). *Reports of the Cambridge Anthropological Expedition to the Torres Straits, 11, 1*, Colour Vision 48–96.

RIVERS, W. H. R. (1901b). Colour Vision of the Natives of Upper Egypt. *J. Anthrop. Inst. Great Britain, 31*, 229–47.

RIVERS, W. H. R. (1905). Observations of the Senses of the Todas. *Brit. J. Psychol., 1*, 326–39.

ROBERTSON, P. W. (1967). Colour Words and Colour Vision. *Biology and Human Affairs, 33*, 28–33.

STREBEL, J. (1933). '*Prolegomena Optica zum Bildnerischen Kunstschaffen.*' *Klinische Monatsblatter für Augenheilkunde, 91*, 258–72.

TREVOR-ROPER, P. D. (1959). The Influence of Eye Disease on Pictorial Art. *Proc. Roy. Soc. Med.* (Ophthalmol.), *52*, 721–44.

WIRTH, ALBERTO (1968). '*Patologie Oculare e Arti Figurativa.*' *Atti della Fondazione Giorgio Ronchi, Anno 23, 4*, Luglio-Agosta, 1968, 445–66.

WYBURN, G. M., PICKFORD, R. W., and HIRST, R. J. (1964). *Human Senses and Perception*. Edinburgh: Oliver and Boyd; Toronto: Univ. Press.

6

Experiments with pictures

Techniques and problems

In contrast with the experiments previously described in Chapters 2 and 4, which dealt with single lines or colours, or pairs of colours, in various ways, many experiments of great aesthetic interest have been carried out with actual pictures or reproductions of pictures and photographs of other material of artistic interest. The experimental techniques, as before, sometimes make use of direct rating scales by means of which the subjects assign a numerical value to a given picture, reproduction or object, for liking, aesthetic quality or other related attribute. These scales are often of five or seven points, sometimes all positive and sometimes running from negative to positive values through a zero point, where the quality considered as bipolar, as with liking/disliking. It is difficult to work with a scale of more than about seven points, and fewer than five may be ineffective.

Another technique is that of giving the pictures or other items numbers representing an order of preference or an order of magnitude of a certain attribute or quality. Thus the least liked may be numbered zero and the most liked given the highest position in the series. If the items are small and can be moved, it is a useful technique for the subject to arrange them in order, and here, as with the numbering technique, it is better to avoid ties for position even if a difference is obtainable only by guessing. When a person guesses, under these conditions, he is more than likely to be actuated by some difference not consciously identified, and ties for position are a disadvantage from the point of view of the statistical study of the results, if they are frequent.

The third important technique is, as before, that of paired comparisons, in which the items are presented in pairs, the first with all the others in turn, then the second with those which remain, and so on, until the two last are seen together. Then the series should be repeated the other way round, so that any effect of the side-to-side position can be eliminated and total preferences for each over the others can be worked out. These preferences, like the numerical positions, can then be treated as scores similar to what might have been obtained on the rating scale technique.

In such experiments the comparison of groups is important, but comparisons of preferences which imply or test presumed racial or cultural differences will be reserved for Chapter 7, and studies of children's art judgments and preferences for Chapter 8 except when it is most appropriate to include experiments carried out both on children and adults together. Correlational techniques and factor analysis have figured in important ways in the researches to be mentioned here, and will be explained where the need arises. Experiments which involve personality and temperamental differences, and which deal with abnormal persons, will be dealt with in Chapter 9.

Valentine's early experiments

Valentine was one of the first to carry out experimental work or judgments about pictures, when he was at St Andrews University. He has given an account of the results of some of this work, carried out in 1912, in which he used 36 postcard reproductions of pictures, deliberately chosen to be of various artistic quality, some famous, some by less famous professional artists, and some which he considered inferior. About half were in colour. He used about 50 men and women students of St Andrews University and Dundee Teachers' Training College (Valentine, 1962, pp. 123–38). Apparently the subjects of the experiments were asked to say whether they liked the pictures and/or thought them good and to give explanations for their judgments.

First Valentine distinguishes three kinds of attitudes by the subjects. The first group expressed liking a picture and added that it was an excellent portrait, for instance, commenting on the quality of the workmanship, or they express disliking a picture but the excellence of the painting seemed to overcome this. The second group would comment on the excellence of the work but say that it displeased or repelled them for various reasons concerning its subject matter or expression.

The third group seemed to be unaffected by the quality of the artist's workmanship, but commented on the person represented in a portrait, for instance, simply treating it as an object about which they expressed their ideas. Valentine comments that the first group showed a more developed kind of aesthetic judgment. Then there were some subjects who had a naive judgment of what was represented, whereas others considered the work of art apart from its subject matter. This leads to an interesting possibility that a picture may be considered beautiful as a work of art, but may show a subject which is considered to be ugly. This problem has been taken up and dealt with more fully in the discussion of the psychology of ugliness (Pickford, 1969).

Another distinction in which Valentine was interested was that some people were affected in looking at a picture mainly by their own feelings—that it made them feel sad or happy, for example—while others were affected by the sadness, happiness or other emotion as something expressed in or by the picture.

This distinction led to a consideration of Bullough's types of experience in relation to pictures or judgments about them, as dealt with first in the consideration of colour in Chapter 4, the objective, physiological or subjective, associative, and character types.

These types came out well in Valentine's experiments with picture-postcards. For instance, the subjective type is represented by the person who commented, 'The picture makes me smell the sea and hear the waves', or, 'I like to feel a tossing motion, and the waves in the picture make me long for it'.

The objective type represented by those who based their judgments on the clearness or obscurity of a picture, on the colour, light and shade, the grouping of objects in it and its composition. The associative type included persons who liked a picture because it reminded them of some memory or incident. The best example of this was the judgment of a picture called 'Thursday', which showed monks fishing for Friday's dinner, by a subject who said she was affected by the memory of an event which occurred the previous Thursday—the only connection with the picture being the name of the day.

The character type was represented by subjects such as those who said, for instance, about a picture, 'The big waves swelling impotently, striving for something and never attaining it', or, 'the nodding flowers give a merry note as contrasted with the sombre majesty of the hills'. Valentine considers a large proportion of the character judgments are made by persons who have a really keen appreciation of pictorial art, and he links the character type of judgment with the importance of true or genuine emotional expression, to be mentioned later in discussing the results of the factor analysis of aesthetic judgments. By a person known to have keen artistic appreciation the following frequencies of judgments of different types were given:

Character judgments		9
Objective	,,	6
Subjective	,,	6
Associative	,,	6
Unclassified	,,	2

Valentine also reports an experiment by a pupil of his, A. L. Mohamed, in which university students at Birmingham were asked to state the extent to which they found each picture in an experimental series pleasing or otherwise, using a seven-point scale. Next they were asked to say how beautiful they found the pictures, also on a seven-point scale, and finally, to give reasons for their judgments according to a pre-arranged scheme, using a five-point scale. In the outcome there was a correlation of $+0.72$ between 'beauty' and 'pleasingness', based on more than 500 judgments. Although this is not a perfect correlation it is high and in an experiment such as this a higher correlation would hardly be expected, owing to the variability of the attitudes to the task inherent in the performances of subjects believing they are making the same kinds of judgments. The conclusion follows that the qualities of beauty and pleasingness tended to go together.

Another very interesting point was that the subjects were most influenced by colour, next by general proportions, composition and balance, then by the artist's skill and by expression and character.

In an experiment with 109 artistically naive subjects, who were students taking psychology courses, 10 reproductions in colour of paintings were used, four of which were 'abstract' and six were 'illustrations'. The subjects were divided into three groups; two experimental groups and one control group. In the experimental groups the students were told the names of the artists and what was thought of the paintings, favourable for one group and unfavourable for the other, by prominent critics, but this was not done for the control group. Valentine says there was evidence of the suggestive effect due to knowledge of the name of the artist and the judgment for seven out of the ten paintings, but in some cases the liking or disliking of the picture was so great that it was not affected by suggestion.

Burt's picture-postcard experiments

The writer has given a short account of Burt's early work with picture-postcard material (Pickford, 1955b, pp. 916–17). Valentine (1962, pp. 146–8) has mentioned this work much more fully. Burt started with fifty picture-postcards, and a general account of the work was given by Burt himself (Burt, C., 1933). The pictures reproduced included the greatest possible variety, 'from classical masters, second-rate pictures by second-rate painters, every variety and type down to the crudest and most flashy birthday card that I could find in a paper-shop in the slums'. The experiment, or test, consisted in arranging the fifty cards in order of preference.

To have a standard with which to compare the performance of the various groups who were asked to take part in the experiment, Burt asked eleven artistic experts to arrange the pictures in order of preference. Apparently most of them said at first that such a standard was impossible, but when the experiment was completed the average correlation between experts was nearly 0·9. This means that there was a very high degree of agreement, because a correlation of +1·0 would mean perfect agreement and of −1·0 would imply complete disagreement.

Burt did not publish full details of his experiment at the time, but he gave Valentine some of the results, which are shown in Table 6.1. Here children's results are included because it would be artificial to reserve them for a separate chapter in this book. It is clear that the orders given on the average by various groups, including adults, and boys and girls of grammer school, elementary school and infants department, correlate positively and quite highly with the standard order of the expert judges. The highest correlations are for applicants for art schools and grammar-school girls of 15–17 years of age and girls and boys of 12–15 years of age.

TABLE 6.1

Correlations of average scores of various groups with judgments of experts in Burt's experiment with pictures

Subjects	Numbers		Correlation with experts	
Adults (students and teachers)	46		0·69	
Applicants for art schools	37		0·76	
Adults (miscellaneous)	23		0·55	
	Boys	Girls	Boys	Girls
Grammar-school children				
15–17 years	52	48	0·63	0·72
12–15 years	68	73	0·61	0·65
Elementary-school children				
Senior depts.				
11–14 years	43	50	0·34	0·46
9–11 years	49	50	0·38	0·57
7–9 years	34	48	0·43	0·40
Infants' dept.				
6–8 years		36		0·59

The lowest correlation is for boys of 11–14 years of age, although the several ages of elementary school boys do not differ widely, but the girls tend to be higher. It is interesting that girls tend to have higher correlations with the experts than boys of the same age groups. This is possibly because their artistic judgment is more developed, and possibly because they are more inclined to conformity with cultural and social standards.

The chief conclusion was that there is evidence of a general factor of artistic judgment or taste. Burt mentions this as the fourth in his list of the special capacities which he set out as well established in the memorandum he drafted for the *Report of the Consultative Committee of the Board of Education, on 'Psychological Tests of Educable Capacity'* (ch. 1 of the *Report, 1924*). This was the first mention of such a factor.

Burt was invited to start a Department of Vocational Guidance and Selection in the *National Institute of Industrial Psychology*

(London) opened by C. S. Myers. As an assistant he had Violet Pelling, who was specially interested in the psychology of art, and she helped to work out tests for artistic ability in somewhat older people than the adults and children for whom the earlier experiment had been devised. The most useful of such tests Burt considered the one he described as the *'Picture Postcard Test'*, mentioned above. The test called upon the examinee to rank certain picture-postcards in order of preference. In working out the results use was made of the technique of factorising correlations between persons, instead of between tests. This technique gave evidence of a general factor of aesthetic judgment applying to all the subjects, and in addition, bipolar factors for certain types of artistic appreciation which seemed to be related to the temperamental differences of the subjects tested. This whole question of the connection between aesthetic judgments and temperament or personality, including its abnormal aspects, will be dealt with in Chapter 9.

Experiments by Kate Gordon, Margaret Bulley, D. A. Gordon and N. Israeli

One of the first to study experimentally the general nature of aesthetic judgments was Kate Gordon (1923). She used colour plates of 50 Oriental rugs, which were first arranged in order of aesthetic merit by three persons and then divided into two groups, Series One and Series Two, by taking the odd numbers of the whole 50 for the first series and the even numbers for the second. There were 207 subjects, all Caucasian except one who was a Negro, and 20 of them had some professional knowledge or experience and were called experts.

Each subject arranged the reproductions of rugs in each series in order of merit. A second trial after at least three weeks was obtained for 38 subjects. Correlations were worked out to show the stability of individual preferences, which was high, but with some exceptions, agreement of individual with group judgments, which was moderately high, agreement of group with group, which was generally high, and agreement of men with women, which was very high. Kate Gordon says that in spite of the general agreement, every rug, without exception, was rated very high by some persons and very low by others, that is to say, it was put within three places of the top and of the bottom of its series. She also stresses the fact that the experts agreed as individuals very little with the group and hardly at all among themselves, while they had only moderate agreement as a group with the non-experts as a group. No large negative correlations were obtained.

The general implications of this interesting and well-planned piece of work seemed to Kate Gordon to be that there was a general agreement on aesthetic value which tended to increase as the size of the group of subjects increased, although there were great individual differences, while the experts did not agree among themselves as much as the non-experts agreed.

Irvin Child (1966), however, points out that there are certain reasons why the opinions of experts are not always in agreement, such as the lack of great differences of aesthetic value of the items. Child also says that, when we look at Kate Gordon's statistics with present-day knowledge, the experts actually showed no less agreement than the other subjects, but possibly more, the apparent difference being an artefact owing to the small number of experts in comparison with the non-expert group. However, it is still true that there was a large amount of general agreement.

Margaret Bulley carried out an extensive experiment with four pairs of pictures of which the person taking part had to choose the 'correct' picture to be right. About 2,000 schoolchildren and 400 adults took part. There were 55 members of the British Psychological Society and 284 Oxford extension students. She also tested 30 women in an English prison and 700 Jewish children in London. It is interesting that the numbers of 'correct' choices made by most of the groups were below the purely chance level of 50 per cent right. Valentine (1962, p. 149) accounts for this by saying that she had no extremes of good and bad art, like Burt, and because of the poor quality of the reproductions (as seen in the *Burlington Magazine,* October 1923). The best group came from Dudley Girls' High School, where girls of 15–17 scored as much as 75 per cent to 85 per cent of 'correct' judgments. Miss Bulley attributed this to the work of the art mistress who had been at the school for 10 years and was especially gifted (Bulley, Margaret, 1934).

Burt had worked with Margaret Bulley as far back as 1910, and in London at a later date they used series of paired designs, which were used in a broadcast talk by Burt in 1933 and were published in *The Listener.* Those who heard the broadcast were invited to give their views on the psychology of aesthetic judgments and a great deal of material was collected from all sorts of people, both men and women who ranged from dock labourers to the Earl Russell. The material used in the experiments included varied types of applied art, such as furniture, dress materials, vases, china, and so on, and the whole series of experiments was described in *The Listener* (Burt and Bulley, 1933). Margaret Bulley also gave an account of the work in two publications (1933 and 1934). In her more recent book (1951) she included a series of pairs of pictorial reproductions of artistic objects and materials to be used as an art judgment test.

The average agreement with the experts in Margaret Bulley's and Burt's broadcast experiment was 70 per cent for men and 74 per cent for women. Other results, arranged according to occupation and education, are given in Table 6.2.

TABLE 6.2

Burt's and Bulley's results: Preferences for pictures arranged according to education and occupation. Maximum score = 9. Pure chance score = 4·5

	Average scores	
	MEN	WOMEN
University education	6·6	6·9
Secondary education	6·0	6·3
Elementary education	5·1	5·3
Artists	7·0	7·5
Musicians	6·3	8·3
Authors	7·5	7·6
Teachers (miscellaneous)	5·8	6·8
Teachers of Art	8·1	7·9
Teachers (arts subjects)	7·2	7·1
Teachers (science subjects)	6·8	6·7
Army and Navy	5·8	—
Other professions	7·0	7·2
Clerks	5·8	6·3
Labourers, servants, etc.	4·4	4·7

A striking point about this table is that women usually score higher than men, but whether this is because of higher artistic taste and judgment or because of great tendency to conformity, it is difficult to say. Another point is that art teachers give the highest scores, while teachers of arts subjects score higher than teachers of science subjects. A third point is that higher scores are given by persons of higher education and superior professions and occupations, male labourers, servants, etc., having the lowest scores.

In an elaborate research Margaret Bulley found similar measures of conformity with her own judgment as the expert, on 750 persons grouped in 50's according to education and occupation.

Another worker who collaborated with Burt was Heather Dewar (1938). She used the series of 50 picture-postcards selected by Burt, and employed the method of paired comparisons, limited to forty pairs. The complete procedure of paired comparisons with 50 items would be extremely laborious and almost defeat the purpose of the research. Her aim was to work out a test of children's aesthetic appreciation. She confirmed the finding of a general factor of aesthetic appreciation and found evidence of specific factors related to the attitudes of Bullough mentioned in Chapter 4.

Burt's studies on children's aesthetic judgments were developed for literary appreciation by Williams, Winter and Woods (1938). They applied five methods of testing literary appreciation to more than 200 children of various ages. The capacity for literary appreciation correlated highly with general intelligence and to a smaller extent with pictorial and musical appreciation. Two factors were found, a general factor positive throughout corresponding to literary appreciation, and a bipolar factor. The latter suggested two antithetical tendencies or 'types', namely a tendency to prefer classical writers and an objective style and a tendency to prefer romantic writers and a subjective style.

Eysenck's experiment on poetry should be mentioned here (1940a). He carried out a factor analysis of the appreciation of thirty-two poems by twelve judges who ranked them in order of liking. All the judges were keenly interested in poetry. Two bipolar factors were found, one of which divided those who preferred simple poems, while the other separated those who preferred emotional from those who preferred more restrained poems. The first factor correlated with a test of introversion-extraversion.

In an experiment by D. A. Gordon (1951–2) ten experts, namely six painters, three museum directors or lecturers and one art critic, together with ten laymen, were used as subjects. They

judged ten untitled oil paintings by students instead of reproductions of accepted works of art. These pictures included a large
variety of styles and kinds of subject matter, but the level of quality
was much more uniform than in Burt's experiment. The subjects
had to rate each work for 'artistic excellence' on a five-point scale
and to give reasons. The comparison between laymen and experts
was very interesting in respect of the reasons given for their
judgment of quality. Laymen strongly preferred realistic to
non-realistic paintings, and mentioned colour, realism, clarity
and content in explaining the basis of their judgments. Colour,
form, composition, shading and lighting technique, style, conception, mood and content were stated to be important by experts.
No sample criterion such as realism distinguished the favoured
paintings. The experts were more concerned with form and colour
relationships than the laymen, and were more aware of the technical aspects of painting. The laymen perceives a painting in
terms of its content—'a painting of a girl', 'a painting of a farm'—
but the expert evaluates it in terms of his likes and dislikes of
that type of painting, and in terms of the artist's success within
that type.

The average correlation between laymen's and expert's judgments was small but negative, −0·27, and Valentine (1962, p. 152)
thinks this was due to the general similarity of the paintings to
one another in aesthetic value, which is very likely to be the
explanation.

In another report on his experiment Gordon (1956–7) found
that the laymen's judgments resembled each other's much more
than the expert's judgment. He factor-analysed the results of the
experiment, and found three factors: (1) a factor representing
disposition to approve or disapprove of modern art; (2) a factor
representing an interest in craftsmanship; (3) a factor stressing
interest in style and originality (displayed by museum directors
and curators). Although Gordon used real paintings instead of
postcards or other reproductions, he did not use the works of the
great masters, or of outstanding artists.

An interesting experiment by N. Israeli (1928) utilised the
judgments of 400 subjects, including sixteen different groups,
some of whom were high-school pupils and others university
students, a section of whom were having training in art. Twenty
reproductions in colour of paintings by well-known artists, such

as Turner, Graham Petrie and George Innes were used. These had been selected as suitable in preliminary experiments. The students were asked to fit verbal 'descriptions' to the pictures. The verbal 'descriptions' included groups of words such as: (1) calmness, peace, serenity; (2) depression, gloom, sadness, dejection, melancholy; (3) solitude; (4) fatigue; (5) excitement, anxiety, restlessness, worry; (6) frenzy, and so on. The percentage agreements in the allocation of adjectives were calculated, with the result that fairly wide differences were revealed, and the combined average percentage agreement for college students was 26·7 per cent; for high-school pupils, 20·7 per cent; and for art students, 20·3 per cent. Thus in spite of the differences there was a considerable core of agreement and in one case the percentage agreement for a given adjective was as high as 68 per cent.

It is clear that in Gordon's experiments the similarity of aesthetic standard of the paintings may have led to disagreement between the experts and laymen because the experts may have been sensitive to important differences not apparent to laymen. Nevertheless the experts differed markedly among themselves in some cases—and this is what is found among experts in such cases as the marking of students' essays and examination scripts. At the same time the laymen may have given many randomly placed assessments. The general result was a lack of positive correlation between laymen and experts. This would be the result also if the laymen were affected by private and personal likings irrelevant to the experts and apparently this was the case, as mentioned above, because the laymen judged by realism, clarity, content, single preferred colours, and so on, while the experts judged by compositional qualities.

In Israeli's experiment, the result of a considerable amount of agreement coupled with fairly wide diversity of judgment in allocating descriptive adjectives to pictures is not altogether surprising. Some pictures are aimed at the creation of a very specific mood or emotion, and with these the degree of agreement might be expected to be high. Many pictures and works of art, however, gain their strength from their tendency to provide opportunities for different people to project into them and to experience in relation to them emotions and moods specially arising in their own lives and specially belonging to themselves. In such cases little agreement would be expected. Perhaps it is not widely realised that this is true, and that many of the greatest works of art may be said to condense into themselves the possibilities of many personalities, emotions and attitudes.

Researches of Eysenck, Peel and Child

In research published in 1940 Eysenck (1940b) pursued the problem of the general factor of aesthetic appreciation. He argued that three conditions had to be fulfilled in order to escape the influences of 'irrelevant associations'. These associations, according to him, would be: (1) The influence of complex effects due to teaching, tradition and general knowledge of cultural background; (2) The influence of technical excellence; and (3) The influence of familiarity. In consequence the pictures used should be such that: 'No tradition or teaching should point to one of them as superior to the others; so far as execution is concerned, they should be roughly of the same degree of excellence; and they should all be equally unknown to the subjects.'

Eysenck fulfilled these conditions as far as possible in the choice of 18 sets of picture material, as follows:

(1) *Portraits*. Thirty-two reproductions of comparatively unknown paintings by modern painters and old masters;

(2) *Emperors*. Fifteen photographs of statues of Roman emperors, taken from the British Museum;

(3) *Bookbindings*. Fifteen coloured reproductions of bookbindings, from the British Museum;

(4) *Claude Lorrain*. Twenty reproductions of pencil drawings by Claude Lorrain;

(5) *Blotters*. Twelve coloured photographs of 'Bathing Girls', used for advertising blotters;

(6) *Vases*. Sixteen coloured photographs of vases from the British Museum;

(7) *Masks*. Eight coloured reproductions of Malayan devil masks;

(8) *Japanese paintings*. Fifteen uncoloured Japanese paintings;

(9) *Ships*. Nine photographs of modern steamships;

(10) *Landscapes*. Twelve coloured landscape paintings by Japanese artists;

(11) *Sets*. Ordering the seventeen sets of pictures in order of liking;

(12) *Embroidery*. Twelve colour reproductions of pieces of embroidery, from the Victoria and Albert Museum;

(13) *Curves.* Twelve curves of mathematical functions, drawn in ink;

(14) *Statues.* Thirty-two reproductions of modern statues;

(15) *Flowers.* Fifteen coloured photographs of various flowers;

(16) *Pottery.* Twelve coloured reproductions of pottery from the East;

(17) *Plate.* Fifteen reproductions of pieces of silver plate;

(18) *Clocks.* Twelve reproductions of medieval clocks.

Eighteen subjects took part, being drawn from various walks of life. They included bank clerks, typists, painters, students, teachers, psychologists and a professor of aesthetics. They were asked to rank the pictures in each set in order of liking, and to rank the sets under item 11.

The intercorrelations between the eighteen rankings were factor-analysed and revealed two important factors. These were, firstly, a general factor accounting for 20·6 per cent and secondly a bipolar factor accounting for 13·7 per cent of the variance. Eysenck says that the first factor may be defined as the general, objective factor of aesthetic appreciation. It covers a large number, of if not all, aesthetic tests, but is not the same as the factor of general intelligence, and it is largely independent of individual taste. The second factor divides such sets as curves, masks and bookbindings from such sets as flowers, statues, plate, clocks and blotters. That is to say, it corresponds to the well-known aesthetic dichotomy between 'formal' and 'representative' art.

In a further research published in 1941, Eysenck confirmed the presence of the general and bipolar factors, and gave them more precise interpretations (Eysenck, 1941). In this research he used five sets of pictures:

(1) *Set A.* Fifty-one postcards of landscapes by artists from Dürer to the present day;

(2) *Set B.* Fifty-one landscapes similar to Set A;

(3) *Set C.* Thirty-two postcard reproductions of paintings from early Italians to Kissling and Modigliani;

(4) *Set D.* Thirty-two photographs of statues of modern sculptors;

(5) *Set E.* Fifty-one landscapes by the Austrian painter Defner, selected to be of about equal aesthetic merit.

Fifteen subjects were asked to rank the pictures in each set in order of liking. They were from a wide range of occupations, as in the previous experiment. Two factors were extracted from the intercorrelations between the ranking of the sets of material, as before, and Eysenck now suggested that the general factor should be called the 'T'-factor, that of good taste, while the bipolar factor should be called the 'K'-factor. He discusses the interpretation of the 'K'-factor and shows that it tends to separate preferences for modern artists' work from that of classical artists. One group of subjects prefers modern, impressionistic, colourful pictures; the other prefers the older, more conventional and less colourful pictures. The effect of this factor was strongest in respect of the pictures in Sets A, B and C, and less marked for the other two sets, D and E.

Eysenck suggests that the 'K'-factor may be linked with five other kinds of psychological variables, namely:

(1) Extraversion—introversion;

(2) Radicalism—conservation;

(3) Youth—age;

(4) Colour preference—form preference;

(5) Preference for bright colours—preference for subdued colours.

He concludes by saying that the results are definite enough to encourage further research into the relation between temperament and aesthetic preferences. The problems of the relationships between personality, temperament and aesthetic preferences and judgments will be dealt with more fully in Chapter 9.

Peel (1945) mentioned the work of Burt, Dewar, and Eysenck, and pointed out that where identification of aesthetic factors had been attempted it had been with reference to temperamental traits, and the emphasis had been upon the person tested rather than upon the qualities of the pictures. He planned a research to compare aesthetic preferences with these artistic qualities and for obtaining an estimate of a person's preference in terms of them. A paper dealing with some of the theoretical considerations was published in 1946 (Peel, 1946).

In his experimental research Peel used two types of aesthetic material. They were: (1) Thirty-one postcard-sized coloured reproductions of landscapes by a wide range of artists from the Middle Ages to modern times; and (2) Thirty-one different watercolour paintings of a still-life group of a coffee pot, a glass decanter, a cloth, a plate containing cheese and tomatoes, and two books.

For both tests expert and non-expert adults were asked to rank the items in order of preference. For the Landscape Test Peel chose the following three criteria in which they were also to be judged by the experts in the experiment: 'detailed naturalism', 'composition' and 'atmospheric light'. For the Still-Life Test he chose as criteria for the experts: 'realism', 'technical quality', and 'spontaneity'. These experts included artists, art teachers and postgraduate art students. The non-expert adults were twelve in number.

Factor analysis of the intercorrelations for liking by the twelve non-experts in the Landscapes Test showed a first factor which was bipolar and a second factor which was in effect a general factor. The 'liking' of each person was then correlated with the three criteria, and finally estimates of the 'liking' of the entire group on each of the factors for each of the criteria were obtained. These showed that the bipolar factor was closely related to a preference for or dislike of landscape paintings executed in a naturalistic manner. The general factor revealed responses of the persons to 'composition'. The influence of 'atmospheric light' was not so much marked.

For the Still-Life Test the three criteria correlated significantly among themselves as follows:

Realism/Technique +0·555
Technique/Spontaneity −0·802
Spontaneity/Realism −0·508

Peel points out that 'Realism' and 'Technique' therefore overlapped to a large extent and 'Spontaneity' was bipolar to them both. Three of the non-expert subjects were less influenced by 'Realism' and 'Technique' than the remainder, but responded more favourably to 'Spontaneity' of drawing.

These researches of Eysenck and Peel may be said to have carried the subject further in two directions. The first was the more adequate establishment of the general factor of ability for aesthetic sensitivity or judgment within the bounds of the material and subjects used, and also of the bipolar factor of temperamental or personality differences in preferences for bright/modern or subdued/older works of art. The second direction was the differentiation of compositional qualities in a work of art on the one hand and representational/technical qualities on the other.

Irvin L. Child (1962) has carried out an interesting experiment which throws serious doubt on the wisdom of assuming that conformity with the average preference is a measure of an individual's aesthetic sensitivity. Two groups of 22 college men (one group from Yale and one from Stanford), unselected for competence in art, gave preferences for 12 sets of 60 pictures of widely varied subject matter and aesthetic quality, by arranging each set into 10 piles of 6 in each pile, according to their appeal to him, from the 6 he liked best to the 6 he liked least. In addition 13 persons of both sexes, mostly graduate students of art or of the history of art, or otherwise competent, also divided each set in the same way. These were considered to give a criterion of aesthetic value for the pictures. They took two or three times as long as the students. Other tests, such as tests of sentence-preference, scholastic aptitude, perception as contrasted with judgment, viscerotonia, and tolerance for ambiguity, were also given.

For the two groups of college men unselected for artistic competence, average preference ratings of paintings bore little relation to the aesthetic value of the paintings as judged by the experts. Those with more knowledge or information about art were in greater agreement with the criterion group. Child asks what this variation in agreement with an aesthetic standard may signify and thinks that much cross-cultural and developmental research will be required before we can confidently judge. Some examples of cross-cultural studies will be reported in Chapter 7.

Aesthetic qualities and artistic appreciation

In a paper published in 1940 Pickford concluded, on general grounds, that, 'If there is a specific aesthetic material dealt with in art, it seems to be the rhythm of pattern, design and colouring, but even this is intimately expressive of the artist's personal life in symbolic ways. Strictly speaking, "abstract" art is non-existent, and all art is really full of meanings related to everyday life, expressed with varied degrees of clarity.' He also concluded, in the same paper (1940 p. 200), that 'the absolute essentials in artistic expression and appreciation are better described in terms of the harmonious working together of other tendencies than as unique aesthetic tendencies themselves'. These ideas were set forth in contrast with the conceptions of Clive Bell (*Art,* 1916) that there is a specific 'aesthetic' emotion, and that it is experienced in relation to objects which have 'significant form', which constitutes them as aesthetic objects.

In a later paper (Pickford, 1948a) the writer reported an experiment based on factor analysis, which was partly due to an attempt to test the ideas just mentioned and partly due to the influence of Eysenck and Peel and the view that their work had not taken adequate account of the emotional aspects of art.

For this experiment a series of eighteen coloured reproductions was selected in such a way as to represent a wide range of artistic and inartistic photographs; realistic, impressionistic, modern, classical and surrealistic paintings; and various degrees of emotional expression, harmony of design and other qualities. The pictures chosen were as follows:

(1) Hornel: 'Spring Roundelay';

(2) Goya: 'The Firing Party';

(3) 'Regimental Red': an almost completely unartistic advertisement for lipstick;

(4) Morland: 'Blind Man's Buff';

(5) Renoir: 'Women in a Field';

(6) Vivien Leigh and Laurence Olivier as Scarlett O'Hara and Maxim de Winter—a coloured photograph with some artistic merit;

(7) Picasso: 'The Dream';

(8) Gauld: 'Contentment';

(9) Bosch: 'The Holy Night';

(10) Manet: 'Peaches';

(11) 'The Victorian Pair'—a partly photographic advertisement for plaid skirts;

(12) Kenelba: 'Pamela Mountbatten';

(13) Derain: 'Le Samedi';

(14) Botticelli: 'Pallas and the Centaur';

(15) Dali: 'Lady Mountbatten';

(16) Gauguin: 'Le Bouquet';

(17) Grünewald: 'St Erasmus and St Mauritius';

(18) Rembrandt: 'The Supper at Emmaus'.

A list of possible aesthetic qualities was drawn up in order to study the influence they exerted on the appreciation of the pictures. The qualities chosen were as follows:

(1) *Liking* or *Disliking*—Interpreted in the simplest way possible, without special analysis;

(2) *Aesthetic design*—Harmony of form, pattern or colouring;

(3) *Sentimentality*—Ineffective, exaggerated, shallow, melodramatic or insincere striving after emotional effect;

(4) *Emotional expression*—Genuine expression of feeling or emotion, whether pleasant or unpleasant;

(5) *Representational accuracy*—Precision, realism or photographic exactness in the rendering of objects and details;

(6) *Symbolic expression*—The manipulation or distortion of normal objects to express feeling or emotion, as in the lengthening of an arm to express stretching for something desired;

(7) *Atmospheric effect*—The impressionistic use of light and shade, and of subtle tones of colouring, to express objects, moods and feelings;

(8) *Religious feeling*—The individual subject's own conception of spiritual quality, whether the painting was intended to be religious in the conventional sense or not.

The subjects were asked to rate each painting for the qualities on a 7-point scale, from +3 (complete saturation with the quality in question), through zero (indifference) to −3 (absence of or negative saturation with that quality). There were two groups of subjects: the university group included 29 graduate psychology students and the WEA group consisted of 30 students of evening classes, all at Glasgow University.

The ratings for the eight qualities of the pictures were added algebraically for all subjects and all pictures and intercorrelations were obtained between qualities by Spearman's rank difference formula. At first separate correlation tables were made up for the university and WEA groups and these were factor-analysed by the simple summation method, without rotation. Since there was little difference between the two groups, the factor loadings were averaged for the final table. The outcome of this analysis was that the first or general factor was mainly represented by Emotional Expression and Aesthetic Design, while the second or bipolar factor contrasted responses to Sentimentality and Representational Accuracy with responses to Atmospheric Effect and Symbolic Expression. The general factor might be the same in essence as Eysenck's and Peel's general factors. The writer called it the 'Aesthetic Factor', as representing the most essential quality in art. The bipolar factor might be related to Eysenck's bipolar factor, although the relationship is not very clear, and to Peel's bipolar factor of realism–technique *versus* spontaneity, which is more likely. The writer called this the 'Technical Factor', because it corresponded to the way in which the aesthetically essential qualities were handled in the art in question.

The writer felt that it would be worth while to carry out a similar experiment with real pictures instead of reproductions. With the permission of the Curator, Mr T. E. Hutchison, and the encouragement of Dr T. J. Honeyman, then Director of the Glasgow Art Galleries and Museums, forty-five pictures were selected in the Eighty-fifth Exhibition of the Royal Glasgow Institute of the Fine Arts, 1946. These were 18 landscapes, 10 portraits, 3 still-lifes and 14 other pictures. The painters were 33 Scottish and 10 English artists, and one French artist. The pictures were all about 3 × 4 feet in size and were, of course, distributed among the 787 exhibits. They were chosen to represent a wide range of styles and degrees of artistic quality. Seventeen judges were selected because of their interest in the psychology of art. They were asked to rate the pictures on a 7-point scale, from 0 to +4, for the following ten qualities: harmony of design, sentimentality, harmony of colouring, atmospheric effect, expression of feeling or emotion, interest of subject-matter, rhythm and/or movement, photographic accuracy or realistic naturalism, sentimentality and distortion or symbolic expression. The ratings were added for qualities, intercorrelated and factor-analysed as before, and the results were broadly the same as in the previous experiment (Pickford, 1948a, p. 141, and 1948b; also 1969a). The mean ratings on each quality showed harmony of design and colouring at the top and impressionism and symbolic expression at the bottom.

In this experiment the factorisation showed that, while harmony of design and colouring were still strong as representatives of the general or 'aesthetic' factor, atmospheric effect and rhythm were also very high, but expression of feeling or emotion was much lower than in the previous experiment. This almost certainly reflected an artistic characteristic of Scottish painting. Many of the pictures were very colourful and harmonious landscapes of high atmospheric quality, but were not either emotional, impressionistic or merely realistic. It was interesting also that distortion or symbolic expression was negatively correlated with the general factor to a small degree.

The second or bipolar factor was again of the 'technical' kind found before. It was strongly represented here by the contrast of photographic accuracy or realistic naturalism and sentimentality on the one hand, against impressionistic effect and distortion or symbolic expression on the other hand. This, again, clearly reflected the essential nature of Scottish art in which these pairs of qualities represent opposite directions of this dimension.

As a result of these experiments a number of similar experiments were carried out in the Psychology Department at Glasgow University. One was by Dorothy Lawson and the writer, with the help of Philip Vernon on music, which gave basically similar results (Pickford, 1948a). Another was by D. G. Gunn, on poetry (Gunn, 1951, 1952). Gunn's experiments will be dealt with briefly here, as the most convenient place, although it was not about pictures.

Gunn carried out a factorial study of aesthetic qualities in the appreciation of poetry, by three forms of schoolboys and a class of University students. A third form of 27 boys, a fourth form of 16 boys, a fifth form of 18 boys and a university class of 52 students took part. Nineteen poems were used, being chosen to give as wide a range as possible of types, styles and degrees of merit. They were rated on a 5-point scale from 0–4 for nine qualities, namely liking, comprehension, rhythm, mental imagery, rhyme, emotional appeal, idea or thought (appeal of subject), word music and suitability of expression.

The results were intercorrelated and factor-analysed for qualities for the four groups of subjects separately. The results supported the previous findings of Pickford. There was a general or aesthetic factor, here mainly represented by emotional effect, mode of expression and appeal of subject-matter, and a bipolar or technical factor which contrasted rhyme, word music and rhythm on the one hand, with emotional effect, appeal of subject-matter, comprehension and mental imagery. The aesthetic and technical factors in these experiments are probably complementary to the general and bipolar factors of Burt, Pelling, Dewar and others.

An experiment by McElroy on sculpture was carried out with the permission of Dr T. J. Honeyman in the 'Sculpture in the Open Air' Exhibition of Modern Sculpture, Kelvingrove Park, Glasgow, 1949. One hundred secondary-school pupils between 16 and 18 years of age were the subjects, and judgments were made upon 40 sculptures on a 7-point scale for hedonic tone.

The first aim of this experiment was to discover whether there was any relationship between the hedonic tone of a piece of sculpture and its readiness of recall. A second aim was to analyse and classify the verbal responses made by children to the sculptures. A third aim was the factor analysis of the intercorrelations between nine aesthetic qualities as judged by the subjects. In general, pleasant items were recalled more readily than unpleasant items. The verbal responses fell into twelve different types, which will not be discussed in detail here. The factor analysis showed a large general factor, but three of the qualities, 'distortion', 'abstraction' and 'vagueness', had negative loadings on it. They are particularly characteristic of modern sculpture, and McElroy suggests that they were probably so strong in these sculptures that they rendered the works less meaningful and masked other aesthetic qualities. Factorising intercorrelations between sculptures rather than qualities supported this view, and it seems that some modern works appeal to good taste only after the adoption of a mental set different from that usually adopted by the conventional viewer. This seemed to support doubts about the universality of the general factor of good taste.

The writer also arranged an experiment using 22 of the works of Van Gogh in the exhibition of his paintings held in the Kelvingrove Art Galleries, Glasgow, in 1948, again with the kind permission of Dr T. J. Honeyman (Pickford, 1955a, 1969a). The pictures were chosen to represent as wide as possible a range of Van Gogh's art in its different phases. The same technique was adopted for this experiment and 10 women subjects and 17 men took part, visiting the Exhibition to view and rate the paintings. A 5-point scale was used, from 0 to +4, because many subjects in previous studies had complained about the difficulty of using negative ratings for some qualities. The following nine aesthetic qualities were rated: expressive distortion, dynamic expression, harmony of colouring, emotional expression, harmony of design, liking, impressionistic effect, sentimentality, and photographic accuracy.

There was a general factor most strongly represented by emotional expression, harmony of design, harmony of colouring and dynamic expression. The first bipolar (or second) factor sharply contrasted expressive distortion, harmony of colouring, emotional expressiveness and dynamic expression, against photographic accuracy, impressionistic effect and liking by the subject of the experiment. There was a statistically significant second bipolar (or third) factor in this experiment which contrasted photographic accuracy and harmony of design with expressive distortion and impressionistic effect. These results are largely the same as the results of the writer's previous experiments and the differences are due to the peculiarities of Van Gogh's art.

Another similar experiment was organised by the writer, this time using the pictures in the Exhibition, 'Aspects of Schizophrenic Art', arranged by the Institute of Contemporary Arts and presented in London. It was presented later in Glasgow under the auspices of the Davidson Clinic, Glasgow, in 1956. This was completed with the help of Maurice Green, and will be mentioned again in Chapter 9 (Green and Pickford, 1968).

A. H. Iliffe (1960) pointed out that little attention had been paid to aesthetic preferences for natural beauty and none for human beauty. He used 12 photographs of women's faces taken in uniform conditions, and these were ranked for 'prettiness' by 4,355 readers of a national daily newspaper (*News Chronicle*). Twenty-two intercorrelations between mean rankings of men and women, in four age groups, and of six regional groups, were worked out. Each was of the order of 0·9. Conformity of opinion within groups was significantly different only for the 55 + age group, who had less tendency to agree than the other groups. Factor analysis resulted in a large general factor and a small bipolar factor. Comparison of mean rankings of five occupational groups showed that social status had little effect. Iliffe points out that the conformity of judgments might be due to the possession by all the faces of some intrinsic characteristic (harmony or balance) common to all beautiful things. A more likely explanation, he thinks, is that culturally determined norms are transmitted through education and familiarity with visual and dramatic arts. While there may be wide differences of cultural influence in the choices by individuals of liked and preferred objects, we still have to understand how culturally determined norms are selected and established. This cannot be assumed to be purely by chance, and some 'intrinsic characteristic' must underlie the social processes. He suggests that the general or 'aesthetic' factor in Pickford's experiments might result from the all-or-none responses of indiscriminating subjects, who rated the pictures they liked highly in all the aesthetic characteristics or qualities. This, however, seems very unlikely to the writer, who planned the experiments, discussed them with his subjects and understood their method of work. In addition, different qualities had different loadings on the general factor, and even on Iliffe's supposition this would imply that they were given higher ratings for some qualities—which always tended to be the same—namely, harmony of design and colouring.

Since the problem of 'photographic accuracy' or 'representational accuracy' has been considered as a possible aesthetic quality, it is interesting to mention the experiment by Francès and Voillaume (Robert Francès and Huguette Voillaume, 1964; and Francès, 1968). They used 20 coloured reproductions of paintings, five under each of four headings: portraits of women; landscapes; portraits of children; pictures of flowers; all by well-known artists. Five groups of children were used as subjects, 6–8 years of age, 9–10, 11–12, 13–14 and 15–16 years of age; and four groups of adults, skilled craftsmen, students of philosophy, students of aesthetics and artists. They were asked to arrange each set of five pictures in order of preference and then, as a subsequent and separate operation, in order of fidelity of representation as it appeared to them.

The most striking results showed that for children there was an increasingly close relationship, with increasing age, between order of preference and order of fidelity of representation, for all four types of picture, but it is least marked in respect of portraits of children and pictures of flowers. For adults the correlation between preference and judgment of fidelity of representation was strong for skilled workmen, and tended to become less or even negative for students of philosophy, students of aesthetics and artists. In general this held for all four groups of pictorial material. For children, therefore, the linkage of preference and fidelity of representation is a function of age, but for adults it is reduced by higher education and artistic occupation.

Many other important points emerged in the research, the most interesting of which was the division of reasons or motifs for their choices of preference by subjects into seven categories, each acting in two ways, either positively, to the advantage of the work of art, or negatively, to its disadvantage. Approximately translated they were: *'realism'* (positive: impression of life; negative: banality); *'originality'* (positive: work of imagination; negative:

eccentricity); *'qualities of technique'* (positive: mastery of composition; negative: maladroitness of design); *'qualities of the model or object'* (positive: beauty of appearance; negative: ugliness); *'use of colour or light'* (positive: harmony of colouring, warmth; negative: too strong, obscurity); *'subjective impressions'* (positive: pleasant feelings; negative: unpleasant); *'expressiveness of the appearance of the object or person'* (positive: innocence, romantic appearance; negative: stupid appearance, gloomy landscape). Francès and Voillaume show that in children and adults, when fidelity of representation is an important element in their judgments, there is an increase in the number of positive motifs with degree of fidelity and a decrease in the number of negative motifs.

Fakhir Hussain (1968) has carried out an experimental study comparing the psychological processes involved in the appreciation of abstract and representational *(figuratif)* art. Five reproductions of pictures of each type were exhibited to three groups of subjects, 20–30 years of age, who included students in the Faculty of Letters and of Art History and craftsmen. They had to say whether or not they liked each picture and to give reasons for their choice. Their comments were classified according to a list of nine categories by six judges acting separately.

The data showed that the same subject made statistically significant differences between the use of the nine categories according to whether he was judging abstract or representational pictures. The subjects made more reference to the subject of the picture in judging representational art, but craftsmen more than students in the Faculty of Letters, and less than students in Art History. In judging abstract art the subject of the painting was not available, and there was a tendency to look for meaning in the works (Category 4, *signification*). Also aesthetic quality (Category 1, *qualité sensible*) and technical quality (Category 2, *qualité technique*) were utilised by the majority of subjects.

Other differences are discussed by Fakhir Hussain, who concludes by distinguishing three levels of development in the response or aesthetic preference:

(a) Emotional evaluation—reception of the impact of feeling produced by the picture;

(b) Perceptual evaluation—grasp of the details of the work and their contribution to its whole impression;

(c) Aesthetic evaluation—integration of the details in the form of a new aesthetic appreciation in terms of (a) and (b), which gives rise to (c), not automatically, but depending on many and complex influences which Fakhir Hussain describes.

After this the third level was reached. Those subjects who had difficulty in reaching this stage, however, were unsympathetic towards abstract art, which presented special problems for aesthetic evaluation, but not with representational art which did not present such great difficulties, because it was always possible to find something pleasing or displeasing in it.

Three experiments should be mentioned here which dealt with the analysis of the dimensional qualities of paintings. Choynowski (1967) carried out a factor analysis of semantic differential data, using 72 bipolar scales, for 21 works of Polish contemporary painters, evaluated by 17 to 23 artists. He showed that there were eight factors, namely (1) artistic value (original-commonplace); (2) interpretation (objective-subjective); (3) mood (serene-gloomy); (4) composition (dynamic-static); (5) tonality (warm-cold); (6) elaboration (sketchy-worked out); (7) content (full-devoid); (8) geometricity (geometric-not geometric). The paintings fell into two large clusters (modern and traditional) and a small cluster with literary content.

Klein and Skager (1967) studied the distinction between 'spontaneous' and 'deliberate' drawing styles due to Burkhart. They showed that one group of artists was very sensitive to this distinction, attributing high quality to the spontaneous paintings. Another group of artists based their evaluations on an unrelated dimension, and apparently preferred more 'deliberate' paintings.

The non-artist group clearly preferred representational paintings. Although they did not agree with the experts on what would be a good painting, they could easily learn to make judgments in accordance with at least one group of experts.

Künnapas and Norman (1970) investigated nine still-life paintings by Cézanne by the method of multi-dimensional similarity analysis. Three groups of subjects took part, namely painters, art pupils and non-art students. Three factors were found as the basis of similarity judgments of the paintings, namely (1) 'complex horizontally arranged motive'; (2) 'vertical central figure'; (3) 'central figure without background'. Among other conclusions, it was shown that differences between painters and non-art students were greater than between painters and art pupils, or between art pupils and students. Also the differences between the groups of subjects were at least partly due to the formal artistic approach, which is most dominant in painters, less dominant in art pupils and found very little in non-art students.

Picture-making and aesthetic judgment of apes

In his book on the picture-making of the great apes, Desmond Morris (1962) has shown that these animals have considerable aesthetic ability. In all 32 apes have been studied as artists by various workers, and these are mentioned by Morris. Mainly chimpanzees were included, but there were also two gorillas, three orang-utans and four capuchins. One chimpanzee, Alpha, studied by Scheller in the years 1941–51, made 200 pictures and Congo, a chimpanzee studied by Morris himself between 1958 and 1959, made 384. Many coloured illustrations and text-figures of their work leave no doubt that these animals were aesthetically sensitive. Many serious artists would have been glad to produce some of the ape's pictures which Morris illustrates. In addition, Morris quotes the results of experiments by Rensch to test various species for aesthetic preference for more *versus* less regular patterns and these showed that a capuchin monkey, a geunon monkey, a jackdaw and a crow showed statistically significant frequencies of preference for the more regular patterns (1962, pp. 159–61).

Morris argues that the following six principles apply to picture-making, 'from Leonardo to Congo' (p. 158):
1. Self-rewarding activation;
2. Compositional control;
3. Calligraphic differentiation;
4. Thematic variation;
5. Optimum heterogeneity;
6. Universal imagery.

The only one of these principles about which the present writer feels any doubt is the sixth, universal imagery. It does not seem, however, that Morris intends to refer to the Jungian concept of universal unconscious imagery. He simply points out that art from many and diverse sources, such as the houses drawn by children from Denmark, France, India, Finland and Germany (p. 166), are similar. They are all rectangular and have windows, a door and a roof, although they are very diverse in other ways.

He also cites the golden section (pp. 166–7), showing that the majority of judges prefer the proportion 1 to 1·618, as explained in Chapter 2.

An experiment of considerable interest in this connection was carried out by Fakhir Hussain (1962, pp. 49, 54–5 and 74). The present writer is grateful for permission of the Goldsmiths' Librarian, University of London, and of Dr Fakhir Hussain, to make this mention of the work, and also two other notes about it, pp. 175, 203. Hussain used coloured slides and coloured postcard reproductions of 16 paintings, in two sets of 8, such that each set contained two pictures from each of four sources, namely, Picasso, P. Reid, a young painter 'of some recognition', children (10 years old and slightly backward), and the chimpanzee Congo (Morris D., 1962). It was postulated that the paintings of Picasso, Reid, children and Congo should be preferred in that order; Picasso being most preferred.

There were 150 subjects in the experiment, in five groups of thirty, as follows:

1. English children—9–10 years old, both sexes;
2. English university students, 20–30 years old, both sexes;
3. Indian university students, 20–30 years old, mostly male;
4. French university students, 20–30 years old, both sexes; and
5. English art students, 20–30 years old, both sexes.

The result of this part of Hussain's experiment was that no group of subjects, under any condition, ranked Picasso, Reid, child art and Congo in that order, as predicted. In addition, the art students did not show any more consistency in their preference judgments under any conditions, in comparison with the other student groups. In other words, there was no support for the theory that so-called better paintings would be more consistently preferred than, for instance, the paintings of children or of a chimpanzee, or that art students would be more consistent than other student groups in such preferences.

Time of decision and eye-movements

As examples of the many other experimental studies of picture material two further researches may be chosen.

The first was an investigation by Genevieve Oleron (1966) of the relationship between the time taken to make a decision about which is the better of a pair of photographs and the degree of difference of aesthetic quality between them. Ten photographs were used, which were first judged, using the method of paired comparisons, while the time taken for each decision by each of 14 subjects was recorded. After this they were arranged in order of preference, and then rated on a 6-point scale by each of the critics, for three aesthetic principles, namely, (1) quality of the subject, photographed, in terms of originality, documentary character, etc.; (2) photographic technique, lighting, etc.; (3) spontaneous response of feeling or personal preference.

It was predicted that those photographs which, when presented as pairs, had a greater difference of aesthetic value or quality between them would take a longer time to be judged and those pairs which were wider apart on the aesthetic scale would take a shorter time. This prediction was confirmed by the experiment and the length of time taken to judge the aesthetic difference between two pictures may be taken as a measure of the magnitude of the difference between them.

As a second example, the study of eye-movements in viewing pictures may be taken. This has excited interest for many years, but, after reviewing the problems and referring to Stratton's work (1903), Valentine (1962, p. 18) comes to the conclusion that, 'Indeed, it is clear that we can take in the beauty of a line or figure without *any* movement of the eye' (original italics).

The subject has, however, found some more recent enthusiasts. For instance, Molnar (Molnar, F., 1964, 1965, 1966 and 1968) has shown that the movements of the eyes in viewing a painting follow the principal objects and forms in the picture and that, from a record of eye-movements, it is possible to reconstruct the essentials of the pictorial composition. It was also shown that fixation points are determined by significant elements in a painting, and it was particularly interesting that colours in stimulus patterns have important effects. When orange, green and yellow stimulus spots were used in irregular order in lines of 10 dots, the number correctly perceived was greater for yellow than for green and for green than orange. In perceiving the correct position of a ring-like stimulus which had a gap variable in position, however, the correct localisation of the gap was more frequent for orange than yellow and for yellow than green.

Molnar asks how it is possible to comprehend the 'unifying power' which is responsible for the assembly of colours in an abstract painting, without knowing the exploratory movements of the eyes in viewing it, when these movements are themselves objective expressions of that 'power'. He also asks whether, without knowing the eye-movements, is it possible to answer the question posed by E. Souriau: how can we know what are the parts we must bring together in a picture, so that it should be an integrated whole, since the movements are as it were the hands of the maker of this ensemble? (1966, p. 146).

Ceccato (1966) has also stressed the significance of eye-movements, saying that in the functions of observation, eyes, hands, etc., are generally very active. He gives an example of the eye-movements and points of fixation in viewing a simple line consisting of two limbs of equal length making a right-angle. The exploratory nature of the eye-movements is clearly evident. However, although Molnar, Ceccato and others have shown that eye-movements occur during aesthetic perception and accord with the organisation of works of art, it is difficult to see that they are essential to it.

Bibliography and References
for Chapter 6

BELL, CLIVE (1916). *Art*. London: Chatto and Windus.

BULLEY, MARGARET (1925). *Art and Counterfeit*. London: Methuen.

BULLEY, MARGARET (1933). *Have You Good Taste?* London: Methuen.

BULLEY, MARGARET (1934). An Inquiry into the Aesthetic Judgments of Children. *Brit. J. Educ. Psychol., 4,* 162–82.

BULLEY, MARGARET (1951). *Art and Everyman*. London: Batsford.

BURT, C. (1924). Psychological Tests of Educable Capacity. Ch. I in *Report of the Consultative Committee of the Board of Education*. London.

BURT, C. (1933). *How the Mind Works*. London: Allen and Unwin; ch. 15, The Psychology of Art.

BURT, C., and BULLEY, M. (1933). *The Listener*, BBC, London, *9;* 8 January, 8 February and 27 December, 1933.

CECCATO, S. (1966). '*Chronique, Art et Genres Artistiques.*' *Sciences de l'Art, Numero Spécial*, 1966, 31–46.

CHILD, I. L. (1962). Personal Preferences as an Expression of Aesthetic Sensitivity. *J. Personality, 30,* 496–512.

CHILD, I. L. (1966). The Problem of Objectivity in Esthetic Value. *Penn State Papers in Art Education. The Pennsylvania State University, Department of Art Education, no. 1.*

CHOYNOWSKI, M. (1967). Dimensions of Painting. *Percept. and Motor Skills, 25,* p. 128.

DEWAR, HEATHER (1938). A Comparison of Tests of Artistic Appreciation. *Brit. J. Educ. Psychol., 8,* 29–49.

EYSENCK, H. J. (1940a). Some Factors in the Appreciation of Poetry. *Character and Personality, 9,* 160–7.

EYSENCK, H. J. (1940b). The General Factor in Aesthetic Judgments. *Brit. J. Psychol., 31,* 94–102.

EYSENCK, H. J. (1941). 'Type'-Factors in Aesthetic Judgments. *Brit. J. Psychol., 31,* 262–70.

FRANCÈS, R., (1968). *Psychologie de l'Esthétique*. Paris: P.U.F.

FRANCÈS, R., and VOILLAUME, H. (1964). '*Une Composante du Jugement Pictural : La Fidelité de la Representation.*' *Rev. Psychologique Française, 9,* 241–56.

GORDON, D. A. (1951–2). Methodology in the Study of Art Evaluation. *J. Aesthet. and Art Criticism, 10,* 338–52.

GORDON, D. A. (1955). Artistic Excellence of Oil Paintings as judged by Experts and Laymen. *J. Educ. Research, 48,* 474–588.

GORDON, D. A. (1956–7). Individual Differences in the Evaluation of Art. *J. Educ. Research, 50,* 17–30.

GORDON, KATE (1923). A Study of Esthetic Judgments. *J. Exptl. Psychol., 6,* 36–43.

GREEN, MAURICE, and PICKFORD, R. W. (1968). A Factor Analysis of Ratings of Schizophrenic Paintings. *Proc. Fifth Int. Congress of Aesthetics.* Amsterdam, 1964. Amsterdam: Mouton.

GUNN, D. G. (1951). Factors in the Appreciation of Poetry. *Brit. J. Educ. Psychol., 21,* 96–104.

GUNN, D. G. (1952). Further Observations on Factors in the Appreciation of Poetry. *Quart. Bull. Brit. Psychol. Soc., 3, 15,* 24–6.

HUSSAIN, FAKHIR (1962). *An Experimental Enquiry into the Phenomena of 'Aesthetic Judgements' Under Varying Time Conditions.* Ph.D. Thesis, University of London (unpublished).

HUSSAIN, FAKHIR (1968). *'Une Approche Psychologique de l'Art Abstrait.'* *Proc. Fifth Internat. Congress of Aesthetics.* Amsterdam 1964. Amsterdam; Mouton, pp. 897–900.

ILIFFE, A. H. (1960). A Study of Preferences in Feminine Beauty. *Brit. J. Psychol., 51,* 267–73.

ISRAELI, N. (1928). Affective Reactions to Painting Reproductions. *J. Appl. Psychol., 12,* 125–39.

KLEIN, S. P., and SKAGER, R. W. (1967). 'Spontaneity vs. Deliberateness' as a Dimension of Esthetic Judgment. *Percept. and Motor Skills, 25,* pp. 161–8.

KÜNNAPAS, T., and NORMAN, MARY (1970). Inter-individual Differences in similarity Estimates of Paintings. *Reports from the Psychological Laboratories,* University of Stockholm, *Number 295.* May 1970, pp. 1–11.

McELROY, W. A. (1950a). Responses to Traditional and Modern Sculpture, and the Factors Influencing its Recall. *Quart. Bull. Brit. Psychol. Soc., 1, 8,* 310–31.

McElroy, W. A. (1950b). The Appreciation of Sculpture. *Scottish Art Review, 3,* 11–15.

MOLNAR, F. (1964). *'Les Mouvements Exploratoires des Yeux dans la Composition Picturale.'* *Sciences de l'Art, 1,* 135–50.

MOLNAR, F. (1965). *'Contribution à l'Étude Expérimentale de la Composition Picturale.'* *Sciences de l'Art, 2.*

MOLNAR, F. (1966). *'Aspect Temporel de la Perception de l'Oeuvre Picturale'.* *Sciences de l'Art, Numero Spécial,* 136–46.

MOLNAR, F. (1968). *'Recherche Experimentale sur le Role des Mouvements Oculaires dans l'Appréciation de la Composition Picturale.'* *Proc. Fifth Internat. Congress Aesthet.,* Amsterdam, 1964; Mouton, pp. 905–10.

MORRIS, DESMOND (1962). The Biology of Art: *A Study of the Picture-Making Behaviour of the Great Apes and its Relationship to Human Art,* London: Methuen,

OLERON, G. (1966). 'Jugement Esthétique et Temps de Décision.' Sciences de l'Art, Special Number, 1966, 47–67.
PEEL, E. A. (1945). On Identifying Aesthetic Types. Brit. J. Psychol., 35, 61–9.
PEEL, E. A. (1946). A New Method for Analysing Aesthetic Preferences: Some Theoretical Considerations. Psychometrica, 11, 129–37.
PICKFORD, R. W. (1940). Social Psychology and Some Problems of Artistic Culture. Brit. J. Psychol., 30, 197–210.
PICKFORD, R. W. (1948a). 'Aesthetic' and 'Technical' Factors in Artistic Appreciation. Brit. J. Psychol., 38, 135–41.
PICKFORD, R. W. (1948b). Form and Expression in Art. Scottish Art Review, 2, 7–11.
PICKFORD, R. W. (1955a). 'Une Expérience avec les Peintures de van Gogh.' L'Année Propedeutique. Paris, 9, 505–10.
PICKFORD, R. W. (1955b). Factorial Studies of Aesthetic Judgments. ch. 37 in Roback, A. A. (Ed.), Present-Day Psychology. Norfolk, USA: Philosophical Library.
PICKFORD, R. W. (1969). The Psychology of Ugliness. Brit. J. Aesthet., 9, 258–70.
PICKFORD, R. W. (1969a). 'Études Expérimentales de Peintures Écossaises et de Tableuax de van Gogh.' Sciences de l'Art 6, 53–63.
STRATTON, G. M. (1903). Eye Movements and the Aesthetics of Visual Form. Philos. Studies, 20, and Experimental Psychology and Culture, 1903.
VALENTINE, C. W. (1962). The Experimental Psychology of Beauty. London: Methuen.
WILLIAMS, E. D., WINTER, L., and WOODS, J. M. (1938). Tests of Literary Appreciation. Brit. J. Educ. Psychol., 8, 265–84.

7

Racial and cultural comparisons

The importance of cross-cultural studies, and studies revealing differences or uniformity between races, is so great that they will justify a separate chapter, although there is not as yet a sufficiently wide range of such studies. This chapter will open with a selection of studies of colour preferences and colour connotations among peoples of different cultural and racial groups, and proceed to the study of shapes and figures and then to picture-material. Some investigations in which children were subjects will be included here, because the significance of these studies in relation to cross-cultural problems is greater than their relevance to children's aesthetic judgments and also an experiment using African masks, although it is really about carving or sculptural material.

Colour preferences of non-white people

Many studies have been made of the colour preferences of non-white peoples (see Burnham, Hanes and Bartleson, 1963, p. 210). Garth (1922) studied the colour preferences of 559 full-blooded North American Indians, aged 7 to 21 years. Most were children. Colour disks of saturated colours were used and the main result was that red was most preferred. Yellow was the least liked. No marked sex differences were found.

A study of 1,152 Mexican children was made by Gesche (1927), who also used coloured disks. The order of preference was: red, green, blue, violet, orange, white, yellow.

Garth and Collado (1929) made an investigation of 1,000 Filipino children from first grade up to high school, ages 6 to 17 years. Milton Bradley coloured papers were used, and the results showed the order of preference to be as before, red, green, blue, violet, orange, white, yellow. Again no marked sex differences were found.

In comparison with these results it is interesting to recall, from Chapter 4, that St George found the order of preference for 500 US college students was: blue, green, red, yellow, orange, violet, white; and Eysenck found: blue, red, green, violet, orange, yellow for 15 men, and blue, red, green, violet, yellow, orange for 15 women, in England. Although cross-cultural comparisons of this kind and those which follow in the next paragraphs are interesting and valuable as experimental results, it is not easy to interpret them and to say how far and in what ways they depend on tradition, convention and fashion.

In an investigation of 1,011 Japanese children by Garth, Kunihei and Langdon (1931) coloured disks of saturated colours were used. The children varied in age from 6 to 18 years. Red was the most popular colour and blue the next. Among children up to 15 years of age, red was most popular with girls, and blue next, but blue was the most popular with boys, with red next.

Chou and Chen (1935) studied 442 middle school pupils in China and 100 university freshmen. They were asked to give the names they preferred for objects or groups of objects. The order of preference was white, blue, red, yellow, green, black, orange, violet, grey. In another enquiry on Chinese children (N. C. Shen, 1937) aged about 15 to 18 years, 1,300 subjects were tested with colours by the method of paired comparisons. Boys gave the order blue, white, red, green, yellow, orange, violet, and girls the order white, red, blue, green, yellow, orange, violet.

Garth, Moses and Anthony (1938) reported a research on 1,078 East Indians attending school in Bijnor, ranging in age from 5–26 years. Omitting younger children in the present chapter, the older East Indians tested by Garth are compared with young Americans in Table 7.1.

The orders of preference are green, red, blue, orange, violet, yellow, white, for East Indians; and blue, green, violet, orange and red, yellow, white for American Whites.

TABLE 7.1

Comparison of High School E. Indians with American Whites
(Garth *et al.*)

Race	WHITE	YELLOW	VIOLET	ORANGE	BLUE	RED	GREEN
			Colour scale value				
E. Indians	0	34	87	132	154	195	210
Amer. Whites	0	22	78	48	194	48	100

As mentioned in Chapter 4, Eysenck pooled the results of sixteen studies of white and ten studies of non-white subjects. He dealt only with those in which saturated colours were used, and confined himself to certain colours which appeared in all the studies and which are shown in Table 7.2. Children's judgments of preference were, however, included and pooled with these for adults. This gave him 12,175 white and 8,885 non-white subjects, in all the 26 studies of colour preferences. The average rankings of colour preferences obtained are shown in Table 7.2. The order of preferences for white people was blue, red, green, violet,

TABLE 7.2

*Average rankings of colour preferences in 16 experiments
on white and 10 non-white people*

Colour Used	White subjects (12,175)	Non-white subjects (8,885)	Weighted total (21,060)
Blue	1·12	1·83	1·42
Red	2·32	2·03	2·20
Green	3·32	2·98	3·18
Violet	3·66	4·28	3·92
Orange	5·30	4·76	5·07
Yellow	5·28	5·12	5·21

yellow, orange, and for non-white it was blue, red, green, violet, orange, yellow. Such a close average correspondence suggests in Eysenck's opinion a general factor, probably of a physiological nature, he thinks, and related to his concept of T or 'good taste' in the appreciation of pictorial and other material. The difficulty about the assumption of good taste is, of course, that while good taste in a narrow sense might be represented by average preferences for colours, its relation to higher aesthetic judgment and the aesthetic quality of pictures and artistic objects and material is an altogether different matter. A picture or work of art least conforming to good taste might easily be aesthetically the best, and if artists assumed that their work would be good if it corresponded to average preferences they would never go far.

McElroy (1952) was very critical of Eysenck's concept of 'good taste' of an interracial kind, based on inherited predispositions. In his research in Australia, which will be mentioned again, he used a battery of 10 ranking tests, including 10 items each of several sets of picture material and also 10 polygons and 10 colours, planned to accord with Eysenck's requirements. The work was carried out in the 1952 expedition to Arnhem Land of Professor A. D. Elkin. The tests were given to forty Aborigines at Old Beswick Aboriginal Reserve and to forty male white students in the University of Sydney. McElroy concludes that his results support the view that the 'beauty' of a visual object is almost entirely determined by the cultural conditioning of perception.

In respect of colour only, it is interesting that average correlations between Whites for the ten colours was 0·28 and for Aborigines it was 0·16, as shown in Table 7.3. All the correlations in McElroy's

TABLE 7·3

Average correlations between preferences for items in McElroy's Tests for Australian Aborigines and Whites

| | Average Correlations | | |
Test	Between Aborigines	Between Whites	Between Whites and Aborigines
Birds	0·34*	0·41*	−0·03
Tartans	0·28*	0·20*	−0·16*
Flowers	0·05	0·29*	−0·04
Fishes	0·16*	0·35*	0·11*
Landscapes	0·00	0·06	0·02
Paul Klee	0·03	0·07	−0·02
Colours	0·16*	0·28*	0·11
Polygons	0·08*	0·09*	0·03
Butterflies	0·31*	0·12*	0·10*
Portraits (Whites)	0·17*	0·36*	0·07
Portraits (Blacks)	0·26*	0·34*	−0·18*

* Statistically significant

tests are shown in this table, and will be discussed again later in this chapter.

Two valuable contributions to the cross-cultural study of colour preferences have been made recently by Kastl and Child on US and Vietnam children (Kastl and Child, 1968) and by Child and Iwao on US and Japanese students (Child and Iwao, 1969).

In the study of Vietnam children the Munsell colour stimuli described in the paper by Child, Hansen and Hornbeck (1968) were used in Saigon. Pairs of colour stimuli were displayed and the students were asked to indicate for each pair which colour appealed more, just as a colour. There was a division at the median age approximately, which gave 131 younger and 174 older girls and 186 younger and 197 older boys. Their results were compared with those obtained with US children and reported in the paper by Child et al. (1968) just mentioned.

With regard to hue, six pairs of stimuli compared colours identical in saturation and brightness, but one was the cooler complementary of the other. For these 76 per cent of the girls and 74 per cent of the boys preferred the cooler hue. Similar preferences were found in US children, namely 63 per cent for each sex.

For saturation differences, eight pairs of stimuli were of colours identical in hue and brightness, but differing in saturation. The Vietnam boys showed 68 per cent preference for the more saturated colour, but the girls were indifferent, only 47 per cent preferring it. US children, on the other hand, showed 67 per cent preference for the more saturated colour among girls, and 82 per cent among the boys.

Six pairs of stimuli differed only in brightness and for these the Vietnam boy students preferred the brighter colour by 74 per cent and the girls by 58 per cent. US boys preferred the brighter colour by 56 per cent and girls by 73 per cent.

The Vietnam children showed the same trend as the US children with increasing age towards consistency of choice along the hue dimension in comparison with the saturation dimension, but less decisively.

In their discussion, Kastl and Child say that their results strongly suggest that universalities of human nature may have a constraining influence towards similarities of preference, but do not always produce it, because the two cultural groups gave considerably different results. The present writer, however, would no more be inclined to think that similarities must be supposed to be due to the qualities of innate human nature, than that differences must be due to cultural influences. Both might or might not be due to either.

The investigation by Child and Iwao (1969) on students of Japan employed a wider range of stimuli, namely 85 pairs of Munsell colour patches mounted on cards of dull white mat. Over 100 subjects took part: male US undergraduates of Yale College, and female undergraduates of Smith College and seven other colleges. The Japanese students were mostly from Keio University and some of the women from other colleges.

Twenty stimulus items contrasted pairs of colours only in brightness. For these both the women of US and of Japan showed no consistent brightness preference. The Japanese men showed a slight preference for brighter colours (56·7%), but the US men preferred brighter colours much less often (39·9%).

Twenty of the stimulus items contrasted colours only in saturation. For these all groups showed an average preference for the more saturated colours. A further 20 items provided contrasts only between complementary hues on 10 evenly spaced diameters of the colour circle. For these there was evidence of preference for cooler colours over warmer colours—65·6 per cent among Japanese women compared with 69·8 per cent among US women, and 60·9 per cent among Japanese men compared with 71·8 per cent among US men. When colours close together on the colour circle were compared there was still a general tendency to prefer the cooler colour, but it is not surprising that the average preference for the cooler of hues close together should be less marked than when they are wider apart, since the two hues differ much less in appearance when near together.

Individual differences in preferences were considered, as revealed by the data, and these proved to show considerable consistency for each individual subject. Individual consistency, however, was decidedly greater for American than for Japanese subjects. Child and Iwao think this may be due to the greater role played in their culture by aesthetic interest and sensitivity.

An experiment of considerable interest, but less closely related to aesthetics than those just mentioned, was reported by Osgood (Osgood, C. E., 1960, especially pp. 163–5). In this research 21

Navajo subjects and 24 Anglo subjects provided semantic differential data upon eight colours (red, yellow, green, blue, purple, brown, black and white) in respect of 27 scales, such as from 'good' to 'bad', 'happy' to 'sad' (evaluative), 'strong' to 'weak' (potency), 'fast' to 'slow' (activity) or 'up' to 'down'. This means that they graded each colour on the various scales to indicate their impression of its proximity to one or other end of each scale, using six intermediate steps, the middle step being omitted to force some directional choice in each case.

Osgood analyses the data to show how far there was agreement or disagreement between Anglos and Navajos. In general there was much agreement, especially in respect of brightness, along the evaluative scales. Thus white was *good, happy, pretty, sweet,* and *clean* for both groups, whereas black was *rougher, angrier* and more *crooked*. Saturation also gave much agreement, especially along the potency scales. Saturated colours were *stronger, harder, heavier, larger* and *thicker* than unsaturated colours. Hue, however, gave rise to some differences between the groups, especially in the activity scales. The Anglos tended more to think of red as being *fast, sharp, energetic* or *young,* and blue or purple as *passive* in comparison. The Navajos tended more to think of green as *cold, quiet, loose* and *unripe,* than as their opposites, although the Anglos agreed with green being *cold* and *unripe* rather than *hot* or *ripe*. In respect of colour connotation some interesting contrasts were that red was *pretty, young, energetic, straight* and *thick* for the Anglos, but the Navajos thought of red as *taut, angry* and *masculine*. Yellow was *small, fast* and *smooth* and green *weak, fast* and *smooth* for the Anglos, but not for the Navajos. There was perfect agreement about white, with one exception, for the Anglos it was 'quite fast' but for the Navajos 'quite slow'. Other colours were judged more diversely, thus blue was more *sad, sour, thick, cold, straight* and *black*; purple more *sad, sour, thick, down* and *black*; brown more *sad, sour* and *dull*; and black was more *sour, dull, down* and *poor,* than for the Navajos. On the whole, it may be said that white was judged more favourably and black less favourably, red as more active and blue or purple more passive, and saturated colours as more potent than unsaturated colours by both Anglo and Navajo groups.

A connection of some of the differences between the Anglos and Navajos with culture, and hence with art, might be seen, as pointed out by Kluckhohn (Osgood, 1960, p. 165, footnote), who said that 'color enters very prominently into Navajo cere-monialism, and therefore the reaction to such a color as red is culturally influenced in a very special way'. Osgood adds the comment that, 'Such ceremonial usages of color undoubtedly account for some of the differences found in this study. The fact that great similarities in color connotation are found despite such ceremonial usage may mean that the significances attached to colors in ceremonies themselves tend to follow the same rule of synesthetic translation'.

Stewart and Baxter (1969) recently reported a research on the colour preferences of three 'ethnic' groups, in which four pictures were used with various combinations of colours. The pictures were: a man, a woman, a house and a car. Four colour combinations were used, namely, monochrome; naturalistic ground and naturalistic object; unnatural object and natural ground; natural object but unnatural ground. Each picture was presented in each of the four combinations. The authors do not specify the colours used.

The experimental population was 162 elementary school children in a large metropolitan district, including 54 children in each of the groups: Negro, Latin, Anglo. In each group there were three age groups: 6–7 years; 8–9 years and 11–13 years, with 9 children of each sex in each age group.

The conclusions from a study of the preferences for the pictures, liking, indifference and disliking, showed that all the children tended to prefer coloured to monochrome pictures at all age groups. There was an interesting change in colour preferences. While the variant colorations were preferred by the younger groups, naturalistic colouring became more important to the older groups. There was also a general pattern of less preference for monochrome and naturalistic combinations and more prefer-ence for colour variations in the human figures rather than the ground, while the unnatural woman figure and the unnatural ground for the man were more often preferred. No difference of colour preference between the Negro, Latin and Anglo groups was found in this study.

In an experiment on a principal component analysis of semantic differential judgments of single colours and pairs of colours, mentioned on p. 79, James Hogg (1969) found that for pairs of colours the main influences on the subjects were (a) 'blatant-muted', or 'active-passive', (b) hedonic effect, (c) 'warmth' and/or 'excitingness' or 'activity' and (d) 'obvious-unusualness', in that order of importance. He points out (1969, p. 138) that in a Japanese research Kansaku (1963) also found four factors in judgments of colour pairs, namely, (a) pleasure, (b) brightness, (c) strength and (d) warmth, in that order. After a brief discussion of some points of difference between his own findings and those of Kansaku, Hogg comments that the overall similarity of results from British and Japanese subjects is quite impressive.

Choungourian (1968) used eight colours in a cross-cultural experiment on colour preferences, namely red, orange, yellow, yellow-green, green, blue-green, blue and purple, on the Ostwald system, and differing only in hue. By the method of paired comparisons he obtained the preference orders for these colours, for 160 adults subjects, all being university students, among whom equal numbers were American, Lebanese, Iranian and Kuwaiti. Highest preferences were red by Americans, green by Lebanese and blue-green by the other two groups. Lowest preferences were blue-green by Americans, purple by Lebanese and Iranese, and blue by Kuwaiti. Choungourian concludes from his experiment that one cannot give a universal order of colour preferences for different cultural groups, but adds that the sex differences are not as obvious as the cultural differences.

Cultural influences on preferences for designs and shapes

One of the earliest and most interesting studies of cultural or racial influences in art was the work of Thouless on the use of divergent perspective in much Eastern Art (Thouless, 1932). He pointed out that in Eastern Art there is often a difference from what we should regard as the true perspective representation of parallel-sided objects receding into space, and circular objects seen in perspective. He linked this with the evidence that a group of 20 Indians had greater size constancy, and greater phenomenal regression for shape, than 49 British subjects. Size constancy or phenomenal regression, as explained in Chapter 2, means that the diminution in apparent size of objects as they recede into space, and their change in perspective shape, is not in proportion to their calculated sizes or shapes according to the laws of perspective, but is much nearer the size or shape they would have if there were no perspective diminution. For this group of Indian people Thouless showed that phenomenal regression was greater than for the British group, and, of course, if an object such as a box or rug is shown actually increasing in size as it becomes more distant, then phenomenal regression would be greater than unity, which would be its measure if for any individual its size remained apparently unchanged in perspective.

The question whether some Eastern artists may have phenomenal regression as great as this is undecided, but Thouless had at least one subject who was not an artist and for whom it was greater than unity. In any case, the representation of rectangular objects with increasing size, reversing our ordinary ideas of perspective, is to some extent a convention in Eastern Art, although it is not invariably done. Indeed it is not confined to Eastern Art, but is also found in Primitive European Art, before 'accurate' perspective was introduced, and in Modern Art, where the artist has apparently reverted to the mode of seeing characteristic of Primitive artists. A well-known example of this is Van Gogh's famous painting 'The Yellow Chair'. It is almost certain that Van Gogh was a paranoid schizophrenic, and it has been shown that schizophrenics often have a breakdown of reality perception, in which phenomenal regression, which is a form of adjustment of perception to reality, is reduced so that they are more affected by perspective than persons with good and normal reality adjustment. Phenomenal regression is greater for paranoids (Raush, 1952). We could not, however, suggest that many or most Eastern and Primitive artists were paranoid schizophrenics. There must be another explanation, and it might be that these artists, and indeed the public for whom they made their pictures, had greater phenomenal regression than we have and found the reversals of perspective natural or even 'realistic'.

One of Thouless's students, W. M. Beveridge (1935), carried out some important experiments on phenomenal regression among West Africans from the Gold Coast, Ashanti and Togoland. In one series of experiments he used 49 African men about 19 years of age, comparable with British university students, who were students of the Presbyterian Training College, Akropong. All were studying drawing. He showed that they had a greater tendency to constancy of shape than 105 British students studied by Thouless. In another experiment he showed that 44 of the

Africans had greater tendency to constancy of size than 35 British students whom Thouless tested. This would tend to support Thouless's views about the art of non-Europeans.

In connection with Thouless's interesting experiment and the hypothesis about the effect of phenomenal regression Zajac (1961) and Wyburn, Pickford and Hirst (1964, pp. 230–1) have suggested, as already mentioned, that at least in certain cases divergent perspective may have some justification. Another possibility, of course, is that the primitive and modern artist often drew what he knew rather than what he saw, and he might sometimes show both left and right sides of a rectangular box because he knew they were there.

In an experiment carried out on 380 boys and 399 girls between the ages of 9 and 16 years in three Scottish schools McElroy (1954) showed that there was a tendency for boys to prefer rounded and curved forms and for girls to prefer angular or elongated forms of comparable designs, such as a circle (rounded) and a triangle (angular). Twelve pairs of designs were used (Fig. 18). He also showed that there was a significant rise in male preferences for rounded forms and a decrease in the frequency of female preferences also for rounded forms, above rather than below the age of 12 years. McElroy calls the rounded forms 'female' and the angular ones 'male', in accordance with his understanding of psychoanalytic unconscious symbolisms. The research suggested strongly that an unconsciously determined sex difference in preference for simple forms was at work, especially in view of the change reported at the age of puberty.

A modified form of this experiment was carried out by Jahoda (1956) on 858 boys and girls from Middle Schools in Accra. He showed that there was a greatly reduced but still statistically significant sex difference of the same kind as found by McElroy. However, while Scottish boys and girls both diverged significantly with increasing age, the Accra boys did not increase their preferences for rounded forms with age, while the Accra girls moved significantly with increasing age towards the preference pattern of the boys. McElroy discussed several hypotheses which his findings might support, but the most likely was that there is a repressed tendency to choose female symbolic shapes by boys, and male symbolic shapes by girls, which is intensified by the increasing repression required to counteract the growing sexuality of adolescents. Jahoda agreed that this general hypothesis would be supported by the Accra results. The difference between Accra and Scottish results could also support subsidiary ideas of a cultural kind, namely that in Accra boys' overt sexual achievement with consequent reduction of tension due to repression occurs

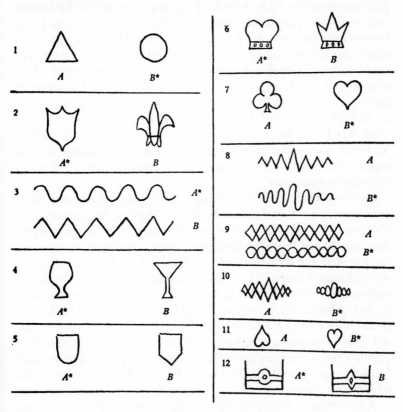

Fig. 18   *McElroy's Figures* (McElroy, 1954).

at a relatively later age, while in girls sexual maturity and overt sexual experiences are achieved after about the age of fifteen, bringing a reduction of tension earlier than in Scottish girls. The general result of a greatly reduced sex difference of shape choices in Accra as compared with Scotland was also understandable in terms of the fact that there is much less sexual repression in Accra.

It will be seen from Table 7.3 that McElroy (1952) showed that there were low but statistically significant correlations between the preferences of Australian Aborigines for certain designs or shapes, namely 0·28 for tartans and 0·08 for polygons. There were similar small but statistically significant correlations between the preferences of the white people of Sydney, namely 0·20 for tartans and 0·09 for polygons. When correlations were worked out between the preferences of Aborigines and Whites, a negative and significant correlation of −0·16 was found for tartans, and a very small and not significant correlation of 0·03 for polygons. This means that, while there was a modest but decided amount of agreement within each of the cultural or racial groups, there was no agreement between the groups themselves. This accorded with what was found for colours and other items in the test battery. McElroy points out that the results of his experiment do not support the concept of an interracial or cross-cultural conformity of design preferences.

McElroy discusses some cultural influences which may have contributed to the differences in preferences for tartans and polygons between Aborigines and Whites. 'An inspection of the data here shows that the Aborigines placed highly multi-coloured tartans near the top, while the whites preferred more "modest" monochrome tartans. The Glen Cameron is a typical Aboriginal preference, while the McAlpine is a typical white preference' (p. 92). Also, in the polygons, 'the Aboriginal subjects in the test situation had shown a large tendency to thrust meaning upon the polygonal figures—a relatively complex and poorly symmetrical polygon often bringing the remark "Star". A poorly symmetrical hexagon was placed much higher by the Aborigines than the whites' (pp. 92–3).

A not unrelated experiment was carried out by R. Davis (1961) in Tanganyika. He asked native children of the isolated Mahali peninsula, on the eastern shore of Lake Tanganyika, to select which of two figures was to be called a man and which a woman. One figure had a square head and the other a round head, as shown in Fig. 19. In Tanganyika 231 boys and 15 girls took part. They were probably about 10 years of age. He reports similar experiments by Miss Helen Ross on 163 East London school children between 11 and 14 years of age, and by Mrs Susie Robinson on 118 school children of 13 to 14 years of age in Wheatley Village,

Oxfordshire. In the East London group the boys gave statistically significant choices (53–24) favouring the square-headed figure for a woman, but the girls strongly favoured the square-headed figure for a man (73 to 13). This unexpected tendency in the boys Davis explains by the inclination of boys of that age to think of women as 'squares'—that is, an 'outside' group with 'wrong' attitudes. On the other hand the Wheatley children all tended on a statistical basis to choose square heads for men and round for women, although the boys (35 to 18) showed a less strong tendency than the girls (65 to 0) in this direction.

Fig. 19   *Davis's Figures* (Davis, 1961).

Among the Mahali children, however, 'man' was consistently allotted to the square-headed and 'woman' to the round-headed figure (153 to 76 for boys and 73 to 12 for girls) on a statistically significant level.

These experiments have an interesting bearing on sex symbolism, because angular, square, rectangular and elongated objects are more often of unconscious male significance, and round objects of unconscious female significance than otherwise, although the writer would not agree with the concept of absolutely universal unconscious symbolism. The symbol which manifests itself on a given occasion depends on the unconscious and conscious mental processes or functions at work. For instance, if in a dream a boy's father were represented and were felt to be very feminine, rounded symbols might appear. A partial deviation from the 'expected' symbolism by East London boys on the conscious level is pointed out by Davis.

A clear-cut experimental result of the same kind was found by Monica Lawlor (1955). She took the opportunity of a period of work in London to compare the preferences for designs of English students and graduates, mostly women, and other English subjects, 56 in all, with those of 56 West African natives of the Gold Coast, 45 of whom were nurses from an Accra training college. The designs chosen were eight patterns taken from decorations on wooden carvings, metal figures and vessels, woven material and cloth and metal earrings and necklaces, all in common use in the southern part of the Gold Coast at the time. One of the designs was included because it was an approximation to the African conception of what the English like. The designs are shown in Fig. 20.

Monica Lawlor's results showed clearly that there was a strongly significant distribution of preferences for the designs in each of the groups, English and African, but while one pattern (H) was favoured predominantly by the Africans, another, (C) was most favoured by the English. Similarly, there was a strongly significant distribution of dislikes for the designs among the Africans, there was but a moderately significant distribution of dislikes among the English. Again, however, the choices were quite different, because pattern C was most disliked by the Africans, pattern H was, interestingly enough, most disliked by the English. In the comparisons of the two cultural or racial groups for liking and for disliking, there was in each case a small but negative correlation.

It was concluded that within each group there was evidence of a considerable degree of agreement and therefore of a central tendency for liking and disliking, but that there was no agreement at all between the groups. This confirms what McElroy had found for Australian Whites and Aborigines. In each experiment, if we admit that the West Africans and the Australian Aborigines had all been somewhat influenced by the impact of Western culture, but probably the Africans in London much more than the Aborigines of Arnhem Land, then the force of the conclusion of no cross-cultural or inter-racial agreement is strengthened. For the moment it must be added that in neither experiment was any attempt made to use the preferences of artistically trained or aesthetically expert judges. It is surprising that many more cross-cultural experiments of this kind have not been carried out.

Three experiments which are perhaps less directly related to art may be mentioned here. The first is a cross-cultural investigation of the Gestalt principle of closure by Michael (1953).

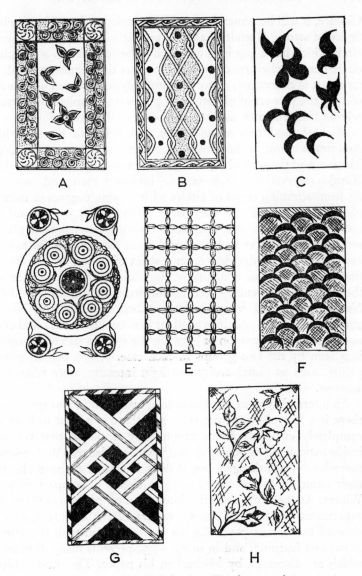

Fig. 20 *Lawlor's Designs* (Lawlor, 1955).

Closure, it will be remembered, is the tendency for an incomplete figure of strong Gestalt quality to appear as if complete. Thus a circle which has a gap in it will tend to be reported as a complete circle readily when perceived with a short time exposure, and, as far as art is concerned, many incompletely represented objects are seen by the viewers of pictures as if they were complete, and artists rely on this tendency as a standard part of their technique.

Michael used two samples, the first being of twenty white Americans from a farming community of Homestead, New Mexico, and the second being twenty members of the surrounding Navajo reservation. Each sample included men and women. As form-stimuli a series of circles with varying degrees of incompleteness was used and they were projected for 0·1 second by means of a lantern and were seen through a translucent plastic screen. Each subject had to record what he thought he saw at each exposure by drawing it on a sheet of paper. It was shown that there were no statistically significant differences between the numbers of openings seen in the circles by the white and the Navajo Indians, or between the numbers of white and Navajo persons seeing any openings at all, or between the mean number of openings seen per person or between the median size of the openings seen by the two groups in each case. A number of special points, such as visual acuity and light intensity, were taken into account.

An interesting point in relation to art was that in Navajo culture there is a fear of closed patterns, and there is a need to have no completely enclosing frame around any works so that the evil inside may have an opening through which to leave. This tendency pervades Navajo designs, but it does not seem to have affected their tendency to see closed or open circles in comparison with Whites. At the same time the interpretation of the results of the experiment in terms of the innateness of the closure tendency claimed by Gestalt psychologists in comparison with the effects of cultural learning, and in other ways, presents many difficulties which are discussed by Michael in his paper. The most evident conclusion, however, appears to be that there was no cultural or racial difference in the closure principle. However, in this experiment it is not possible to make any decisions about the relative influence of cultural learning and innate tendencies to closure. An imponderable possibility is that the Navajo tendency to resist closure in patterns compensated for an innately determined tendency to closure hypothetically greater in them than in American Whites. One cannot agree to assume, as Michael apparently does, that similiarities in closure tendencies must be of innate origin, while differences would be culturally determined.

The second experiment was by Osgood, and part of it was mentioned previously in connection with colour connotations, in a research on cross-cultural similarities and differences in the relationships between words and pictorial alternatives.

In this research the subjects were 40 Navajos, 10 Mexican-Spanish subjects, 20 Japanese in the University of Illinois, and 27 Anglos, graduate and undergraduate students of psychology in the University of Illinois.

The words used were: heavy, good, fast, happy, *up, *energetic, *loose, strong, excitement, *quiet, blue, bad, light, *down, black, woman, *lazy, *tight, green, *noisy, *grey, slow, white, calm, man, yellow, weak, and sad. The pictorial alternatives, illustrated in Fig. 21, were: up-down, vertical-horizontal, homogeneous-heterogeneous, colourless-colourful, thick-thin, dark-light, crooked-straight, hazy-clear, *blunt-sharp, rounded-angular, *diffuse-concentrated, large-small, *near-far. The words and pictorial alternatives marked with an asterisk above were omitted for the Mexican-Spanish subjects.

The results of the choices of a word to fit one or other of each pair of alternative pictures may be summed up in the following way. If a confidence level of 1 per cent is chosen, then 52 per cent of all items for Anglos, 30 per cent for Navajos, 50 per cent for Mexican-Spanish and 44 per cent of all items for Japanese reach this conservative criterion. In other words, when 28 verbal concepts were judged against 13 different pictorial alternatives, about half the items give consistent evidence for similarity of inter-cultural meaning. Osgood calls this similarity of meaning 'synaesthesic' but that term is usually reserved for a much stronger identity if two (or more) sensations, such as a sensation of colour, for instance, are experienced at the same time as or instead of a certain sound sensation. However, it is the cross-cultural similarity which is the point of central interest here.

If the percentage of items yielding the same direction of choice is calculated, for Anglo *versus* Navajo groups 65 per cent of 364 items agree in direction; for Anglos *versus* Mexican-Spanish 72

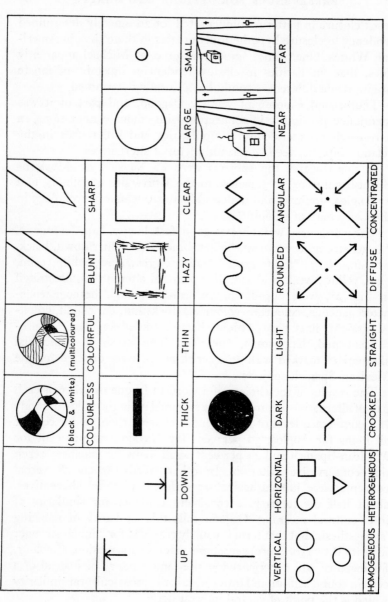

Fig. 21 *Osgood's Figures* (Osgood, 1960).

per cent of 190 items agree; for Anglos *versus* Japanese 78 per cent of 364 items agree; for Navajo *versus* Mexican-Spanish 61 per cent of 190 items agree, for Navajo *versus* Japanese 71 per cent of 364 items agree; and for Mexican-Spanish *versus* Japanese 69 per cent of 190 items agree in direction. All these percentages are beyond the 0·005 level of confidence. Osgood analyses his data in much greater detail, but these extracts are sufficient to indicate the nature of the results.

There is an impressive degree of inter-cultural agreement, which has considerable interest in relation to problems of inter-cultural uniformity of artistic feeling and taste. However, the central difficulty for this experimental work is that these groups of subjects must be regarded as having been open to a general influence of the American-Anglo culture, although it does not seem likely that this would account for the uniformities fully.

The third experiment was another by R. Davis (1961). In this research, associated with his work on the masculine/feminine symbolism by Mahali children of Tanganyika, Davis tested the tendency of these children to attach the nonsense names 'uloomu' and 'takete' to a rounded and an angular figure. This was based on Kohler's well-known work with a rounded and an angular figure to which the names 'maluma' and 'takete' were to be attached (Kohler, 1947). He showed that the smooth-sounding word 'maluma' was more readily attached to the rounded figure and the harsh-sounding word 'takete' to the angular figure. This is the tendency generally attributed to 'physiognomic' aspects of the auditory and visual stimuli, which made them appropriate (see Wyburn, Pickford and Hirst, 1964, and Figs. 22 and 23).

Davis wanted to find out whether the children of the isolated groups on the Mahali peninsula, almost completely separated from Western cultural influences, would show the same physiognomic tendencies as Western Whites. He used a different word, 'uloomu', instead of Kohler's 'maluma' because in the Swahili language, used in the Mahali peninsula, 'maluma' means 'mother's brother' and is not a nonsense word.

Among the Mahali children studied by Davis there was a very strong and statistically significant tendency for 'uloomu' to be attached to the rounded figure and 'takete' to the angular figure. The frequencies were 75 to 32 for boys and 21 to 3 for girls, in an experiment in which the nonsense words were written down,

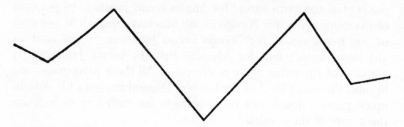

Fig. 22 *Physiognomic Properties of Designs: 'Kipotik'* (Wyburn, Pickford and Hirst, 1964).

and 82 to 33 for boys and 50 to 39 for girls in another experiment in which the words were spoken only. The last difference mentioned, 50 to 39 for girls, was not statistically significant.

In comparison with these results, Davis points out that East London children studied by Miss Helen Ross, and children of Wheatley Village, Oxfordshire, studied by Mrs Susie Robinson, gave essentially the same results, but they did no experiment in which the nonsense names were written. In these experiments the girls' results were statistically significant to a strong degree.

Fig. 23 *Physiognomic Properties of Designs: 'Olulo'* (Wyburn, Pickford and Hirst, 1964).

There is a strong tendency to associate smooth-sounding words with rounded and harsh-sounding words with angular figures.

Davis draws the general conclusion that 'purely structural factors do have some influence in naming objects', for the African as well as for the British children. From the point of view of the cross-cultural study of art, this is important in so far as it indicates that the difference in physiognomic quality of rounded and angular designs or figures is essentially the same for African children from Tanganyika as for East London and Oxfordshire children.

Cultural influences on preferences for picture material

As part of his study of phenomenal regression among West African students of the Presbyterian Training College, Akropong, and his comparison of them with Scottish students, Beveridge carried out a picture preference experiment (Beveridge, 1939, especially pp. 59–60).

The aim of the picture preference experiment was to discover whether the African's greater tendency to phenomenal regression affected his appreciation of pictorial art. He points out that Thouless showed that certain features of Oriental art, 'the absence of shadows, and the partial or total absence of perspective', are possibly due to the larger tendency to phenomenal regression in Orientals (Thouless, 1932). Beveridge says that these features are found in the drawings of African school children and students and in the work of African artists.

The subjects of Beveridge's experiment were about 100 male Gold Coast students. The material used was a set of 80 coloured postcards, forty of famous European pictures and forty of Japanese, Indian and Persian pictures. They were paired roughly according to subject and exhibited on a board, eight at a time, the European picture being sometimes to the right and sometimes to the left of the Oriental picture. The subjects were asked to state which picture of each pair he liked better and which of the eight he liked best of all.

The results showed that Western pictures were preferred to a marked degree, since 86·5 per cent of the choices were for them and only 13·5 per cent for Oriental pictures. Only two of the Oriental pictures were more popular than their Western pairs. 'Ten Thousand Acres' by Hiroshigi was preferred to Farquharson's 'Dawn', and the Persian Miniature from the Fable of Kalilah Wa Dimnah was preferred to Margaret Tarrant's 'Sylvan Melody'. No Oriental picture was the favourite on a board of eight pairs.

Beveridge points out that the African students had been used to seeing European pictures, whereas Oriental art was new to them. The Africans also gave some interesting reasons for liking the pictures. Of these the most important seemed to be the illusion of reality and naturalistic representation. Another reason was admiration of the artist's technique and, while some pictures were liked because they told a story, others were liked because they seemed to represent ideal conditions—Vermeer's 'Little Street in Delft'. It would have been interesting if Beveridge could have divided the Oriental pictures into Japanese, Indian and Persian groups, and compared them with various groups of the European pictures. Another interesting extension of the research would have been to compare preferences for European and for African paintings with which the students of the Gold Coast were equally familiar.

As part of an extensive research on children's aesthetic appreciation at the Cleveland Museum of Art, Betty Lark-Horovitz published a report on a comparison of the art judgments of white and Negro children, 13 to 15 years of age (Lark-Horovitz, 1939–40). This research, fuller details of the other parts of which will be given in Chapter 8, dealt with children's judgments of preference concerning (a) 12 carefully chosen subject pictures, (b) 51 portraits for the younger children and 43 for the older children, and (c) 39 textile patterns (13 of which were Oriental, one American-Indian, three Moroccan and one of African Negro origin). The children were asked to pick out their first, second, third or further choices (or none at all), and to answer questions about the reasons for their preferences.

In (a), the subject picture experiment, there were 62 white boys, 64 white girls, 46 Negro boys and 58 Negro girls. In (b), the portrait experiment, the subjects were 81 white boys, 81 white girls, 44 Negro boys and 54 Negro girls. In (c), the pattern experiment, there were 106 white boys, 114 white girls, 71 Negro boys and 97 Negro girls. Detailed frequency tables of the children's preferences are given, together with analyses of their reasons for choices. Betty Lark-Horovitz summarises her results in the following ways (pp. 284–5).

Negro and white children differed widely in their picture preferences and in their choices of most preferred portraits, but they showed similar interests for the whole group of portraits preferred, and they showed great similarity in their choices of textile patterns.

In respect of (a), subject pictures, white children were much more inclined to suggest changes they would like to make than were Negroes. In (b), the portrait experiment, colour and subject were mentioned more than twice as often by Negro than by white children, while facial expression, reality of the picture and tech-

Fig. 24 *Expanding Perspective on a Mogul Picture*, about 1585 (Thouless, 1932).

nique were far more important to white children. Both groups of girls were higher in emotional reaction than boys. Portraits chosen remind Negro children much more than Whites of people they know. Negro children do not want to change the portraits, while Whites were more likely to do so. In (c), the textile pattern experiment, colour arrangement and subject were most often mentioned as reasons for choice by both groups. There was no group difference in preference for abstract or geometrical patterns, or in respect of colour in general. However, white girls preferred delicate and subdued to bright colours, while the reverse was true of Negro girls. Interest in the use of chosen textile patterns was different in kind with white and Negro children, and both groups claimed to have patterns at home similar to those in the test series, but Negro children were much more inclined to prefer patterns not like any they had at home.

The difference in response to colour, subject, reality and technique disappeared when Negro children were compared with the younger group of white children. This suggested the possibility that the difference was due to a difference in mental development. However, Betty Lark-Horovitz thinks that this could not be accepted as fact unless the same results were found with groups which had the same median of Probable Learning Rate. This was determined by group tests used in Cleveland schools and was unequal for the groups in question, namely, 83 for Negroes and 108 for white children. Another possible interpretation mentioned with respect to colour was that Negro children retained their colour sensitivity to a greater extent than Whites at the expense of other factors.

In considering the results it may seem less significant that there was a marked difference in the preferences of white and Negro children for subject pictures and for portraits than for textile patterns, because all the subject pictures were Occidental, as also were almost all the portraits, while 18 out of the 39 textile patterns were Oriental, African or of American Indian origin. Another point is that the Negro children of Cleveland would have been subject to considerable Occidental influence, and it is not known whether this would have made them suggestible or contra-suggestible to Occidental standards of pictorial art.

If we look again at Table 7.3, which gives the average correlations between Whites, between Aborigines and between Whites and Aborigines in McElroy's experiment in Australia (McElroy, 1952, p. 92), we see that several of his tests used picture material. The most notable of these, perhaps, were Australian *Landscapes*, pictures by *Paul Klee* and *Portraits*. The Landscapes gave zero correlation between Aborigines, and almost zero between Whites, and between Whites and Aborigines. The pictures by Klee gave very low positive correlations between Whites, and between Aborigines, and a very low negative correlation between Whites and Aborigines. The portraits of Blacks and of Whites both gave significant positive correlations between Whites, and between Aborigines, and a very low correlation between Whites and Aborigines, for portraits of Whites and a significant negative correlation for portraits of Blacks.

The tests based on coloured drawings of English flowers, of British butterflies, of British fishes, and of British birds, are, in a sense, tests of picture material, and in general they gave small but significant positive correlations between Whites and between Aborigines (with the exception of flowers, which was not significant for Aborigines), and small negative but non-significant correlations were found between Whites and Aborigines for birds and flowers, while fishes and butterflies gave small but positive and significant correlations.

The general outcome of these data is essentially the same as that for cross-cultural comparisons of colour preferences in the same experiment, mentioned previously. It is that, while on the whole there was agreement within each cultural group, there was little or no agreement, or perhaps actual disagreement, between these groups. Only the pictures of British fishes and butterflies gave statistically significant positive correlations between Whites and Aborigines. Perhaps this was because their somewhat geometrical patterns may have appealed to the Aborigines, whereas the British birds and flowers may have been more unrelated in appearance to their own flowers and birds or cultural objects.

In an experiment already mentioned Fakhir Hussain (1962, p. 75) showed that, in their rankings for preference of paintings by Picasso, Reid, children and by the chimpanzee Congo, Indian, French and English students showed clearly different orders of ranking, which supported the hypothesis that different cultural values would have their effect on preferences for such paintings.

Recently Child and his collaborators have found some evidence of cross-cultural agreement in aesthetic judgments, provided artistically competent and experienced judges were used as subjects.

In one experiment Child and Siroto (1965) compared the aesthetic evaluations of 13 US experts of New Haven, Conn., with various groups of Ba Kwele judges, upon 39 photographs of Ba Kwele masks. The American experts were advanced art students and others able to make such judgments. The Ba Kwele are a Bantu-speaking people, living in the Republic of the Congo, and the Gabon, Western equatorial Africa. They used ceremonial masks at rituals on various occasions and this use was probably discontinued during the 1920s as a result of European contacts. Child and Siroto think there is no reason to believe Ba Kwele evaluations of their own masks would have been influenced by European traditions.

The field worker used an interpreter with whom he spoke in French. The subjects were asked to pick out from the 39 masks the four he considered best, then the four next best, and so on, until the last photograph had been judged. This procedure was not always followed absolutely. For instance, four subjects did not complete the series, and one of them selected masks in groups of eight. However, the method was well suited to the special difficulties owing to the field-work conditions.

The results were computed by correlational and factorial techniques, the Ba Kwele judges being divided into three groups, namely 4 carvers, 4 cult leaders and 8 others, while all 16 judges were considered together. Individual judges were also studied from the point of view of their age, which varied from 35 to 65 for carvers, 55 to 65 for cult leaders, and 17 to 70 for the others. The photographs were also grouped in the following way: all 39; 31 remaining after 8 poor photographs had been abstracted; 27 remaining after 4 of doubtful origin had been omitted; 16 of these 27 which were play masks; and 8 of the 27 which were fierce masks. Separate statistics were calculated for the various groups of judges and masks, showing the resemblance in evaluation between US experts and Ba Kwele tribesmen.

Child and Siroto show that for all 39 photographs each of the groupings of Ba Kwele judges agrees with the US experts by a correlation of 0·48 for carvers, 0·44 for cult leaders, 0·38 for others, and 0·44 for all 16 judges. These correlations are all statistically significant at the 0·01 level of probability. For the 31 photographs after the 8 doubtful ones were removed, the correlations were slightly higher. When the number of masks was reduced and the Ba Kwele judges were taken singly, the correlations tended to be lower and less strongly significant or not significant at all, and for the 8 fierce masks and individual Ba Kwele judges, there are three negative correlations, which are not significant.

The agreement between Ba Kwele judges is, however, much greater than the agreement between Ba Kwele and US judges. For instance, for all 39 masks the four carvers agree with the four cult leaders by a correlation of 0·84, and with 8 other Ba Kwele by a correlation of 0·93, while the cult leaders and the others agree to the extent of a correlation of 0·86.

The conclusion from this particular study is that, while there is a very marked degree of agreement between competent US judges and competent Ba Kwele judges with respect to the quality of Ba Kwele ceremonial carved masks, the agreement between the Ba Kwele judges themselves is very much higher.

In an experiment with Iwao (1966) Child studied the judgments of 60 Japanese potters, in comparison with those of 14 expert judges in one group and 17 in another from New Haven, Conn., in respect of 36 pairs of black and white photographs of works of art, each pair chosen to be similar in kind, style and subject-matter, one better than the other, and 16 pairs of coloured postcard reproductions of abstract paintings.

The sixty potters comprised 36 from Tanba, a small village where pottery has been made for centuries, 14 from Izushi, where there were five ovens; and 10 from the city of Kyoto. Only 4 had less than five years, and some had up to 50 years of experience.

Among the results Iwao and Child report that 30 potters judged 21 pairs of black and white reproductions, another 30 judged 15 of these reproductions; and all 60 judged 12 of the pairs of coloured abstract paintings. Agreement with the US experts was found in 62 per cent of the judgments on the first batch of black and white pairs, in 59 per cent of the judgments in the second batch and in 57·5 per cent of judgment on the coloured pairs. These are statistically significant at the 0·02 level of probability. In addition, 26 of the pairs of black and white pictures were shown to several hundred suburban New Haven high-school students. Their average agreement with the US experts was 47 per cent, whereas the Japanese potters agreed to the extent of 63 per cent for these pairs. Yale undergraduates, however, agreed to the extent of 64 per cent with US experts over 31 of the pairs of photographs, while Japanese potters agreed 61 per cent concerning the same pairs.

A further research (Iwao, Child and Garcia, 1969) was carried out on 31 residents of Tokyo, all of whom were practitioners or teachers of flower arranging, tea ceremony or other traditional arts. They judged which was the better of each of the 51 pairs of black and white photographic prints used in the previous research and 24 pairs of coloured postcards of modern abstract paintings. The Japanese subjects agreed 58·5 per cent, which is significantly higher than chance agreement with the US experts on the black and white photographs. For the coloured postcards, however, their agreement was only 51·5 per cent, which is not above chance expectation.

The same sets of black and white and postcard reproductions were also shown to 40 working-class residents of Puerto Rico, and for them there was 43 per cent of agreement over the black and white pairs and 45·5 per cent for the coloured postcards. Both these results are statistically significant in respect of disagreement. Thus, it is pointed out by the authors, the Japanese expert subjects may have shown a relative tendency to agree with the US experts, while the Puerto Rico non-experts tended to show disagreement.

In another investigation (Ford, Prothro, and Child, 1966) five men and one woman, all engaged to some extent in craftwork, in a remote Fijian village, expressed preferences within eleven trios of photographs of works of art, and two men and two women craft workers in the Western Cycladic Islands of Greece similarly expressed judgments within five trios of pictures.

Statistically significant agreement was found between the Fijians and US experts of New Haven, Conn., but the agreement, although positive, between the Greek craft workers and the US judges was not statistically significant. These results tend to support the results of previous researchers which show that among experts and persons active and interested in art and in crafts there is agreement in aesthetic judgments.

Bibliography and References
for Chapter 7

BEVERIDGE, W. M. (1935). Racial Differences in Phenomenal Regression. *Brit. J. Psychol., 26,* 59–62.

BEVERIDGE, W. M. (1939). Some Racial Differences in Perception. *Brit. J. Psychol., 30,* 57–64.

BURNHAM, R. W., HANES, R. M., and BARTLESON, C. J. (1963). *Color: A Guide to Basic Facts and Concepts.* New York: Wiley.

CHILD, I. L., HANSEN, J. A., and HORNBECK, F. W. (1968). Age and Sex Differences in Children's Color Preferences. *Child Development, 39,* 237–47.

CHILD, I. L., and IWAO, S. (1969). A Comparison of Color Preferences in College Students of Japan and the United States. *Proc. 77th Ann. Convention, APA,* 1969, 9 pp.

CHILD, I. L. and SIROTO, L. (1965). Ba Kwele and American Esthetic Evaluations Compared. *Ethnology, 4,* 349–60.

CHOU, S. K., and CHEN, H. P. (1935). General versus Specific Preferences of Chinese Students. *J. Soc. Psychol., 6,* 290–314.

CHOUNGOURIAN, A. (1968). *Percept. Motor Skills, 26,* 1203–6.

DAVIS, R. (1961). The Fitness of Names to Drawings. A Cross-Cultural Study in Tanganyika. *Brit. J. Psychol., 52,* 259–68.

EYSENCK, H. J. (1941). A Critical and Experimental Study of Color Preferences. *Amer. J. Psychol., 54,* 385–94.

FORD, C. S., PROTHRO, E. TERRY, and CHILD, I. L. (1966). Some Transcultural Comparisons of Esthetic Judgment. *J. Soc. Psychol., 68,* 19–26.

GARTH, T. R. (1922). Color Preferences of Five Hundred and Fifty Nine Full-Blooded Indians. *J. Exptl. Psychol., 5,* 392–418.

GARTH, T. R. and COLLADO, I. R. (1929). The Color Preference of Filipino Children, *J. Comp. Psychol., 9,* 397–404.

GARTH, T. R., KUNIHEI, IKEDA, and LANGDON, R. M. (1931). The Color Preferences of Japanese Children. *J. Soc. Psychol., 2,* 397–402.

GARTH, T. R., MOSES, M. R., and ANTHONY, C. N. (1938). The Color Preferences of East Indians. *Amer. J. Psychol., 51,* 709–13.

GESCHE, I. (1927). The Colour Preference of 1,152 Mexican Children. *J. Comp. Psychol., 7,* 297–311.

HOGG, J. (1969). *J. Gen. Psychol., 80,* 129–40.

HUSSAIN, FAKHIR (1962). *An Experimental Enquiry into the Phenomena of 'Aesthetic Judgements' Under Varying Time Conditions*. Ph.D. Thesis, University of London (unpublished).

IWAO, S., and CHILD, I. L. (1966). Comparison of Esthetic Judgments by American Experts and by Japanese Potters. *J. Soc. Psychol.*, *68*, 27–33.

IWAO, S., CHILD, I. L., and GARCIA, M. (1969). Further Evidence of Agreement between Japanese and American Esthetic Evaluations. *J. Soc. Psychol.*

JAHODA, G. (1956). Differences in Preferences for Shapes: A Cross-Cultural Replication. *Brit. J. Psychol.*, *47*, 126–32.

KANSAKU, J. (1963). *Jap. J. Psychol.*, *34*, 11–12 (abstract).

KASTL, A. J. and CHILD, I. L. (1968). Comparison of Color Preferences in Vietnam and the United States. *Proc. 76th Ann. Convention, APA*, 1968, 437–8.

KÖHLER, W. (1947). *Gestalt Psychology* (2nd ed.) New York: Liveright.

LARK-HOROVITZ, BETTY (1939–40). On Art Appreciation of Children: IV. Comparative Study of White and Negro Children 13–15 Years Old. *J. Educ. Research*, *33*, 258–85.

LAWLOR, M. (1955). Cultural Influences on Preference for Designs. *J. Abnor. and Soc. Psychol.*, *51*, 690–3.

McELROY, W. A. (1952). Aesthetic Appreciation in Aborigines of Arnhem Land: A Comparative Experimental Study. *Oceania*, *23*, 81–94.

McELROY, W. A. (1954). A Sex Difference in Preferences for Shapes. *Brit. J. Psychol.*, *45*, 209–16.

MICHAEL, D. N. (1953). A Cross-Cultural Investigation of Closure. *J. Abnor. and Soc. Psychol.*, *48*, 225–30.

OSGOOD, C. E. (1960). The Cross-Cultural Generality of Visual-Verbal Synaesthetic Tendencies. *Behavioral Science*, *5*, 146–69.

RAUSH, H. L. (1955). *J. Personality*, *21*, 176–87.

SHEN, N. C. (1937). The Color Preferences of 1,368 Chinese Students, with Special Reference to the Most Preferred Color. *J. Soc. Psychol.*, *8*, 185–204.

STEWART, R., and BAXTER, J. (1969). Color Preferences of Three Ethnic Groups of Elementary School Children. *Art Interpretation and Art Therapy. Psychiatry and Art*. vol. 2, Ed. Irene Jakab, pp. 186–90. Karger: Basle/New York.

THOULESS, R. H. (1932). A Racial Difference in Perception. *J. Soc. Psychol.*, *4*, 330–9.

WYBURN, G. M., PICKFORD, R. W., and HIRST, R. J. (1964). *Human Senses and Perception*. Edinburgh: Oliver and Boyd, Toronto: Univ. Press.

ZAJAC, J. L. (1961). Studies in Perspective. *Brit. J. Psychol.*, *52*, 333–40.

8

Children's aesthetic judgments

In this chapter a review of the literature on children's aesthetic judgments and preferences will be made, showing the history of the subject since the earlier years of the present century, and taking into account numerous researches on children's preferences for colours, and their judgments and aesthetic preferences for patterns and designs, sensitivity to compositional unity and balance, and then dealing with children's choices of pictures and preferences for them. This is a very large field, because the interest of aesthetic education has stimulated many studies of children's attitudes to art and the illumination which has been thrown upon methods of teaching art and art appreciation has been very valuable. The chapter ends on a somewhat guarded note because of Child's recent work showing how little the in-artistic can be taught or even passively influenced to appreciate art. This, however, is hardly surprising. Just as we have limited power to teach children to be intelligent, or to be musical, so also we have limited power to teach them to be artistic if it is not in them to start with.

Three examples of child art are given, namely, (1) the *Frontispiece,* 'Driving Out the Demon', by a girl of 8 years of age, from a calendar illustrated by children in Rikkyo Primary School, Tokyo (1968), by permission of Professor William A. Sakow; (2) 'A House', by a boy aged 14 years, with permission of Sister Jude

(Plate 8); (3) 'A Little Girl', by a girl aged 4 years 10 months, with permission of Mr Robin Gilmour (Plate 10). These illustrate (1) the brilliant use of colour and dynamic expression of a Japanese girl aged 8 years; (2) a powerful painting by a boy of 14 years of age who had no training or experience in art; and (3) a most expressive picture, probably an unrealised self-portrait by a girl of 4 years of age during a period of great enthusiasm for drawing and painting.

Preferences of children for single colours

Many experiments and tests have been applied to children in order to discover how well they can discriminate colours and what preferences they show. C. S. Myers (1908) reported his own and those of McDougall on infants a year or less of age. Two coloured blocks or pieces of paper, for instance, were placed at equal distance from the infant and a note was made which object he reached for first. The right and left sides were alternated.

Other experiments involving this choice technique or a matching technique were carried out by various workers such as Holden and Bosse (1900), Winch (1909), Valentine (1914), Dashiell (1917), Staples (1932) and Chase (1937). These have been reviewed very thoroughly by Valentine (1962, pp. 33–7 and 64–5) and it is not necessary to report all the details about them here especially because, in most or all cases, saturation and brightness were not controlled, which means, of course, that it is difficult to know whether the children or infants were responding to hue, saturation or brightness. There is also the difficulty that the children were not given efficient tests for colour vision and its defects. Lakowski (1958) has shown that the efficiency of colour vision varies considerably in relation to age. The best age group, according to his work, was that of 25–35 years, and there was an average improvement in normal colour sensitivity up to this age group and a decrease after. Fewer anomalous trichromats (certain kinds of major defectives explained in Chapter 5) were found in this age group, and after 45 years of age there was a steady increase in blue/yellow deficiency which could be quite important for art and aesthetics.

However, it is interesting that Valentine (1962, pp. 35–7) claims that there is a change in the average colour preferences of children about the age of 5 or 6 years. For example, Garth (1924) said that at about 6 years of age red came first, slightly above blue, but after this age red and orange both fell and blue became first choice. Garth was, however, unable to separate the effects of age and of education. He says that education seems to produce a suppression of preferences for all colours except blue in white subjects. For 498 boys of all ages, red was a close second to blue, but for 502 girls red was only fifth. This confirmed Winch's (1909) results on 2,000 children aged 7–15 years. He asked them to write down the following colour names—white, black, red, green, yellow and blue—in the order in which they liked the colours best. With the youngest children red was the most popular colour, but blue took its place after about six years of age. Valentine gives a summary of the findings for the older girls and boys:

	Boys' order	Girls' order
Blue	1	1
Red	2	2
White	5	$3\frac{1}{2}$
Green	3	$3\frac{1}{2}$
Yellow	4	5
Black	6	6

Another extensive enquiry, on 2,500 children, showed that blue was the most frequently chosen as best-liked, even by five-year-olds, there was a rise in the preference for short-wave length colours (blues and greens) and a decrease for long-wave length colours (red, oranges and yellows) with increasing age (Katz and Breed, 1922).

Hildreth (1936) reported a study of the picture and colour choices of young children. Seventy-eight boys and sixty girls between the ages of 3 and 5 years were asked to name ten colours, to name their preferred colour, to express preference for picture subjects among a series of sixteen pictures and to express preferences for reproductions in four forms: monotone, outline, colour and silhouette. Nearly a third of the group below five could name ten colours and another third nine colours. Above 5 years of age 75 per cent could name ten colours and 17 per cent nine colours. Orange was the favourite colour of both groups, pink second and red third. Both groups liked the coloured pictures best and the silhouettes next best.

A study of children's actual use of colours in their own free paintings was made by Alschuler and Hattwick (1947, pp. 104–6 and 175). Their conclusions were based on objective and statistical analysis of paintings and by personality studies of 88 boys aged 2 years 3 months to 5 years 8 months and 82 girls aged 2 years 9 months to 5 years 8 months. A decreased preference for red and an increased preference for blue were found at 4 years 6 months and 5 years. There was also a decrease in the use of warm colours in general and an increase in emphasis on cold colours between the ages of 3 and 5 years. 'The period of greatest transition from warm to cold emphasis tends to be between three and three and a half—a period already described as nodal in the transition from emotional to controlled behaviour.' 'In contrast to the use of red, emphasis on blue was found to parallel just such attempts at control as tend to occur repeatedly during the latter part of the nursery years.' The authors found that there was also an increase of interest in green with increasing age, and that, while blue often expresses or symbolises responses which have been learned, yellow was frequently used when more infantile drives continued to be present.

Interest in mixing colours or in the use of a variety of colours also increased with increasing age. In respect of colour placement, in the impulsive stage of 'unbounded interest in self-expression', the children were more concerned with sheer use of colour than with its placement. In the transition period to controlled behaviour there was an increased interest in colour placement and, when controlled behaviour was attained, rather rigid attempts to express control in colour placement tended to be replaced by more free usage and purposive mixing of colours. Also, prior to 5 years of age there was a high incidence of overlay of colours, and this was shown by the data on the children's personality problems to express repression and to reflect inadequate adjustment. Many of the children were not making an easy transition from impulsive to adaptive and reasoned behaviour and 39 per cent of them came from homes which offered evidence of excessive demands. Alschuler and Hattwick say, however, that their statistics do not support the possibility that home pressure towards control might be considered as a factor which contributed to the lack of adjustment reflected in overlay in painting. 'The conflicts reflected by consistent overlay have apparently been too highly individual and too varied to have been caught in our statistical analysis' (p. 106). This would accord with the view which the writer would support, namely that discipline by itself is not a cause of children's neurotic maladjustments. Other references to Alschuler's and Hattwick's work will be given in Chapter 9, on personality in relation to art.

In an experiment on 'the objectivity' of colour, André Coupleux (1968) used ten colours of standard physical properties obtained with Kodak colour filters projected with a standard light source. His subjects were 91 boys and 104 girls, 15 to 22 years of age. They were asked to give associations or preferences and to assign to the colours emotional qualities from a list of 14 affective tonalities. The general results showed that sex was a most important factor, as indicated in Table 8.1.

TABLE 8.1

Affective tonalities related to colours (André Coupleux, 1968)

	Garçons	Filles
Alimentation	Brun (chocolat)	Rose (bonbon)
Textiles		choix plus large
Revêtement	Jaune	Brun
Affectivité		choix très large
Préférence	Vert	Blue-clair
Rejet	surtout Brun	surtout violet
Agréable	Jaune, Rose, Bleu-clair	surtout Rose
Instinct	Rose	Rouge

Other interesting associations and emotional meanings of colours to the children are given in Table 8.2.

TABLE 8.2

Emotional meanings of colours to children (Coupleux, 1968)

Rouge	{ Biologie animal (sang), 68·51% Puissant, fort, impérieu, 47·56%; instinct, désir, amour, 42·70% Excitant, stimulant, 37·29%; haine, jalousie, aggressivité, 30·81%
Brun	Mechante fée, 35·63%; découragement, déprimant, 35·13%
Parme	Craintif, 26·48%; faible, débile, 66·48%
Bleu Clair	Calme, sécurité, 33·48%; bonne fée, maman, 30·81%
Violet	Douleur, malheur, 42·70%; Maladie, mort, 41·05%

These correspond to a great extent with what has been found by other workers. Coupleux suggests that colour will become a means of revealing mental conditions, and an instrument of analysis. Whether the results given truly represent an objectivity of colour meaning, however, or whether they are the products of circumstance, remains an open question.

A very efficient experiment is reported on the colour preferences of children by Child, Hansen and Hornbeck (1968). More than 1,100 children in the public school system of a small middle-income suburb within a metropolitan area of about 250,000 were the subjects. All children in two primary schools (grades 1–6) and five classes at each grade level in the junior and senior high schools (grades 7–9 and 10–12) were given the test. They were shown pairs of colour patches in class-room groups. No tests of colour vision were applied. They had to record whether they preferred the left- or right-hand patch. All saw thirty-five pairs of patches in a standard order by which similar pairs were separated and two occurrences of an identical order were avoided. Each pair showed two colours differing in one of the three basic dimensions of colour, drawn from four evenly spaced diameters of the colour circle, from four chroma (saturation) levels and from four levels of value (brightness). Each pair was shown for ten seconds. The patches were Munsell papers $5\frac{1}{2} \times 8\frac{1}{2}$ in., and each had a flat black surround. Other details are given in the original paper.

The experimenters found that cooler (bluer or greener) colours were preferred by all children of school age, under these conditions. Higher rather than lower degrees of saturation were preferred, and higher rather than lower values of brightness. The average preference for cooler hues was stronger for girls than for boys, but sex differences varied from one pair of colours to another. In saturation preferences, boys and girls were similar in the fourth grade, but by the twelfth grade there was a large difference, fewer than half the girls now choosing the higher saturation, whereas 75 per cent of the boys continued to make the higher saturation choice. In respect of brightness or value, the girls at all ages chose the higher brightness more often than the boys.

These results are at considerable variance with those of other workers, but it appears to the writer that all such results may be greatly affected by cultural standards and conventions, even when very large groups are efficiently sampled. It is hardly surprising that there are differences, as, for example, between England in the 1950s and USA in the 1960s, the 1920s or earlier in the century.

The problem is one at least in part for the social psychology of factors influencing colour preference and depends to some extent on fashions and patterns of sexual display and reticence.

In an experiment on 308 American and Lebanese male and female subjects of differing ages and educational levels, Choungourian (1969) used eight colours, namely red, orange, yellow, yellow-green, green, blue-green, blue and purple, on the Ostwald system and differing only in hue. The children and adults expressed their preferences by the method of paired comparisons. There were subjects at the ages of 5, 9, 10, 14, 15 and 20 years. Red was most preferred at the ages of 5, 14 and 15, but blue at the ages of 9 and 10, and green at 20 years. Green was least preferred at 5, 9 and 10; green-blue at 14 and 15, and purple at 20 years. At the age of 5 years American children preferred red most and green least, but at the same age Lebanese children had no statistically significant differences of colour preference. Apparently no sex differences were found.

Children's preferences for combinations of colours

Dashiell (1917), one of the earliest workers, reported an experiment in which certain pairs of colours using Milton Bradley coloured papers were judged by more than 200 children of kindergarten age. The colour pairs were: red/green, red/blue, orange/yellow, orange/green, yellow/violet and blue/violet. The general result was that one colour combination was liked as much as another by children of this age. However, when the same colour pairs were used with university students there was a sex difference. The yellow/violet pair was placed highest by the women students but lowest by the men students.

Studies by Williams and Walton (1933) upon about 500 children and 100 adults was carried out by a doll-dressing technique. A large number of nine-inch squares of silk were dyed, two at a time, in various shades of red, orange, yellow, green, blue, purple and intermediate hues. Twelve pairs of colours were then chosen according to a rule of modified complementaries, each of the six main colours being represented four times in its various shades, and they were identified according to the Ridgway colour system (Ridgway, 1912). One colour from each of six pairs was used to dress a small doll, and a scarf was made from the other colour of the pair. Three other scarves were then made for each doll from colours which have as poor an aesthetic effect as possible with the dress colour. The child had to choose from the four scarves the one which looked 'prettiest' with the doll's dress.

About 50 children were used as subjects in each of the following ages: 4, 5, 6, 7, 8, 9, 10, 11 and 12 years. Two groups of about 50 adults were also used. The average number of 'correct' choices dropped from score 2·03 at the 4th to 1·25 at the 7th year and, after the 7th year, it gradually rose again to 2·50 at the 12th year. The adult level, 3·98, was much higher than that of the 4th year. However, although sensitivity to colour harmony was found in certain individuals as early as the 4th year, averages for the groups were not above a chance score until after the 8th year. By the 12th year the children had not reached the adult level. Intelligence, single colour preferences and time spent on the test did not appreciably affect the scores. Artistic children made little better performances on the test than unselected children, but definitely better than non-artistic children—the criteria of artistic ability being teacher's ratings and various tests made in the University of Iowa Psychological Laboratory.

A more recent experiment on the effect of age on preferences for colour combinations has been reported by Woods (1956). Since this employed a technique more related to real art than the use of very simple colour stimuli, such as colour chips or skeins of wool, it is worth reporting in some detail. Nine cards or plates were prepared on each of which the same pattern was presented, but in different colour combinations. The colours were chosen with a view to their probable or possible attractiveness and emotional effects. Unfortunately Woods does not illustrate the basic pattern, but says that it was chosen to hold the attention of the observer and to eliminate as far as possible the visualisation of symbolic forms in the pattern.

The experiment was carried out on more than 3,500 individuals, but the report deals with the results for 2,076 of them. The method was to present each individual with all nine cards at the same time and ask him to pick out the most preferred, the next and the next most preferred again, and then to deal with the three least attractive in a similar way. There were more than 100 individuals in each year group from 6- and 7-year-olds and 8- and 9-year-olds up to 16-year-old children. Then there were 201 non-college adults, 488 freshmen and 167 college upper-class adults. In addition there were 24 male mental defectives, below 40 IQ, and 118 adult mental defectives, IQ 40–70, and the upper and lower 20 per cent of the male college freshmen were picked out as they were classified on ACE Q scores.

The cards were as follows:

Card 1. Two shades of grey—'adaptable and flexible'. This was rarely considered attractive, but often unattractive up to age 12 years. After this it was regarded as increasingly attractive.

Card 2. Two tertiary colours—yellow-green and purple 'flamboyant'. No age trends were found for this card.

Card 3. A 'tint' of orange and blue primaries—'quiet'. This was often considered unattractive by those under 12 years, but not much after that age until adult ages were reached.

Card 4. Orange-red and blue-violet, maximally saturated— 'primitive or impulsive'. This card was favoured by 6-year-olds, and increased in popularity until age 13 years. After that it declined in popularity.

Card 5. Red and green, darkened to reduce intensity, variety and contrast—'contemplative'. This card was never regarded as attractive by children under 11 years of age, then slightly, but usually it was among the three worst, although it was attractive to 20 per cent of adults, 17 per cent of college freshmen and 19 per cent of upper-class students.

Card 6. Orange and green—'offensive'. No age trends were found for this card.

Card 7. Polychrome—six sets of complementaries with triadic interruptions—to appeal to those responding impulsively to colour. It was among the most attractive to 94 per cent of the 6-year-olds and then declined in popularity.

Card 8. Red and blue primaries at maximum saturation— 'considerable sensory appeal'. It was of less popular appeal among younger children, but increased in popularity to about 37 per cent among all the older groups.

Card 9. Orange-red and red-purple—'vibrating reds'. This card was liked by half the 6-year-olds, but then declined in popularity.

Sex differences. These did not appear until age 11 years. Card 1 was preferred by women and found unattractive by men. Card 4 was more liked by men; card 5 was considered unattractive by males, especially of age 14, 15 and 16; card 9 was more often regarded as unattractive by females than males over 12 years of age.

Intelligence differences. The 24 males of IQ below 40 failed to make differential reactions to the nine cards. Defectives of IQ 40–70 selected cards much as did the 7-year-olds. Among college freshmen those in the lowest 20 per cent more often disliked Cards 1, 2 and 6, and liked Card 5, while the upper 20 per cent more often liked Card 3.

In his summary Woods says that the general findings of the study support the hypothesis that responses to differentially composed colour combinations vary with age, intelligence and sex, and that those who are more 'primitive' in their behaviour tend to regard as attractive those colour combinations in which variety, intensity and contrast prevail, while those who are more highly developed and socially oriented tend to select on the basis of more subtle colour relationships.

Valentine (1962, pp. 67–70) carried out experiments with combinations of three colours, using coloured skeins of wool from a wools test of colour blindness, the skeins being about eight inches long and three-quarters of an inch thick. This suggests that they were not taken from the well-known Holmgren Wools Test, in which the skeins are much smaller. The subjects were asked to arrange the skeins in sets of three, either upright or horizontal. The principle of 'weight' played a large part in the horizontal combinations, the 'heaviest', that is the darkest colour —according to Bullough's interpretation—or most saturated being placed at the bottom, then the next darkest and the lightest at the top. Sometimes this principle was entirely overthrown, either in order to separate colours which did not go well together, or to keep together colours which did go well. In the vertical combinations a principle of 'balance' was at work, since a light colour would be placed between two dark and heavy ones, with various exceptions and modifying influences. Valentine stresses the great variety of factors at work and the importance of individual differences.

This is obviously a subject which would deserve much further research, especially in view of the practical interests of decoration and the colouring of everyday objects, and in view of the abstract principles of pure aesthetics. Also better definition of the colours combined in threes, or other combinations and patterns, could be

Plate 1 *'Composition: Black and Red'* 1954 by Kenneth Martin (Morris M., 1957).

Plate 2 *The Start of the Experiment* (Morris, M., 1957).

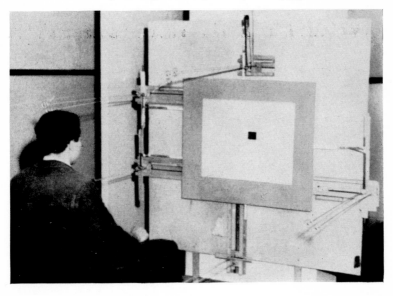

Plate 3 *The Conclusion of the Experiment* (Morris, M., 1957).

Plate 4 *'Moses Strikes the Rock that Water may Flow'* by a normal sighted subject, visual type (Lowenfeld, 1939, Plate 1).

Plate 5 *'Moses Strikes the Rock that Water may Flow'* by a normal sighted subject, haptic type (Lowenfeld, 1939, Plate 2).

Plate 6 *'Being Throttled'* by a weak sighted subject, 23 years of age, haptic type (Lowenfeld, 1939, Plate 8).

Plate 7 *'Longing for Sight'* by a congenitally blind subject, visual type (Lowenfeld, 1939, Plate 9).

Plate 8 *'A House'* by a boy, aged 14, who had no experience or training in art.

Plate 9 *'Inner Decay'* by a congenitally blind subject, haptic type (Lowenfeld, 1939, Plate 68).

Plate 10 '*A Little Girl*' by a girl aged 4 years 10 months who was very enthusiastic about drawing.

Plate 11 *Design no. 1* (Daniels, 1933).

Plate 12 *Bird-bath Test* (Whorley, 1933).

Plate 13 *Entrance Planting Test* (Whorley, 1933).

Plate 14 *Pictorial Design Materials* (Jasper, 1933).

obtained by the use of definitely specified colour chips or cards from the Munsell series. This could be done either by offering the subject the choice of what colour chips to select and combine quite freely, or by making up pairs or trios of colour chips beforehand, according to principles by which hue, saturation and brightness were controlled systematically. For instance, in one set hue and saturation would be held constant and brightness varied, in another hue and brightness would be held constant while saturation was varied, and in a third set saturation and brightness would be held constant but hue would be varied. Then the subjects would be asked to make their choices, or to arrange each set in order of preference.

Conclusions relating to children's colour preferences

Children's colour preferences have been extensively investigated, and the earlier work tended to show a change from red as the most popular colour to blue before or about the age of six years. Recent work also suggests that the blue/green colours are most preferred by all children of school age. For the older age group both boys and girls prefer more saturated colours, according to Child and his colleagues (1968) who showed, however, that the preferences of girls tended more towards lower saturations, cooler hues and greater lightness (brightness) than boys.

Experiments on pairs of colours showed that in young children one pair was liked as much as another, whereas by women students the yellow/violet pair was placed highest but by men students lowest. Later experiments showed that where the choices of children for colour combinations were compared with choices based on aesthetic principles, there was a drop in 'correct' choices from the fourth to the seventh year and then a rise again towards the adult level. However, some of the youngest children's sensitivity is found even among the youngest children, so that artistic children are evident very early.

An experiment with a standard pattern presented in different colour combinations showed that there were some age and sex differences and some varying with intelligence, and that the more 'primitive' prefer variety, intensity and contrast of colours, while those who were highly developed and socially oriented preferred more subtle colour relationships. In an experiment with three-colour combinations 'weight' in the sense of darkness and saturation led to dark saturated colours being placed lowest, but a wide range of influencing factors was observed.

Children's judgments of compositional balance and patterns

In the University of Iowa *Studies in the Psychology of Art* there are three investigations of children's sensitivity to compositional balance, rhythm in visual patterns and compositional unity, with special attention to very young children, and a fourth concerning aesthetic design of costumes in which the judgments and preferences of older girls are compared with those of women.

In the first of these studies, Parmely C. Daniels (1933) sets out the purpose of her investigation as being to devise and apply a technique for determining the child's sensitivity to compositional balance, suitable as far as possible for 2-year-old children; and for those up to the six-year level. She wanted to determine whether this sensitivity does exist at such an early age and to discover whether individual differences exist and whether, if they do exist, they are related to intelligence and performance ability.

She points out that the term 'balance' as applied in the graphic and plastic arts most frequently refers to an unsymmetrical form of equilibrium, but this, called occult balance, was too complex to investigate in this study. Symmetrical balance is found in three general forms, namely bilateral, or symmetry of right and left, radial as in the shape of leaves, trees, etc., and vertical balance, as in rocks, ant-hills and the like.

The apparatus, illustrated in Plate 11, consisted of sets of wooden blocks specially devised for the purpose, and two display cabinets. In each cabinet a design was built with the blocks, one symmetrical or balanced, the other of identical blocks but unbalanced. Set A was made with six blocks; Set B, seven; Set C, eight; Set D, eighteen; and Set E with twenty-five. The balanced and unbalanced designs were presented right and left in irregular order, set by set. The child was supplied with the same number of identical blocks for each set and asked to build one of the designs for the experimenter. When he had finished he was asked to indicate his preference. The subjects were 38 children, 2 years 1 month to 5 years 8 months, of IQs from 65 to 149, from average Middle West homes. Spontaneous building activities were also studied for many of the children.

A child's construction of one of the models was rated 3 for perfect reproduction, 2 for average, 1 for poor reproduction and 0 for attempted construction without sucess. The experimental records also dealt with (a) which compositions were balanced or unbalanced, (b) the child's preference, and (c) his own free compositions.

The results of this experiment showed that pre-school children tended to a statistically significant extent to prefer balanced to unbalanced three-dimensional designs.

Individuals differed greatly in their capacity to discriminate three-dimensional balance, however, and in their ability to reconstruct such designs from the models. Ability to reconstruct the models was not correlated with balance discrimination and balance discrimination was not correlated significantly with general intelligence as measured with the Stanford Revision of the Binet–Simon test ($r = \cdot197 \pm \cdot105$).

The third study, which will be mentioned next, because it seems to be more closely related to the first than is the second, concerned children's sensitivity to compositional unity (Whorley, Katherine S., 1933). In order to study pre-school children three tests were developed which would reveal sensitivity to compositional unity, which was defined as, 'The just adaptation of the parts to each other, in any system or combination of things intended to form a connected whole; such an agreement between the different parts of a design or composition as to produce unity of effect' (*Webster's International Dictionary*).

The test materials were as follows:

I. *Bird-bath*. A toy bird-bath and four toy evergreen trees arranged on a toy grass plot with a wall-corner of wooden blocks behind (illustrated in Plate 12);

II. *Entrance-planting*. Eight toy trees and a symmetrical toy entrance or doorway of wooden blocks (illustrated in Plate 13);

III. *Room arrangement*. A doll's house with cut-away side facing the child. Furniture for a music room and a living room were provided.

For the bird-bath test the child had to choose which to imitate of two models before him, one having compositional unity and the other not unified, the bird-bath itself being fixed in position in the set of material he had to handle. For the other two tests the child had to make the arrangements himself.

One hundred unselected children were subjects, 40 from the Pre-School Group III, 29 from the Junior Primary and 31 from the Elementary School Grade I, ranging in age from 3 years 6 months to 7 years 6 months. Of these 51 were boys and 49 girls. Repeat tests results to determine reliability were obtained for a considerable number of the children, and this was reasonably high; mean square contingency being from 0·24 to 0·71 for various comparisons. Fifty unselected adults from university summer school classes, 17 to 51 years of age, also did the first two tests.

A scale of values from 1 to 7 for classifying the children's results was developed for the bird-bath and entrance-planting tests, by agreement of a number of expert landscape architects. The results of the experiment showed that while the majority of the children showed little or no consistent appreciation of unity of arrangement, a few appeared to be sensitive to a high-degree. Between ages 4 and 7 years of age unity-sensitivity increased slightly and the adult results supported the idea of a maturation, because the proportion of adults sensitive to unity was higher than for children, although no adults were more sensitive than some of the children. There was no relationship between sensitivity to compositional unity and mental age, but there was a tendency to suggest that girls were more sensitive than boys. Fitness, the main factor in the room-arrangement test, seemed to be independent of outdoor arrangement as in the other two tests.

The second study was reported by Constance C. Jasper (1933). In order to have apparatus suitable for children about 2–6 years of age, after trying out some preliminary forms for the experiment, the following material (illustrated in Plate 14) was adopted: A. Six pictorial border designs in colour, having as motifs rabbits, ducks, children, birds, dogs and boats; B. Six abstract border designs in black on cream paper; C. Twelve pairs of abstract border designs in black on cream paper, one rhythmic and one unrhythmic in each pair; D. Two rows of wooden blocks cut in abstract designs and lacquered in red, one row rhythmic and one unrhythmic. For A and B, the child had to choose a suitable figure to fill a space in the set in a way consistent with the rhythmic pattern. For C he had to say which design of each pair he liked best, and for D he had to look at the row of blocks and make a design of his own. A composite score was worked out for the four tests together.

The children comprised 21 aged 3 years; 22 aged 4 years; 29 aged 5 years and 40 aged 6 years; total 112. The correlation between chronological age and sensitivity to design rhythm was r = 0·69 ± 0·036. There was a definite increase in composite score with chronological age, which rose from 160/250 at age 31 months to about 200/250 at age 72 months, showing that there was a fairly steady increase in visual rhythm sensitivity with increasing age. There was no correlation of rhythm of design sensitivity score and intelligence as measured by the Stanford–Binet and Kuhlmann tests. Sex differences were negligible, the average score for girls being 200·8 and for boys 201·7, a trifling difference in favour of the boys.

The fourth study on the Iowa monographs was by Wilhelmina E. Jacobson (1933) and concerned the basic aesthetic factors in costume design. In the first phase of this study twenty paired designs adapted from *Vogue* (October 1928 to June 1929) was obtained by taking twenty designs and making a copy of each modified to be of lower aesthetic quality. The material was shown to 198 women and 126 girls, ranging from 10 to 81 years of age. It was assumed that a high percentage of preferences for one design and a low percentage for the modification showed that the first was beautiful and the second ugly, and that approximately equal preferences showed that the test items were faulty in not presenting a clear-cut problem. Wilhelmina Jacobson does not state the implication of preference for the altered and so-called inferior version, which occurred in about 7 or 8 of the 20 comparisons. However it is important that there was a correlation of 0·805 between the choices of women (age range 18 to 80 years) and girls (age range 10 to 18 years). The factors influencing choices were classified into (1) aesthetic, (2) economic, (3) hygienic and (4) miscellaneous.

The second phase of the research was directed to the isolation of the aesthetic factors which are basic in costume design, and the third phase was an investigation of the reasons why these factors are basic. As the main purpose of summarising the research here is to show the high correlation between girl's and women's choices, the second and third phases will not be reported in detail. Girls, however, were less analytical than women. 'The aesthetic impulse', says Wilhelmina Jacobson 'finds, satisfaction, (a) in certain space relationships when they tend to create a sense of balance or lessen tension; (b) in balance in that it creates an experience of stability and equilibrium; (c) in rhythm when it directs attention or favours perception by unifying; (d) in emphasis when it lessens the strain of attention by attracting, fixing, directing, or holding attention' (p. 182).

In Chapter 7, where the comparison of Negro and white children's art preferences by Betty Lark-Horovitz (1939–40) was reported, three studies by her of white children's preferences for subject pictures, portraits and textile patterns were mentioned. In the research on textile patterns, which is most relevant to this section on composition and balance, there were 521 children, aged 6–15 years and a group of children who were specially gifted artistically, aged 11–15 years. The group of average children included 259 boys and 261 girls, and the special group included 26 boys and 17 girls. The textiles used in the experiment consisted of 11 modern and 28 historical patterns. The results showed a preference for three of the 39 patterns enduring through all age groups. These three patterns were: no. 7, brocaded silk, grey ground with black elephant heads, French, by Bianci Ferrier; no. 19, leaves and flowers and stylised plums, hand painted in colours on a lemon silk ground, Chinese, 18th century; no. 34, design for Navajo weaving, dark red ground, diamond shapes, continuous pattern, diamond border of white and black steps, insertions in green, black and red crosses. Pattern no. 7 was also preferred by the children of special ability. Boys were influenced in their choices by special interest in the subject represented (as in nos. 7 and 34), while girls shared the subject interest of the boys, but to a larger extent showed a more static type of interest in decoration which was embodied in a reality (as in the flowers of no. 19). Younger children were attracted by brightness, variety of colours and favourite colours. Older children preferred fewer colours in more subdued shades. Children of special ability picked out qualities to support their choices which are important in artistic achievement, such as techniques, line and shape, texture, originality, and reduce the importance of associations of various kinds. They interpret their pattern preferences in terms of aesthetic qualities, while average children interpret their choices in terms of qualities which are general, personal and associative.

Children's aesthetic judgments of pictures

A very interesting and significant book on the psychological and educational aspects and problems of children's aesthetic judgments was published by Littlejohns and Needham (1933). They were largely interested in the teaching of art in schools, and improving it from the point of view of understanding better than before what kinds of art children liked and disliked at various ages, and the teacher's equipment in the classroom and technique in the art lesson.

In order to discover more about the attitudes and interest in art of the children, they began with three assumptions (p. 6):
 (1) That children are likely to have preferences;
 (2) That there is a natural evolution of taste; and,
 (3) That the evolution of taste can be fostered and developed.

Altogether they dealt with about 3,000 children from 11 to 18 years of age in many schools of different types, and they collected data in the hope of solving the following three questions, which correspond to their assumptions:
 (1) What kinds of pictures do children naturally prefer?;
 (2) What is the natural evolution of their tastes?; and,
 (3) How can this natural evolution be fostered and developed?

The first study reported by Littlejohns and Needham was on the immediate reaction of children to pictures (ch. 2). They took three sets of four pictures each, the first set being of landscapes, namely, 'Landscape' by Poussin, 'Salisbury Cathedral', by Constable, 'Sheltered Pastures' by Waterlow, and 'Break of Day' by Angus Angrave. These were chosen to form a series of varied aesthetic merit, the Poussin being the best and the one by Angrave the least good. The other two series were similarly constituted. The second series of pictures was of interiors and the third was of subjects (people). The children, 11 to 16 or 17 years of age, in two age groups, younger and older, were asked to view the pictures and to say which they liked or disliked and why.

The most general results of these experiments were to show a growth of aesthetic taste with increasing age. For most of the children the subject of the picture was the first consideration, then colour, while generally only the older children appreciated light and shade, and only a few felt that arrangement of the objects in a picture had anything to do with its aesthetic merit.

The second study reported the effects of experience (ch. 3). For this three pairs of pictures were used, one of each pair being 'good' and the other being brightly coloured and having a strong sentimental appeal. The first pair was two landscapes, and the second of horses and figures and the third of agricultural labourers. The children were asked to make a choice between the pictures and to give their reasons. Some classes of boys in a London school, the younger being about 11 years of age and the older ones 14 to 15 years of age, acted as subjects.

After making their selection the boys were allowed to see the pictures several times a week for about six weeks and then to see whether their opinions changed, and to say why. Some changed their opinions after a week, others after two weeks and a few did not change until after the fifth week. No boy went back to his original choice. In the landscapes the young boys at first greatly favoured the brightly coloured picture (no. 2), but a large proportion went over to the other (no. 1). Older boys who liked no. 1 best at first later gave such reasons for changing their minds as: 'On examining the pictures more closely I have noticed that no. 2 looks very artificial.' Many other examples are quoted.

Several classes of boys were shown coloured reproductions of Dutch pictures at the time of the 1929 Exhibition of Dutch art at the Royal Academy, and also coloured reproductions of School pictures by English artists. They were allowed to examine them thoroughly and asked to answer the question, 'If you had to select a picture for your room at home, from which group would you choose one, the Dutch group or the School group?'

Out of 86 boys from 12 to 15 years of age, only seven of the younger, and only eleven of the older boys, would have preferred one from the Dutch group. The most popular Dutch pictures were Hals's 'Laughing Cavalier', Hobbema's 'Landscape with a Mill' and Rembrandt's 'Mill'.

After this they were asked to choose which group of pictures they would use if they had to decorate all the rooms in their houses. Only nine of the 86 boys preferred the Dutch group, and they gave such reasons as 'Dutch pictures show life in the olden days and so contrast to modern times'. Of the majority, who preferred the School group, the following kind of reply was typical, 'Colours are not so sombre; unless the Dutch pictures have a lot of light on them, you can hardly see them, whereas the School ones give out light.'

When questioned whether they preferred outdoor or indoor subjects, all 86 preferred outdoor subjects. As they were London boys, landscapes and seascapes forming a contrast to their drab surroundings might be more attractive than the rather dark interiors.

In another experiment about 50 boys of 14 to 15 years 6 months, in a secondary school, were shown reproductions of 21 pictures published in the Board of Education's pamphlet *School Pictures* (Pictorial Education). They were told to imagine themselves as a committee to consider the suitability of the pictures for their school. The pictures were all in monochrome, and colour could not be considered. The boys, however, were asked to discuss the pictures freely and express their likes and dislikes frankly without considering whether a picture was 'supposed' to be a good one or not. Some interesting conclusions emerged: (1) older boys liked the simpler form of picture as much as younger ones; (2) the desire for clearness, realism and action was strong; (3) a portrait was not regarded as a picture; (4) pictures of women did not interest the boys; (5) the work of the great painters could not be appreciated without a larger experience of life; (6) there was little interest in design; (7) nothing in the types of picture shown was of interest to quite young children, which seems to point to the non-existence of 'good' pictures for infants and juniors in the adult sense and the need of specially designed pictures for them.

Littlejohns and Needham devoted another study (ch. 4) to the 'considered opinions' of girls and boys, in order to find out in what ways and to what extent there were differences between boys and girls of various ages. In the replies of 400 girls from various schools, giving reasons for liking or disliking pictures shown to them, a gradual change from 7–8 years up to 12–13 years in the development of taste can be found, beginning with excitement about things and movement, passing to sentimental interests and then to appreciation of arrangement. Compared with boys, girls were more emotional and appreciative; boys were more analytical and destructive, but insisted upon realism and exactness. Girls preferred pictures in which dress predominates, but boys were attracted to landscapes, seascapes and vigorous action. All preferred coloured pictures to monochromes.

In a study of children's reactions to modern art (ch. 5), four pictures by modern artists were selected and four showing similar subjects by old masters. They were: *First pair:* 'Boulevard in Spring' (Renoir), and 'Grand Canal' (Canaletto); *Second pair:* 'The Village Way' (Cézanne) and 'The Avenue at Merdervort' (Albert Cuyp); *Third pair:* 'Montmartre' (Renoir) and 'The Bent Tree' (Corot); *Fourth pair:* 'Red Horses' (Marc) and 'The Horse Fair' (Rosa Bonheur). In another test three pictures were used, representing realism (Constable—'Bridge over the Stour'), impressionism (Murray Smith—'The Bridge') and post-impressionism (Van Gogh—'Landscape with a Bridge'). The four pairs of pictures and the trio of pictures in the fifth set are named here because they might help another worker in choosing material for a further study.

The outcome of this research, however, showed that, as far as the trio of pictures was concerned, among 200 boys in a secondary school, there was a sternly critical attitude towards the non-representational character of recent painting. The preference for realism was overwhelming, but among those who preferred the modern works there was a hint of appreciation of colour and arrangement.

In respect of the four pairs of pictures, 200 younger and 200 older boys of a secondary school expressed their preferences, and there was no doubt that normal children, 11–15 years of age, disliked the pictures of unaccustomed style intensely. There was no evolution of taste with age. The result, say Littlejohns and Needham, appears to dispose of the contention of some enthusiasts for modern art, who have tried to show that because children's drawings are often incompletely realistic they will prefer the same kind of expression in pictures by artists.

Other chapters in Littlejohns and Needham's book deal with experiments based on poster art, on lettering and on various kinds of crafts; and with the teaching of art in schools.

In comparison with the work of Littlejohns and Needham just mentioned, it is interesting that Gertrude Hildreth (1936) found, in a study already discussed in the section on colour preferences, that, among sixteen pictures including a wide variety of subjects, the two most preferred by both under- and over-five-year-olds included animals. The first choice was a picture by S. Glücklich called *'Die Kleinen Tierfreunde'*, which showed a girl seated on a bench holding a white rabbit being fed by a boy seated on the ground. The second was Landseer's picture of a large Newfoundland dog, and the third choice was a picture called 'Little Brother' by M. O. Kobbé, which showed a girl about 12 years of age holding her baby brother.

At the Cleveland Museum of Art, as already mentioned, Betty Lark-Horovitz (1937–8) studied children's preferences for subject-pictures and for portraits. The results of her observations and many other interesting aspects and problems of art appreciation and art abilities of children are reported by Munro, Lark-Horovitz and Barnhart in the report on their work at the Department of Education, Cleveland Museum of Art (1942).

In the study of children's preferences for pictures, 561 children aged from 6 to 16 years, and 72 specially gifted children aged from 11 to 16 years, acted as subjects. There were 227 boys and 234 girls in the group of average ability, each year age group comprising about 20 girls and 20 boys, and there were 34 boys and 38 girls in the special group. Out of 70 pictures 12 were chosen by a preliminary experiment, and they were as follows: (1) Denis Etcheverry—'Portrait in Pink'; (2) H. Fantin-Latour—'Tannhauser'; (3) Hans Thoma—'Dancing in a Ring'; (4) W. Bouguereau—'The Bathers'; (5) Carl Hofer—'Muzzane'; (6) C. Corot—'Evening'; (7) J. Bastien Lepage—'Joan of Arc'; (7a) N. C. Wyeth —Illustration from *The Black Arrow* by Stevenson; (8) Bruno Liljefors—'Swans'; (9) G. Courbet—'Apples'; (10) A. Renoir—'Flowers'; (11) H. le Sidanier—'The Dessert' (Interior).

The children were asked to choose their first, second, third and further preferences, and a questionnaire was used to investigate reasons for choices. The interest and majority of votes centred about the Hans Thoma, 'Dancing in a Ring', the Carl Hofer, the Wyeth, *The Black Arrow*, and the Bruno Liljefors, 'Swans', which held first place for 8 age levels. The Etcheverry, 'Portrait in Pink', carried a majority of votes through ages 6, 7 and 8, mainly supported by girl's votes. The Wyeth was mainly supported by boys.

Reasons for preference were first subject or content and second colour. The average group centres on the subject; the special children were influenced by design, colour and knowledge gained from a picture and they gave more reasons relating to emotion and imagery than the average group. They were not so desirous as the average group to own their favourite picture or to want to paint just such a picture, and fewer of them offered suggestions for changes in the pictures. Numerous other interesting points are mentioned in the original paper.

In the portrait preference study Betty Lark-Horovitz used 237 boys and 242 girls in the average ability group, 6–15 years of age, and 23 boys and 21 girls in the group of special ability, 12–15 years of age. The pictures were chosen systematically from 261 arranged in five groups: young women, young men, old people, children, and family pictures. The choices of pictures consisted of 51 for the younger children (6–10 years old), 25 per cent un-coloured, and 43 for the older group (11–15 years of age), 32 per cent uncoloured. Pictures 1 to 21 were the same for both groups. A comparison of two pictures (no. 10, K. W. Leighton: 'Sun Dance' and no. 14, Georg Buchner: 'Erica') shows a fading of interest with age for the first and mounting interest for the second with increasing age.

At the age of 9–10 uncoloured pictures began to be preferred to coloured ones, and this preference, increasing with age, exceeded the number, in proportion, of uncoloured pictures in the exhibits. The younger group chose only pictures of younger people, with the exception of no. 38, William Orpen: 'General Foch'. Girls preferred pictures of women and children, while boys almost exclusively preferred pictures of men, but no. 26, A. Graff: 'Self-Portrait', a man's portrait, was a favourite of both girls and boys.

The choices of the younger children suggests identification with their hero or with what he is likely to do, but older children identify themselves with individual 'character' traits, sentiments, and emotions. Thus the younger children want to be included in the doings of their hero, but the older ones want to look like him or her.

Colour was of secondary interest, but the choices of the older group were influenced by technique. The comparison of specially gifted with average children showed few differences, except that the average boy and girl differ markedly in their taste, while the taste of the specially gifted boys and girls is much the same. The specially gifted have less interest in the person portrayed, and are more influenced than the average children by qualities of an aesthetic nature.

An experiment by James P. Cranston (1952) was designed in an attempt to discover the type of art preferred by primary and secondary-school children at various ages from 8–17 years, and to enquire into the bases of children's aesthetic judgments. Twenty postcard reproductions of widely divergent types of paintings were used, and 96 boys and 96 girls from two Glasgow schools differing widely in social and cultural background were the subjects. They were asked to rate the postcard reproductions on a seven-point scale for general liking, colour and emotion, to say which they liked best and which least and to write down any associations to the picture.

It was evident that the youngest group preferred bold general outlines to painstakingly careful detail. Older children, above about the age of 11 years, however, become more interested with increasing age in more or less photographic reproductions of some pleasing or interesting subject. Impressionist and classical works each had their following, but Cubist and Symbolist works had no appeal to the children in this experiment. There was a marked difference between 'boys' ' pictures, such as Gibb's 'The Alma or Forward the 42nd', and 'girls' ' pictures, such as Dégas' 'Dancing School'. One picture, 'Red Squirrels', by Margaret W. Tarrant, was highly rated on all criteria by children of both sexes and of all ages. This picture is one of a series of illustrations of animals and birds.

Second to content, colour played an important part in appreciation, and the experiment confirmed the finding of other workers, that younger children prefer bright, primary and contrasting colours, while older children prefer colours which blend harmoniously and give a quieter effect. Colour preference differences between the sexes were not marked.

Cranston's most general conclusions were that, although the child's attitude to different types of painting undergoes a change with increasing age, he does not really develop a true awareness of the intrinsic value of any work of art. 'To arrive at a stage of truly critical appraisal of any work of art it would seem that the children must follow some definite course of instruction in aesthetic appreciation' (p. 23).

Hussain's experiment already referred to in Chapters 6 and 7 (1962, p. 76) showed that children of 9–10 years of age did not vary any less or have more consistency in their judgments for preference of paintings by Picasso, Reid, children or the chimpanzee Congo, than adult subjects, nor did it show that the responses of children were more stereotyped than those of adults to these paintings.

Some of the results obtained by workers previously mentioned were confirmed by an experiment conducted by Rump and Vera Southgate in the Whitworth Art Gallery, Manchester (1967). These investigators studied the pictorial interests and preferences of 20 boys and 21 girls aged 7 years; 14 boys and 20 girls aged 11 years; 28 boys and 21 girls from two technical high schools, aged 15 years; and 7 men and 11 women teachers attending a conference connected with the picture exhibition. This was of 76 items, including 13 oil paintings and 6 other paintings by contemporary artists of repute, 21 original prints, 8 reproductions of 15th to 18th century works and 10 of 19th and 20th century works, 11 paintings by local pupils and 7 textiles by contemporary designers.

Some concordance was found, using three measures of appreciation: 'approving comments', recorded 'interests' of the groups and individually expressed first and second choices. The 7- and 11-year-old children strongly preferred pictures realistically depicting familiar objects. Brightly coloured items were preferred by all age groups. Abstract paintings preferred by some older children were liked for their colouring. Comments mainly referred to objects represented, or were expressions of approval. Seven-year-old children made some ego-centric remarks. Sex differences, especially marked for younger children, were found for some pictures and the preferences expressed by an interviewer had a positive effect of suggestibility while the purported preference of a teacher had a negative effect on the children's preferences.

Irvin Child (1966) and Irvin Child and Rosaline Schwartz (1966, 1968) have dealt with some important problems concerning picture preference studies and the teaching of aesthetic appreciation. In the first paper Child reviews the experimental and statistical evidence for objectivity of aesthetic taste and points out the weakness of researches which assume that the opinion of the majority is a sound objective criterion. He also discusses the evidence concerning degrees of agreement among experts, showing that one reason why experts differ is that sometimes the works compared do not in fact vary greatly in aesthetic value. Another reason is that they are distracted by other aspects, such as unfamiliarity with a new style or artistic invention, and some of the disagreement between judges in different cultures must be ascribed to the fact that they have different experiences even though looking at the same objects.

Child was interested in studying, 'In what kinds of people we especially expect to find personal preferences or aesthetic judgments which agree with those of experts?' and in experimentally produced variations in experience that might lead to measured agreement with them.

In the second paper Child and Rosaline Schwartz (1966) report an experiment on the training in art appreciation of 130 sophomores at Yale College, and the entire 4th, 5th and 6th grades of children in a public elementary school in a well-to-do suburb, and portions of the 7th and 8th grades in the regional secondary schools of the three-town region to which the suburb belongs. The results did not support decisively either the view that aesthetic value is based entirely on convention or that the judgments an art expert makes on aesthetic value depend mainly on careful study of art and of his own reactions to it. For some college students the training opened a new realm of experience. Others found no such new meaning, except the superficial effect of identifying clues leading to prediction of what someone else would say about each work. The results on the children were more telling against the extreme study-and-understanding position. On the whole Child and Schwartz say that, 'The ability to learn to recognise by relatively superficial cues what experts consider better or poorer art does not necessarily result in increased understanding'.

The third paper (1968) reports an investigation of the effects of exposure to poorer and better art among 19 college students and three schools, A, B and C, within a city of moderate size (population about 150,000). Nearly 60 per cent of the pupils in the third school, C, were Negroes. For these subjects the effects of seeing pairs of lantern slides, up to a total of 960 pairs being used, for the college students all 960 in 8 sessions of one hour each spread over several weeks, and for the school children 900 pairs in 9 sessions for school A, a shorter series for school B and 900 pairs in 11 sessions for school C. The results were analysed to discover whether there was an increasing tendency to prefer the better picture of each pair as the training proceeded, as a result of the experimenter's comments and explanations, although he avoided at all times any suggestion that art can or should be evaluated in any other way than that requested of the children—the expression of personal preference. No artist's names were mentioned.

Child and Schwartz say that the results of this exposure to many pairs of works of art differing in aesthetic quality were negative. There was no suggestion of a consistent change for the groups as a whole, either among school children or college students. The authors say, 'Should one conclude that mere exposure to good art contributes nothing to the development of aesthetic sensitivity? This seems too broad a generalisation from our particular procedures' (p. 117). They then discuss the implications of their results for art training and in the light of other experiments, Mendenhall and Mendenhall (1933), for instance, found that the influence of familiarity on children's preferences for particular pictures and poems was that it led them to like better what they already liked and to dislike more intensely what they already disliked.

Some interesting and unusual points concerning children's art judgments about children's paintings have been brought out in a study by Huguette Voillaume (1968). She obtained 200 paintings by boys and girls from 4 years 6 months to 16. They were provided with gouache paints in 12 colours and standard sheets of paper and were asked to make a picture of '*Une dame se promene avec son chien*'. A group of artists classified the paintings, and put numerous works of the youngest group of children, aged 4 years 6 months to 6 years 5 months in the first rank. Those of children of the next age group, 6 years 6 months to 9 years 5 months, were placed second, while those of the next two age groups, 9 years 6 months to 12 years 5 months and over 12 years 6 months, were placed either third or fourth in rank. The children themselves, 365 in number, however, reversed this order, placing the works of the two youngest groups either third or fourth, those of the third age group, second, and those of the fourth or oldest age group first in rank.

More precisely, it was shown that children of 7 to 12 years of age are above all appreciative of the skill of execution of the older ones. Those less than 7 years of age were too unstable in their judgments for anything decisive to be stated about them, except that they never placed in the first-rank pictures by children of their own age which were considered very good by the artists. Among the children over the age of 12 years individual differences due to personal and socio-cultural factors were observed. The majority of children continue, says Huguette Voillaume, to appreciate art in the manner of the youngest, but some develop in their taste and class certain pictures in the same way as artists. Among the young ones however, in certain rare cases, children have been found who differed from the whole group.

In a recent research Eysenck and Maureen Castle (1970) asked 369 male and 408 female art students, and 176 male and 180 female non-art students, to rate 90 polygons for aesthetic pleasingness on a scale from 7, the most pleasing down to 1, the least pleasing. The subjects also completed the Eysenck Personality Inventory, Form A, and scores for extraversion, neuroticism and a lie scale were obtained. The age range was about 16–25 years, with a majority at about 20 years of age.

A factor analysis was carried out for 90 factors and the 12 factors having the highest latent roots were rotated by the Promax method. Examples of the polygons corresponding to the various factors are given in the article. Most of the factors were similar for the artist and non-artist groups, but artists preferred simple and non-artists complex polygons. Birkhoff's formula $M = O/C$ had little predictive value, although it correlated slightly better with the artist's than the non-artist's rankings. Artists were higher on neuroticism than non-artists, but the two groups did not differ on extraversion. Women were higher than men on neuroticism, and non-artist women were lower on extraversion but artist women were not.

Eysenck and Castle point out that they might be dealing with the effects of art training, and/or with a process of selection that those who prefer order and simplicity are more likely to choose art courses, to be accepted for them and to make good in them. In view of recent evidence of the ineffectiveness of teaching art values (Child and Schwartz, 1966) and of exposure to better and poorer art (Child and Schwartz, 1968) a fuller study of the effects of art training, selection for art courses and fundamental aesthetic judgment, sensibility or capacity in ranking polygons, would be particularly valuable.

Eysenck has recently (1972) suggested that maturation was probably more influential than teaching in producing 'correct' judgments on the tests he used.

Bibliography and References
for Chapter 8

ALSCHULER, ROSE H., and HATTWICK, LA B. W. (1947). *Painting and Personality: A Study of Young Children.* Chicago: University Press. 2 vols.

CHASE, W. P. (1937). Colour Vision in Infants, *J. Exptl. Psychol., 20,* 203–22.

CHILD, I. L. (1966). The Problem of Objectivity in Esthetic Value. *Penn State Papers in Art Education,* no. 1, pp. 1–25. Dept. of Art Education, Pennyslvania State University, USA.

CHILD, I. L., and SCHWARTZ, ROSALINE S. (1966). Exploring the Teaching of Art Values. *J. Aesthetic Education. 1,* 41–54.

CHILD, I. L., HANSEN, J. A., and HORNBECK, F. W. (1968). Age and Sex Differences in Children's Color Preferences. *Child Development, 39,* 237–47.

CHILD, I. L., and SCHWARTZ, ROSALINE S. (1968). Exposure to Poorer and Better Art. *J. Aesthetic Education, 2,* 111–24.

CHOUNGOURIAN, A. (1969). *Percept. Motor Skills.* 28, 801–2.

COUPLEUX, ANDRÉ (1968). 'L'Objectivité Psychologique de la Couleur'. *Proc. Fifth Internat. Congress of Aesthetics,* Amsterdam: Mouton, 1964, pp. 877–80.

CRANSTON, J. P. (1952). The Nature and Development of Aesthetic Appreciation in Children. *Brit. Psychol. Soc. Quart. Bulletin, 3, 15;* 21–3.

DANIELS, PARMELY C. (1933). Discrimination of Compositional Balance at thePre-School Level. *Psychol. Monogr., no. 200,* 1–11.

DASHIELL , J. F. (1917). Children's Sense of Harmonies in Colours and Tones. *J. Exptl. Psychol., 2,* 466–75.

EYSENCK, H. J. (1972). *J. Child Psychol. and Psychiatry, 13,* 1–10.

EYSENCK, H. J., and CASTLE, MAUREEN (1970). Training in Art as a Factor in the determination of Preference Judgments for Polygons. *Brit. J. Psychol., 61,* 65–81.

GARTH, T. R. (1924). A Color Preference Scale for 1000 White Children. *J. Exptl. Psychol., 7,* 233–41.

HILDRETH, GERTRUDE H. (1936). Color and Picture Choices of Young Children. *J. Genet. Psychol., 49,* 427–35.

HOLDEN, W. A., and BOSSE, K. K. (1900). The Order of Development of Colour Perception and of Colour Preferences in the Child. *Arch. Ophthal., 29,* 261–77.

HUSSAIN, FAKHIR (1962). *An Experimental Enquiry into the Phenomena of 'Aesthetic Judgements' Under Varying Time Conditions.* Ph.D. Thesis, University of London (unpublished).

JACOBSON, W. E. (1933). An Experimental Investigation of the Basic Aesthetic Factors in Costume Design. *Psychol. Monogr., no. 200,* 147–88.

JASPER, CONSTANCE C. (1933). The Sensitivity of Children of Pre-School Age to Rhythm in Graphic Form. *Psychol. Monogr., no. 200,* 12–21.

KATZ, S. E. and BREED, F. S. (1922). The Color Preference of Children. *J. Appl. Psychol., 6,* 255–66.

LAKOWSKI, R. (1958). Age and Colour Vision. *Advancement of Science, 59,* 231–6.

LARK-HOROVITZ, BETTY (1937–8). On Art Appreciation of Children. I. Preference of Picture Subjects in General; and II. Portrait Preference Study. *J. Educ. Psychol., 31,* 118–37 and 572–98.

LARK-HOROVITZ, BETTY (1939–40). On Art Appreciation of Children: III. Textile Pattern Preference Study. *J. Educ. Psychol., 33,* 7–35.

LITTLEJOHNS, J. and NEEDHAM, A. (1933). *Training of Taste in the Arts and Crafts.* London: Pitman.

MENDENHALL, J. E. and MENDENHALL, M. E. (1933). *The Influence of Familiarity upon Children's Preferences for Pictures and Poems.* New York: Bureau of Publications of Teachers' Colleges, Columbia University.

MUNRO, THOMAS, LARK-HOROVITZ, BETTY and BARNHART, E. N. (1942). Children's Art Abilities: Studies at the Cleveland Museum of Art. *J. Exptl. Education, 11,* 97–184.

MYERS, C. S. (1908). Some Observations on the Development of the Colour Sense. *Brit. J. Psychol., 2,* 353–62.

RIDGWAY, R. (1912). *Color Standards and Color Nomenclature.* Washington: Ridgway.

RUMP, E. E. and SOUTHGATE, VERA (1967). Variables Affecting Aesthetic Appreciation in Relation to Age. *Brit. J. Educ. Psychol., 37,* 58–72.

STAPLES, RUTH (1931). Color Vision and Color Preference in Infancy and Childhood. A Summary of Investigations from 1890 to 1931. *Psychol. Bull., 28,* 297–308.

STAPLES, RUTH (1932). The Responses of Infants to Color. *J. Exptl. Psychol., 15,* 119–41.

VALENTINE, C. W. (1914). The Colour Perception and Colour Preferences of an Infant during its Fourth and Eighth Months. *Brit. J. Psychol., 6,* 363–86.

VALENTINE, C. W. (1962). *The Experimental Psychology of Beauty.* London: Methuen.

VOILLAUME, HUGUETTE (1968). '*L'Art et l'Enfant.*' *Proc. Fifth Internat. Congress of Aesthetics,* Amsterdam 1964. Mouton, 1968, 911–15.

WALTON, W. E. (1933). The Sensitivity of Children and Adults to Color Harmony. *Psychol. Monogr., no. 200,* 51–62.

WHORLEY, KATHERINE S. (1933). An Experimental Investigation of the Sensitivity of Children to Compositional Unity. *Psychol. Mongr.*, no. 200, 26–45.

WILLIAMS, EILEEN J. (1933). A Technique for Testing Colour Harmony Sensitivity in Young Children. *Psychol. Monogr.*, no. 200, 46–50.

WINCH, W. H. (1909). Colour Preferences of School Children. *Brit. J. Psychol.*, 3, 42–65.

WINCH, W. H. (1910). Color Names of English School Children. *Amer. J. Psychol.*, 21, 453–82.

WOODS, W. A. (1956). Some Determinants of Attitudes Towards Colors in Combinations. *Perceptual and Motor Skills*, 6, 187–93.

9
Personality and aesthetic preferences

The study of temperament and personality in relation to aesthetic preferences and judgments links up with several other aspects of the whole subject of psychology, art and aesthetics. For example, it links up with personality tests, some of which depend wholly or partly on responses to colour (Rorschach Technique, 1942; Pfister Colour Pyramid Test, 1951; Lüscher Test, 1949). It also links up with art judgment tests, which depend on responses to form and colour because artistic ability is in some degree a personality attribute. It links up with tests of creativity, and with Bullough's studies of perceptive types. There are related problems in studies of psychiatric types and psychiatric art.

Recently excellent surveys of the problems of personality and aesthetic judgments and preferences have been made by Francès (1968) and by Child (1969). In this chapter the central aspects will be considered. Some of the psychiatric aspects have been mentioned elsewhere (Pickford 1967), and in many cases it is not easy to say exactly where a given study or experiment should be placed.

Artistic and non-artistic children and students

Four studies of the differences in behaviour, background experiences, personality qualities and psycho-physical capacities of children were published together (Mildred Dow, 1933; Frances Rodgers, 1933; Carolyn Tiebout, 1933; and Hildegarde F. Dreps, 1933).

Mildred Dow asked two questions: (1) whether there is a difference in the 'reaction patterns' of an artistically superior group of children compared with an artistically inferior group; and (2) whether there is a difference in the amount of 'progressive activity' between two such groups. By 'reaction pattern' she meant a typical adjustment to the environment based upon native constitution and systems of habit. By 'progressive activity' she meant movement by which a child covers territory, goes from place to place. She utilised the free-play period in the school ground as a suitable opportunity to bring out the differences. The subjects were children from the Preschool of the Iowa Child Welfare Research Station and the Iowa University Elementary School. Eleven children were selected, namely, the six most and the five least artistically talented. Full details of the playground are given in Mildred Dow's monograph.

The general conclusions of this study were stated as follows:

(1) Statistically significant differences were found in types of reaction in free play in a playground containing much play equipment and in one containing little;

(2) These differences were primarily dependent on the presence or absence of equipment;

(3) Artistic children engaged less in physically active and social play and more in play involving equipment than non-artistic children, and these differences tended to disappear in a playground possessing no equipment;

(4) Differences in types of reaction and amount of activity between boys and girls within an artistic or non-artistic group increases in an unequipped as compared with an equipped playground and, in particular, there is a great increase in sociability and activity in the artistic boy.

The object of Frances Rodgers's study was to find out whether high artistic 'intelligence' was directly related to highly aesthetic environment and low artistic 'intelligence' to aesthetically poor environment.

Two groups of subjects were chosen, namely, seven artistically superior and seven artistically inferior children from Detroit, an urban community, and six artistically superior and five artistically inferior children from Iowa City, a small city community. The children were all over 5 years of age. They were compared in terms of an *Environmental Analysis* form and a *Qualititive Index of the Relative Aesthetic Opportunity in the Environment* (122 items).

In general the study brought out the following points:

(1) Artistically more competent children had better environments, and less artistic children had less aesthetic environments;

(2) These differences were more marked in respect of children's books and exterior surroundings and less definitely marked in respect of interiors;

(3) Transient environments had little effect, and travel apparently had none;

(4) Since children in the artistically inferior groups frequently had books of high grade and other aspects of their immediate environments equal to or even better than those of some of the artistically superior children, environment as studied in this research could not be considered a vital factor in the explanation of the variation in artistic competence of the children.

The groups of children studied by Frances Rodgers were also studied by Carolyn Tiebout in order to determine experimentally psychophysical traits—the superior development in which characterises the artistically superior as compared with the artistically inferior child. The subjects were 11 artistically superior and 12 artistically inferior children varying in age from 5 years 2 months to 10 years 1 month. Seventeen psychophysical tests were used, and the results showed that the artistically superior children gave a better performance than the artistically inferior children in the following functions, in so far as they were measured by the tests: (1) completeness and accuracy of observation; (2) recall of observed material after 10 days and six months; (3) uniqueness in construction of objects and situations in images from meaningless forms; (4) originality, as expressed in line drawings; (5) form discrimination or apprehension of the main forms of objects; and (6) feature discrimination involving observation and comparison to determine variant items in a series of visual stimuli (Tiebout, p. 131). Differences found in favour of artistically superior children on tests of recognition memory and apperception or completion of an object from visual imagery of the whole were doubtfully significant. Tests of motility and precision of movement showed no significant differences. The two groups were practically equal in colour sensitivity on the *Lewerenz Recognition of Color Test* (Tiebout, p. 117).

The problems studied by Hildegarde Dreps were to discover if certain capacities are closely correlated with success in graphic art, and what psychophysical characteristics artistically superior individuals possess in comparison with those showing little or no promise. She used 27 subjects in 3 groups as follows: nine Liberal Arts College students, nominated by their Department of Graphic and Plastic Arts as having superior ability; nine designated as 'non-art', and nine rated as having average ability or less. Each subject was studied for 16 hours, normally one hour per week for 16 weeks, and they were given 23 psychophysical tests grouped under six headings, namely aesthetic judgment (3 tests), imagination (3 tests), visual memory for form (6 tests), accuracy and steadiness of movement (4 tests), fundamental abilities, such as colour sensitivity (4 tests), and miscellaneous, such as emotional sensitivity (3 tests).

Dreps concludes her study by saying that there is no one psychophysical characteristic present in all persons gifted in graphic art, and superior degrees of some skills or capacities may be found in individuals not involved in art. In certain capacities, such as aesthetic judgment or visual memory for form, those choosing art may have a superior degree of ability. In other functions there is no apparent advantage possessed by the art student. Prognosis of eventual success in graphic art must be based on other factors than skills in certain capacities, possibly upon temperamental and attitudinal factors, or upon the interaction of a high degree of aesthetic judgment with certain combinations of other capacities and abilities.

Children's paintings and personality

The research by Alschuler and Hattwick on children's paintings and personality characteristics was mentioned in Chapter 9, where some of their conclusions about the development of colour choices and their significance were discussed (Alschuler and Hattwick, 1947). These authors, as mentioned already, analysed the paintings of 88 boys aged 2 years 3 months to 5 years 8 months and 82 girls aged 2 years 9 months to 5 years 8 months. The children were not equally distributed in all the seven half-year age groups, but most were in the three middle groups. The first volume of the book reports and interprets the findings in general terms, but in the second volume biographical summaries about all the children are given, and there are full statistical data concerning all the points presented in the first volume. Here it will be useful to give brief notes summarising findings which are of particular interest, but these notes cannot do adequate justice to these findings.

Alschuler and Hattwick point out that young children tend to express a primary interest in colour at a stage when they are in a largely impulsive level of development. Colour tends to be a more intense and persistent interest among girls than boys, and girls have been found to manifest emotion more than boys. A group of children who emphasised colour was compared with a group who mainly used line and form, and it was found that the second group showed greater self-control, concern with external stimuli and higher frequency of reasoned behaviour. Those children who consistently preferred warm colours tended to manifest free emotional behaviour, whereas those who consistently used cold colours tended to be controlled and over-adaptive, and to be critical and assertive towards others.

Those children who preferred red used it either to express affectionate feelings, or to express hostility or aggression. Those who preferred blue tended to be in a phase of development from impulsive towards controlled behaviour, and the authors distinguished the 'controlled anxiety' use of blue from 'sublimated' blue. In the former, for instance, blue is used to overlay red. In the latter blue is used for constructive outline patterns. Children who emphasised yellow tended to show emotional dependence on adults, to have good relations with them, to seek adult attention and to be disregarded by other children, whereas those who emphasised blue showed more mature objective orientation and self-control. Green was preferred by children who tended to show a lack of strong, overtly expressed emotions. They were more restrained than children who emphasised red. They were self-reliant and content to play by themselves, but accepted social relationships when opportunities for social activities were given to them. Orange was found, in a group analysis, to characterise a number of children who had good adaptation to the environment. In individual case studies it was used by children who feared strong emotion, or those who took refuge from life in imaginative play. Brown was associated with the desire to smear and was contrasted with blue. The children who showed most persistent use of purple were rejected, unhappy boys, and some tended to use purple during unhappy periods. Black was consistently used by children who tended to show a dearth of emotional behaviour in group analysis, and in individual cases they were afraid of individuals or situations with which they felt unable to cope.

Certain points about colour placement were important. Those who consistently overlaid one colour with another tended as a group to be hiding strong personal feelings under an assumed pattern of behaviour. Various other interpretations of overlay centred round the existence of conflicts and emotional stresses in those who used it freely. As a group those who used colours with separated placement tended to direct their energies outward and to be adapting themselves to the environmental expectations. Intermingling of colours was found among children who, as a group, were more free in emotional expression than those with separate colour placement, and more outgoing than those with persistent overlay of colours. Indiscriminate mixing of colours occurred among very young and immature children who were still at the manipulative, smearing level, and had not yet fully developed sensitivity to colour differences. In addition to these general points, individual choices and placements of colour often seem to give clues to personality, mood and passing phases of development.

The study of dynamics of personality expressed through line and form revealed some points which deserve mention here. Emphasis on circles tended to tie in with immaturity, and the change from circular to vertical patterns tended to increase with age during the nursery school years. Children who emphasised verticals were likely, as a group, to be assertive and outgoing. There was also a sex difference, because circular emphasis reflected feminine tendencies, those who used vertical patterns more often were more masculine.

Many other points emerged as a result of the study of individual cases, for details of which the reader must consult the original book. Several kinds of problems about the types of usage of verticals are mentioned, for example, 'cut off' verticals were used most markedly by children who were feeling strongly competitive and hostile concerning masculinity in someone of the opposite sex, and crossed verticals were consistently made by children who showed anxiety about their own sexuality. Alternating emphasis on verticals and circles was found in the paintings of children who showed alternations in submissive and assertive feelings and behaviour.

Further aspects of line and form emerged in the study of the use of symbolic material. Container patterns, for instance, especially when filled with smaller oval or circular forms, were often made by children who were concerned about a new baby in the family. Children whose designs showed horizontal emphasis were likely to be self-protective, fearful or overtly co-operative.

Like the use of line and form, space usage and spatial patterns proved to be of great interest in relation to the children's personality dynamics. Again, the reader must be referred to the original book and its many illustrations and statistical tables, but the following aspects of space usage in the paintings were significant.

1. *Extent of space used*—(a) Painting beyond the border of the page reflected immaturity in some, but defiance against authority in other children.

(b) Painting spread all over the page reflected general immaturity, in some children, but an outgoing, assertive and self-reliant personality in others.

(c) Painting in isolated areas reflected withdrawal and dependency.

(d) Painting proportionately to the page reflected adaptive behaviour.

2. *Space usage with special concern for placement*—(a) Concentration of painting at the top of the page characterised physically small children.

(b) Children who painted mainly at the bottom of the page tended to be 'firmly rooted' and stable.

(c) Differential use of right and left sides of the page was not associated definitely with right- and left-handedness; but

(d) Predominant placement on right or left sides tended to reflect conflict between basic personality drives and overt behaviour; and the dominant hand might be, but is not always, the one which expresses overt behaviour rather than repressed feelings.

(e) Centering on the page reflected self-centered and also affectionate and adaptive tendencies.

(f) Balance accorded with adequate adjustment of behaviour.

3. *Method in space usage*—(a) Scattered strokes occurred in the paintings of less controlled and more assertive, immature children.

(b) Full-page painting might be a by-product of inadequate control, but, if it was done with deliberate controlled stroking it reflected out-going, self-reliant, assertive and adaptive tendencies.

(c) Working over the same area reflected self-control, repression, fearfulness and emotional dependency, but if it amounted to shading, then it reflected emotional problems.

(d) Those children who did little re-tracing were relatively self-reliant, outgoing, self-confident and adaptive. They tended to be friendly with both children and adults and to show initiative in play and to have many interests.

Introversion and extraversion in relation to aesthetics

The concepts of introversion and extraversion were applied in an experimental research to the appreciation of pictures by Burt (1939). In his experiment 80 picture-postcard reproductions of romantic, realistic, impressionistic and classical art were judged by 276 persons, chiefly children over 12 years of age or students aged 20 to 23 years. The pictures were divided into those 'liked' and those 'not liked'.

The subjects of this experiment were divided into four main temperamental or personality types, which followed from Burt's factorial analysis of emotional traits. These types were stable *versus* unstable and introvert *versus* extravert which, by cross-classification, gave the following: (a) unstable extravert, (b) stable extravert, (c) unstable introvert, (d) stable introvert. The majority of the unstable extraverts liked emotional, dramatic or romantic scenes, and preferred human subjects to landscapes or still-life pictures. The majority of stable extraverts expressed their preferences in terms of representation, function or ability, and liked realistic pictures best. The unstable introverts liked impressionistic or romantic art, and wanted a picture to arouse emotions in themselves rather than to represent emotions, while they also wanted a picture to realise some private day dream. The stable introverts tended towards an intellectual attitude to art and liked live or black and white better than colour, while they were interested in landscapes rather than portraits.

The great interest of this analysis is evident, although the

numbers of subjects in Burt's study were not great enough to
justify highly reliable statistical confidence in all cases. The data
are given in Table 9.1. While the association Unstable-Extravert/
Romantic, Stable-Extravert/Realistic, Unstable-Introvert/Impres-
sionistic, Stable-Introvert/Classical is clear from this table, it

TABLE 9·1

Temperamental type and choice of type of picture (Burt, 1939)

Group of subjects	Number of subjects	Style of picture chosen			
		Romantic	Realistic	Impressionistic	Classical
Extravert					
Unstable	18	14·4	8·9	11·1	5·9
Stable	32	10·4	12·5	7·9	9·2
Introvert					
Unstable	16	11·3	5·6	15·6	7·5
Stable	33	4·6	9·1	10·2	16·1
Others	177	11·9	10·3	11·1	6·7
Males	120	13·3	12·9	7·4	6·4
Females	156	9·5	7·7	13·5	9·3

also shows that 'other' subjects whose type was less extreme or
more normal had fairly evenly distributed preferences, while males
tended to prefer romantic and realistic paintings, and females
tended to prefer impressionistic pictures. It should be noted that
the proportions of stable and unstable introverts and extraverts
to the total do not represent the numbers found in a strictly
random population.

Eysenck's first contributions to the problems of personality
and temperament in relation to aesthetic preferences have been
mentioned in Chapter 6, but they call for further mention here.
In his research on factors in the appreciation of poetry (Eysenck,
1940a) he showed that there were two bipolar factors. 'The first
of these divided those who preferred poems which were complex
in expression and content from those who preferred simple poems.
The second factor divided those who preferred highly emotional
poems from those who preferred poems which were more restrained.' The first of these factors correlated with a test of
extraversion-introversion. Eysenck says that these results were in

agreement with Burt's theory of the relationship of aesthetic responses with emotional and temperamental qualities.

In his research on 'type-factors' in aesthetic judgments (Eysenck, 1941) he showed that there were two factors in the appreciation of a wide range of pictures, statues and photographs. The first he had in a previous article (Eysenck, 1940b) called the 'T'-Factor, and the second the 'K'-factor. The second of these divided the population into two types, the one preferring modern, the other older kinds of paintings, and it correlated with extraversion, like the second factor in his poetry experiment.

In a research, presumably on Indian subjects, D. P. Rakshit (1946) asked 150 persons between 20 and 45 years of age to arrange cartons made from 10 different colours of cardboard in order of preferences, and also to do the Neymann–Kohlstedt New Diagnostic Test for Introversion-Extraversion. The colours were in two groups: (a) *lighter*, namely green, yellow, orange, violet and red and (b) *deeper*, namely, violet, yellow, blue, red and green. The subjects fell into the following classes in the introversion-extraversion test: introverts, 69; neutroverts, 10; extraverts, 62. For extraverts the first place of colours chosen in the order of preference test was for three deeper colours, namely, blue, red and green. For neutroverts the first place was for two lighter colours, namely, orange and violet. For introverts the first place was also for the light colours, orange and violet. Thus the general conclusion was that extraverts preferred deeper colours, excluding violet and yellow, while neutroverts and introverts preferred lighter colours, excluding green, yellow and red.

McElroy (1953) reported an experiment aimed at obtaining information about individual differences in tone-form attitudes, and the study of their relationships with colour-form attitudes. The subjects, 43 adults, were also given the Heidbreder test of introversion-extraversion.

The subjects first established their orders of preference for ten polygons, and then for ten colours. Then they were presented with the ten polygons again, the least liked being in the best liked colour, and so on, the best liked being in the least liked colour. The method of paired comparisons was used. A subject was classed as a colour reactor or a form reactor according to whether his final ranking of coloured polygons correlated more with his ranking of colours or polygons alone.

Similarly a test of tone-form attitudes was made with ten tones five semitones apart, and ten rhythmical patterns. First he obtained the order of preference for the ten tones, then for the ten patterns, and then the patterns again, the least liked being in the best liked tone, and so on, the best liked being the least liked tone. The subject's tone-form attitude was established according to whether his preference order for the tone-rhythm combinations correlated more with his order for tones or for rhythmic patterns.

Nineteen out of 43 subjects were colour reactors, and 10 subjects were tone reactors. The subject's scores on the three tests were assigned ranks and correlated, but none of the correlations was statistically significant, although the highest correlation, 0.25 ± 0.16, between colour-form and tone-form, suggested that these attitudes had a common emotional basis. No relationship was found between introversion-extraversion on the Heidbreder Scale and tone-form or colour-form attitudes. In spite of its rather negative conclusions, this experiment suggests unexplored possibilities for future research, and well deserves repetition.

Cardinet (1958) carried out a very thorough research using a final selection of 195 pairs of pictures contrasting 22 categories, namely 4 aspects of colour, 7 aspects of form and composition, 3 aspects of treatment and 7 other characteristics such as movement, emotional effect or the presence or absence of human subjects.

A personality questionnaire was used, employing questions from the *Thurstone Temperament Schedule* bearing on seven characteristics, such as activity, dominance and sociability, together with questions dealing with nine other qualities, such as depression, independence and dynamicism.

There were 180 subjects, 100 being students of a College of the University of Chicago, 50 from the University itself and 30 from Wright's Junior College.

The results may be paraphrased as follows: persons tend to project themselves in their choices of pictures, but compensation rarely occurred. The practical type of person preferred naturalistic representations. Introverts preferred modern and more abstract paintings. The expansive or manic character disliked rigid forms, but especially liked emotional expression. Sociable persons rejected pictures with rigid forms. People looking for warmth in personal contacts rejected coldness and rigidity in pictures. A relationship appeared between preference for good form and introversion. Stable introverts liked peaceful scenes and disliked any overt appeal to their feelings. Liking for paintings with straight line strokes indicated an assertive social attitude, but liking for curves indicated a more affectionate disposition towards people. Neatness and order in paintings were appreciated by self-control-led people, while impulsive people preferred lifelike impressions gained by the use of hasty strokes. Liking for movement correlated with lack of restraint and with self-assertion and drive. Emotionality was generally manifested by a liking for paintings expressing a definite mood (Cardinet, 1958, p. 68).

Knapp and Green (1960) reported a study in which a factor analysis was made of preferences for various types of abstract art as well as the personality correlates of these preferences. Five factors were identified and a major dichotomy was suggested within the paintings, namely the geometrical abstract paintings and the non-geometrical. It seemed that preference for the first group might be identified with extraversion and preference for the second group of paintings with introversion.

The following hypotheses were tested experimentally by Wallach and Gahm (1960):

1. When overt adaptation of social introverts is accompanied by high anxiety, graphic expression will be more expansive than that of social extraverts and non-anxious social introverts.

2. When overt adaptation of social introverts is not accompanied by high anxiety, graphic expression will be less expansive than that of social extraverts and anxious social introverts.

The hypotheses were suggested by a consideration of the functions of graphic expression in relation to social introversion-extraversion tendencies. The authors suggest that moving towards other people may be covertly expressed by an expansiveness in graphic movements, while moving away from others and back to the self may be expressed by a constriction of graphic movements. Thus degree of graphic constriction, which would be a covert indication of social tendencies, could function either to express attitudes accepted at the conscious level, or as a channel for the displacement of consciously denied attitudes.

The subjects were 76 women students of Simmons College, who devoted one session to a doodling procedure and another to taking a personality inventory. The doodles were assessed for graphic constriction and expansiveness by a precise technique. The personality inventory consisted of the Neuroticism and Extraversion scales from Eysenck's Maudsley Personality Test and the Emotional Extraversion scale from the Minnesota T-S-E Inventory.

The main results showed that social introverts high in anxiety level were more expansive graphically than non-anxious social introverts, while social extraverts high in anxiety were more constricted graphically than non-anxious social extraverts. Non-anxious extraverts were also more expansive graphically than non-anxious introverts, while anxious extraverts were more constricted graphically than anxious introverts. Thus, while the predictions were verified for graphic expansiveness for anxious and non-anxious social introverts, the prediction for extravert groups was not borne out. The anxious social extravert group was in the middle of the constriction-expansion continuum, but the non-anxious social extravert group was at the high expansiveness extreme.

In a research on 49 arts students (18 men and 31 women) aged about 19–20 years, Kathleen Currie (1966) used 12 coloured papers supplied by the Geigy Company. These were spaced as evenly as possible round the spectrum and were of equal luminosity. For each hue there were also five papers of differing saturation evenly graded in half-tones. The subjects chose the colour liked best from a circle of the 12 colours laid out in spectral order and then the least liked colour. Following this they chose the best and least liked of the six degrees of saturation for each of the pairs chosen at first as most and least liked.

The *Cattell Sixteen Personality Factor Questionnaire* was used for each of the subjects.

The most liked colour choice was blue for men and green-blue for women; the overall greatest preference being for green-blue. The order of choices for liking of colours for both sexes together was: 1. green-blue; 2. blue; 3. Violet; blue-green, light yellow and light red; 4. magenta, green, dark yellow, orange and dark red; 5. yellow-green. Men preferred orange and dark yellow to light yellow, but women preferred light yellow to dark yellow and orange.

The most disliked colour choice was violet for both sexes. The order of disliking for both sexes together was: 1. violet; 2. magenta;

3. yellow-green, dark yellow, orange and dark red; 4. green-blue; 5. green and light yellow; 6. blue, blue-green and light red.

Subjects who had a high score on the tough-sensitive scale liked blue-green, and disliked violet to a statistically significant degree. No significant differences were found in relation to the extraversion-introversion scale, either with regard to hue or to saturation. Subjects with a 'medium' score on anxiety tended to like colours in the blue-violet range with a low degree of statistical significance (p between 0·10 and 0·05).

Kathleen Currie suggests that there is no 'reliable' or constant relationship between colour preference and personality, but, in spite of the rather negative results of her study, would still hold that there may be a tendency towards relationship, which is mediated by the dictates of fashion in various ways.

More recently Eysenck has taken up the problems of personality and temperament in relation to aesthetic judgments again. In a paper with Olive Tunstall (1968) he reported a research in which forty-one subjects were given a test in which they were asked to rank in order of preference fourteen rectangles with sides of different proportions, varying from the ratio of 0·25 to 1·0 up to that of a square. The eighth of these had sides in the proportions of the golden section, namely 0·62 to 1·0. This test was given twice, and the subjects also did the Eysenck Personality Inventory (Eysenck and Eysenck, 1965) which measures introversion-extraversion. Re-test reliabilities were high and the golden section rectangle was the most generally preferred. On re-testing, however, there was a slight tendency for the subjects to prefer thinner rectangles. Introverts preferred thinner rectangles than extraverts and this tendency increased significantly from first to second testing (Eysenck and Tunstall, p. 9). Among extraverts, the golden section rectangle was simply the one preferred to all other figures. Among introverts, however, the extreme preferences for thick and thin rectangles annulled each other and gave an average preference for the rectangle of the golden section (Eysenck and Tunstall, p. 8).

Since the rectangles were varied by altering the width only and not the height, Eysenck and Tunstall think the changed appearance which this gives may have been partly responsible for the results just mentioned. It is possible to vary the ratio by altering both height and width, which does not change the appearance so much.

A further experiment is in progress with series of rectangles of both types to investigate this possibility.

Other personality studies related to aesthetics

It is clear that some experiments, like the work of Cardinet, just mentioned in the previous section, dealt with other temperamental and personality factors besides introversion and extraversion and therefore a section dealing with more general problems of personality is desirable.

One of the first researches which dealt with the relation of personality to colour and form sensitivities was that of Oeser (1932), who used a tachistoscope to expose figures of various types in several different colours for perception and recognition. These figures included the following: 'weak' forms in a 'weak' colour (yellow or blue); 'weak' forms in a 'strong' colour (red or green); 'strong' forms in a 'weak' colour; and 'strong' forms in a 'strong' colour. 'Weak' forms were, for instance, a circle or rectangle, but 'strong' forms were such as a five-pointed star or an arrowhead.

The subjects were asked to look carefully at one of the figures exposed for two seconds, in order to be able to recognise it. Then eight similar figures in the form of a circular arrangement were presented for $\frac{1}{10}$ second, including the one already presented but not necessarily in the same colour. The aim of the experiment was to find out whether the subject was more influenced by form or by colour in his attempt to identify the figure just presented.

Oeser used 19 women and 13 men subjects. Six women and 3 men were students at a school of arts and crafts. One subject, who was a colour vision defective, had been excluded. One conclusion was that the men tended to be more influenced by form (9/13) and women more by colour (10/19). These frequencies were recalculated from Oeser's percentages. If more subjects had been used this difference would have been statistically significant. He divides the subjects into the form dominant and the colour dominant, with two mixed groups, those usually influenced by form but partly by colour, and those usually influenced by colour but partly by form.

The subjects were studied by the Rorschach Technique, which showed that the colour dominant and form dominant were in many ways very different in personality. The colour dominant were more influenced by feeling, and were better able to interpret the Rorschach ink blots as wholes, while they give more kin-aesthetic responses and were all 'extraversive'. The form dominant interpreted the blots on the basis of form, selected small, clear details and were more 'introversive'.

An interesting attempt to study the relationship of personality characteristics to colour preferences was made by Thomaschewski (1935), who reported a study based on experiments with over 200 school children. Each child had to make three choices of preferred samples from an assortment of twelve crayons, and also to choose and put in order of preference five pieces from twenty-five small sheets of coloured paper. Co-operativeness, mental capacity, outstanding gifts, interests, temperament, initiative and intelligence were all studied in relation to the colour choices.

The author notes 12 points about the significance of colours in relation to personality. They are, briefly, as follows:

(1) Peace or calm (blue, black, violet);
(2) Friendliness (orange);
(3) Seriousness (white); depression, sorrow (black);
(4) Amorous feelings (orange);
(5) Dirty (or unfair) children like brown;
(6) Instability (light blue);
(7) Reserve (dark green);
(8) Preference for the concrete (grey);
(9) Sensitivity (green and violet side by side);
(10) Weakness of mind (red hues);
(11) Sound self-feeling, playful impulses, zest (strong red);
(12) 'Closeness', 'togetherness' (violet and orange combined).

Also Thomaschewski says that separation of colours expresses clarity of thought; the more strong red is ranked at the end (3rd, 4th or 5th) the more free the chooser is from manic tendencies; and that the position in which dark tones are placed shows mascul-ine (dark tones first) or feminine tendencies (dark tones last).

It is difficult to estimate the scientific adequacy of these interest-ing conclusions from the data given, because the author gives no statistical evidence, but the paper suggests a number of possibilities and deserves attention as one of the earliest researches on colour preferences in relation to personality.

Among the most interesting pieces of research in this field was that of Anne Roe (1946a, b, c, d) because it concerned practising artists. This study consisted of an extensive investigation of 20 American painters and the significance of their use of alcoholic drinks in relation to their personalities, their habits and their work. One to four interviews of not less than two hours were conducted with each painter and personality tests were also given to them. All took the Rorschach Test, and 18 of them took Murray's Thematic Apperception Test. The subjects were all men, 38 to 68 years of age, residing in or near the New York metropolitan area. Four were born abroad of foreign parents, and several were second-generation Americans. Their professional standing was attested as follows: six were members of the National Academy of Design, six had been Guggenheim fellows, 12 had paintings in the Metropolitan Museum of Art, 18 were included in the Whitney Museum permanent collection, 16 of them had pictures bought by the *Encyclopaedia Britannica* for its Collection of American Art and 18 were noted in *Who's Who*. They were divided into the following groups: five were moderate users of alcohol, nine were steady social users and six were excessive users.

In summarising the influence of alcohol Anne Roe says that, with one exception, all the men found that alcohol was not a good stimulus to creative work and did not use it consciously for this purpose. There were some indications, however, that alcohol may have an indirect influence on painting because of its effect in inducing relaxation, and many of the men used it for this purpose, consciously or unconsciously. Also, it was notable that in the case of all the excessive drinkers but one, art had been a primary interest of their fathers. This was not true of the other groups. It seems that the excessive use of alcohol by these may have had some relationship to the need to face professional rivalry with the father.

In discussing the problems of personality in relation to artistic work, Anne Roe (*Artists and their Work*, 1946a) points out one interesting problem. She takes Angyal's concept of two basic drives, the *trend toward autonomy*—to master the environment by conquest and achievement and the *trend toward homonomy*—to share, to participate and fit in with and conform to the family social group, and so on (Angyal, 1941). She discusses the ways in which these drives, which are at least superficially antagnostic, must both be satisfied, and shows how they are indeed both satisfied in different ways by creative artistic work, especially the homonomous drive, as most of the men seemed to have a type of social and sexual adaptation which was of a markedly non-aggressive kind, which, however, did not exclude vocation and social success. From the use of the Rorschach Technique an outstanding result emerged, namely, that there was no personality pattern common to the group, and it was, in fact, extremely heterogeneous (Roe, 1946c, pp. 401 and 406). For fuller details of Anne Roe's work the original four papers must be consulted.

Precker (1950) gave a useful summary of the study and use of painting and drawing in personality assessment. After a thorough review of the literature he mentions four points concerning the uses of these techniques, which may be summarised as (1) diagnosis, (2) understanding inner dynamics, (3) study of developmental changes over a period of time and (4) prognosis. He also mentions six suggestions for future research, namely, the study, (1) of cultural factors, (2) of psychiatric classification, (3) of different personality pattern in normal groups, (4) of age, sex and socio-economic background, (5) of longitudinal changes, and (6) of relationships of painting and drawing with other projective techniques.

Significant ideas about art in relation to personality characteristics and problems were put forward by McElroy, who showed that there is a positive relationship between certain types of orderliness and the dislike of special shades of green and brown which might have infantile anal significance (McElroy, 1955, and 1957; Pickford, 1957). In his study positive correlations were found between three tests of orderliness and a summed score for dislike of six shades of green and brown in a matrix of twelve tests. A general factor related to geometrical orderliness and orderliness with mosaics accounted for 13·2 per cent of the variance, and orderliness of mosaics correlated +0·36 (± 0·18) with dislike of these colours.

McElroy also raised the question whether orderliness and compulsive and repetitive tendencies in the art of Australian Aborigines of Arnhem Land might be related to anal erotic character traits. He compared the construction of patterns using Lowenfeld's Mosaics Test by 30 Aborigines with those of 30 New South Wales adults. This test consists of 228 pieces in four colours, red, green, yellow and blue, together with black and white, distributed among five shapes, namely, squares, right-angled triangles, diamonds, scalene triangles and equilateral triangles. The Aborigines remade their patterns, lifted pieces and then rejected them, and produced compact designs, much more frequently than the NSW adults. This accords with their compulsive orderliness in tribal ceremonials and in their native art, and McElroy discusses the question whether or not their compulsive behaviour had its origins in the anxiety connected with excreta, arising from anxiety associated with the use of excreta for 'bone pointing' in sorcery, although it would seem that in Arnhem Land there is an absence of guilt concerning excretion. He also raises the question whether the attachment of Aborigines to ochre colours for aesthetic expression depends upon unconscious anal factors, or reflects a number of different variables, one of which might be the availability of certain pigments and lack of others.

A different kind of study related to the problems roused by McElroy was carried out by Barry (Herbert Barry III, 1957). He considered eleven art variables as measures of complexity in art style, and studied art of thirty cultures, not including the Australian Aborigines of Arnhem Land. In all, 549 works of art were studied. The cultures were rated on a scale of severity of 'socialisation' in terms of the 'five universal systems of behaviour: oral, anal, sexual, dependence, and aggression' of Whiting and Child (1953). There was a biserial correlation of $+0.47$ ($p < -0.05$) between a combined measure of complexity of art and an overall measure of severity of socialisation.

Barry concludes by saying: 'A possible interpretation of the results is that a personality characteristic is related to severity of socialisation and complexity of art style in the individual, and that the cultural custom which perpetuates a pattern of socialisation and art style is an adjustment to the personalities of the individuals in the culture' (p. 283).

It will be remembered that the observations of Alschuler and Hattwick (1947) showed that some children who are socially isolated tend to make spatially constricted paintings while some who have many social ties produce expansive pictures and that some children who conceal their true feelings in overt behaviour express them in their paintings. Thus paintings may express tendencies concealed or tendencies expressed in overt behaviour.

Wallach, Green, Lipsitt and Minehart (1962) carried out a

research in order to study these points. Four hypotheses were tested. (1) Among defensive subjects those who had extensive social ties should be more constricted in graphic expression than those who are socially isolated. (2) Among non-defensive subjects, however, those with extensive social ties should be more expansive in graphic expression than those who are socially isolated. (3) Among subjects with extensive social ties those who are more defensive should be more constricted in graphic expression than the non-defensive, while (4) among the socially isolated the more defensive should be more expansive in graphic expression than the non-defensive.

The subjects were 120 first-grade girls. Defensive tendencies were assessed through a scale developed for the purpose. Social interaction was assessed through a scale of sociometric status and independent ratings of popularity in school. Graphic constriction or expansiveness was estimated through a task of drawing abstract designs, repeated three times, and was assessed by an objective technique.

The basic hypotheses were confirmed with a high degree of statistical significance, and the individual differences expressed in the abstract drawings were highly stable throughout the three repetitions of the task. There were control data concerning age, socio-economic status, general intelligence and verbal productivity, which showed that graphical constriction and expansiveness were not at all related to any of these factors.

Two researches by Child (1962 and 1965) throw light on the problems of personality or temperament in relation to aesthetic judgments and preferences. The first of these papers, already mentioned in Chapter 6, involved the grading of 12 sets each of 60 pictures of various types, according to personal preference, by two groups of 22 college students and 13 judges of aesthetic value. Certain personality or temperament tests were used with the subjects. Child reports (1962, footnote on p. 508) no significant correlations with either preference measure and the following 8 variables: (1) extraversion *versus* introversion and (2) feeling *versus* thinking on the Myers–Briggs Type Indicator (a questionnaire distributed by Educational Testing Service, Princeton, NJ, USA); (3) extraversion *versus* introversion, (4) somatotonia and (5) anxiety, on a questionnaire assembled for this research; (6) time required to express the preferences; (7) mathematical score on the Scholastic Aptitude Test; (8) human movement score on the Barron Inkblot Test (Barron, 1955).

In the second of these papers Child (1965) reported a research on 138 young men, one a graduate student and the others all undergraduates at Yale University. They attended for two group sessions and a further individual session for aesthetic judgment and personality tests. The aesthetic test consisted of 120 pairs of pictures, chosen from about 3,360 pairs, which represented those pairs on which 14 competent judges were almost always unanimous in agreeing with selectors who had chosen them so that the members of each pair were of the same type and subject-matter but decidedly different in aesthetic value.

Measures other than the aesthetic test were of background in art, skill in perception of visual form, finding human meaning in ambiguous stimuli, and a questionnaire on cognitive style. The latter involved tolerance of complexity, tolerance of ambiguity, ambivalence and unrealistic experience, scanning (a tendency towards broad deployment of attention), sharpening (keen awareness of differences), narrowness of equivalence range (tendency to react distinctively even to stimuli which are only slightly different), flexibility, field independence (ability to maintain a set in perception), independence of judgment, regression in the service of the ego (a capacity to fuse the more infantile with the more mature) and Jungian measures of cognitive orientation (measured with the Myers–Briggs Type Index). There were also behavioural measures of cognitive style, and other variables of personality such as introversion *versus* extraversion, anxiety, Sheldon's variables of temperament (viscerotania, somatotonia and cerebrotonia), measures of scholastic attitudes, masculinity-femininity, originality, colour preferences, and other visual preferences, among which were sexual connotative meaning in pictures, and preference for Baroque *versus* Classical Art. A partial replication of the study was made which confirmed the main findings.

The most outstanding results and conclusions may be summarised as follows: firstly, aesthetic judgment was related to amount of background in art; secondly, skill in perceiving visual form and in perceiving human meaning in ambiguous stimuli, masculinity *versus* femininity, originality and behavioural measures of cognitive style, were not consistently related to aesthetic judgment; thirdly, tolerance of complexity, scanning, independence of judgment, regression in the service of the ego, intuition rather than sensation, and perception rather than judgment (on the Myers–Briggs Type Index) were positively related to aesthetic judgment; fourthly, several other measures were also positively related to aesthetic judgment, namely, anxiety, viscerotonia (love of comfort and relaxation), verbal aptitude, and certain visual preferences such as liking colours of lower brightness, for abstract designs and for Baroque rather than Classical art. This remarkable research cannot be dealt with adequately in a short summary and the reader who wishes to study it in detail must consult Child's original paper.

Another significant investigation of personality attributes in relation to aesthetic judgments and preferences was reported by Knapp (1964). For this study selections of 16 paintings representing each of four stylistic varieties were chosen from 120 colour slides of paintings by ten judges by suitable statistical procedures. The four types were: realistic, fantastic, geometric and expressionistic. This material was then presented to 78 male freshmen, of superior intelligence, at Wesleyan University. The subjects also took the *Allport–Vernon Study of Values* (theoretic, economic, aesthetic, social, political and religious), the Myers–Briggs Type Index (extraversion-introversion, intuiting, sensing, thinking, feeling, judging, perceiving), and the Terman Concept Mastery Test. Correlations were worked out between preference scores for each of the four styles of painting and the other eleven test items mentioned above.

Knapp interprets the patterns of correlations as showing that individuals preferring realistic art were 'practical', 'worldly', 'uncomplicated' and 'naive'; those preferring geometric paintings were 'intellectual', 'systematic', 'theoretical' and 'inhibited'; and those preferring expressionistic paintings were 'subjective', 'imaginative', 'impractical' and 'sensitive'. The fantastic group of paintings, he suggests tentatively, represents merely a less effective version of the realistic because its pattern of correlations parallels that for the realistic scores. He makes the comment that there is a statistically significant positive correlation between preferences for realistic art and extraversion and the polarity of extraversion-introversion is best measured by the preference for realistic rather than expressive art, not by a preference for geometrical in contrast to non-geometrical abstract art. The preference for realistic rather than expressive art is more correlated with the sensing-intuitive than with the extraversion-introversion scale. He concludes by suggesting that the representational in art may be identified with the Appollonian, the geometric with the Pythagorean and the expressionistic with the Dionysian tradition.

A study of colour-form dominance was made by Margaret Carruthers (1970), who used a version of Eysenck's colour-polygon ranking test, namely 10 polygons in each of 10 different colours. She also tested her subjects with the *Burnham-Clarke-Munsell Colour Memory Test,* and screened them for defective colour vision with the *Ishihara Test.* She used 19 men and 21 women subjects who were students in Glasgow University, and their age range was 19–26 years.

The subjects were divided into (1) colour dominant (n = 14); (2) form dominant (n = 12); and (3) intermediate (n = 12). No significant differences were found between these groups on the Colour Memory Test. More women were colour dominant than men, in the proportion of 42·85 per cent of women and 27·7 per cent of men and more men than women were intermediate. There was one red/green defective man, excluded from the subjects just mentioned, and he had the lowest score of any on the Colour Memory Test, as would be expected.

Aesthetic preferences of abnormal and psychiatric subjects

It is convenient to separate the studies of abnormal and psychiatric subjects from other studies of personality and temperamental differences in relation to aesthetic judgments and preferences. However, there is no intention to suggest that there is a sharp difference between abnormal and psychiatric persons on the one hand and normal persons on the other. Many characteristics of the normal are seen in extremer forms in the abnormal and the normal often have traits not dissimilar to those recognised as abnormal in psychiatric patients.

One of the researches, by Katz (1931), sought answers to the following questions:
(1) whether certain colours are generally pleasing to the insane; (2) whether similarities exist between colour preferences of the insane and of children; (3) whether colour preferences of the insane vary with age; (4) whether they vary with length of hospital residence; (5) whether they vary with diagnosis; and (6) whether

any relation exists between colour preference and sex in the insane.

In order to provide data on the basis of which to answer these questions 433 patients in the Hudson River State Hospital were studied. They were fairly representative of the ages, lengths of residence, diagnoses, education and social status of patients in similar hospitals. Six colours from the Bradley coloured papers in 1 in. and ½ in. squares were used, the colours being red, orange, yellow, green, blue and violet. The subjects indicated their first, second and other choices.

The outcome of the experiment showed that blue was most preferred by the majority, 40·9 per cent of males and 40·4 per cent of females giving it first choice, as compared with 47 per cent of school and college pupils. Green was a distant second, and red a close third with the patients as with the children, but unlike the children, the male patients put green second and the females red. The other colours were violet fourth and yellow and orange last, as with the children.

The other results may be summarised more briefly. Males of 25 years of age and below gave 60 per cent of first choices to blue, but this figure decreased with increasing age. Younger females, apparently, did not give such great preference to blue, but the frequency of choices of blue for both sexes dropped to 37 per cent for ages of 46 years and older.

Blue-green and violet were preferred more by patients of shorter length of residence, and red, orange and yellow by those of longer residence. Red, orange and yellow were more pleasing to manic–depressive patients than to dementia praecox (schizophrenic) and other patients. Green was liked best by dementia praecox patients and violet by those of other diagnoses.

A more adequate investigation of colour preferences of psychiatric patients, using more efficient materials, was carried out by Warner (1949). He used Munsell standard colour papers in the form of 5 in. by 8 in. rectangles mounted on 12 in. by 20 in. neutral backgrounds. The colours were exposed in a plywood enclosure and illuminated by a 25 watt daylight-blue Mazda lamp. Other details may be found in Warner's Monograph. The colours were presented in pairs and the subject expressed his preference for one of each pair by switching off the light illuminating the other. Each pair was presented four times.

The following colours used were red, yellow, green and blue. They were presented in six pairs differing in hue, and for each hue three pairs differing in lightness, and three more differing in saturation, making 30 pairs altogether. Munsell specifications for the colours are given in the Monograph.

Four groups of psychiatric patients were studied, namely, anxiety neurotics, catatonic schizophrenics and patients in the manic and the depressed phases of manic-depressive psychoses, from various State hospitals and clinics. There were 120 schizophrenics and 60 patients in each of the other groups.

The results were complex, but may be summarised as follows:

A. The colour preferences were highly reliable;

B. Anxiety neurotics preferred green to yellow more than any of the other groups. They also preferred the lighter colours, but no significant differences were found for saturation;

C. Males tended to prefer the cool hues more than did the females.

Females preferred lighter to darker colours more than did males, where the comparison was between high and low lightness, but males preferred the lighter to the darker more than did females where the comparison was between high and medium lightness, and females preferred the lighter to the darker colours more than did the males when the comparison was between medium and low lightness.

Males preferred the more saturated colours to a greater extent than did the females except when the comparison was between medium and low saturation.

Lastly, males preferred colours more extreme in lightness and saturation to more medial colours to a greater extent than did females; but females preferred extremely high lightness to extremely low lightness colours more than males, although males preferred extremely high saturation colours to extremely low saturation colours more than did females.

While the researches of Katz and of Warner dealt with colour preferences of psychiatric patients when choices were required in an experimental setting, using six colours seen together by Katz, and pairs of colours by Warner, another kind of study dealt with the colours used by such patients in actually making paintings. Thus Robertson (1952) studied various points in relation to the use of colours in the painting of 176 patients at

Netherne Hospital. They were divided into schizophrenics (diagnosis of schizophrenia or paraphrenia) and non-schizophrenics (depressives, psychopaths and psychoneurotics). Consideration was given to the frequencies with which the following colours were used: red, yellow, green, blue, purple, mauve, black, brown, grey and white. Only a patient's first ten paintings were studied. Statistically different frequencies were found in the following comparisons. Red was used more abundantly by male than by female recent schizophrenics; yellow was used more by chronic than recent non-schizophrenic females; green was used more by male than female non-schizophrenics; purple was more used by chronic than recent schizophrenic and non-schizophrenic females, and by male more than by female schizophrenics; mauve was more used by chronic than recent schizophrenic females; grey was used more by non-schizophrenic than schizophrenic recent males, more by recent than chronic schizophrenic and non-schizophrenic females, and more by male than female recent non-schizophrenics. No significant differences were found for blue, black, brown or white.

In addition it was found that chronic patients had significantly fewer dull and pale paintings, and significantly more thickly coloured paintings and paintings with 'displeasing' colour-combinations.

Another part of the research involved colouring a standard drawing. In this 36 schizophrenics were compared with 36 non-schizophrenics, all females, and 18 student nurses as controls. In this the schizophrenics had a significantly higher tendency to use unrealistic colours than the other groups, and a higher score for 'indifference' as a 'reason' for liking such colours.

Investigation of likings of isolated colours showed that schizophrenics liked dark green more and white less than did the non-schizophrenics; mauve more and white less than did the nurses; and non-schizophrenics liked dark green less than did the nurses.

Liking for colours in combination was also studied, with the findings that schizophrenics liked combinations including mauve less and those including white more than did the non-schizophrenics; that they liked combinations including dark red or mauve more and those including white less than did the nurses; and that non-schizophrenics liked combinations including dark red more and those including dark yellow less than did the nurses.

In a test of strength of feeling aroused by colours, schizophrenics differed significantly from the other two groups in giving fewer affirmative and more negative answers to the question, 'would you say that colours arouse strong feeling in you or not?'

A word association test to give in one word what was associated with each of the fourteen colours showed that schizophrenics associated more body-parts, fewer religious references, more feelings, valuations, symbols and irrelevant or peculiar references and had fewer failures to respond than non-schizophrenics. Schizophrenics associated more clothing references, more body parts, more irrelevant references and had fewer failures to respond than did the nurses. Non-schizophrenics associated more clothing and religious references and fewer feelings, valuations and symbols than did the nurses.

In his discussion of these results Robertson considers that 'the central factor underlying all the peculiarities in the use of colour in painting by seriously disordered patients is a diminished feeling for colour or a weakened reactivity to it'. He takes up each statistically significant difference and shows that it can be made understandable on the basis of this generalisation.

The *Pfister Colour Pyramid Test* (Pfister, 1951) was used by Conticelli (1963) in a study of the colour preferences of Italian boys. In this test, which is essentially a personality test, the subject uses squares of coloured paper to make a coloured pyramid by sticking them on a printed outline pyramid with five spaces in the bottom row, four in the next, three next, then two and lastly one space at the top. The choice of colours available was blue, red, green, yellow, violet, orange, black, maroon, white and grey; and this was the order of preference for twenty-three normal boys, blue being most preferred.

The subjects were:

Group A. 23 mid-school boys with no abnormality of mental or scholastic attainment; with no irregularity of relationships with other people and with normal physical development; their average age was 13 years and 8 months.

Group B. 12 boys of various scholastic levels and deficiency of intelligence. Their average age was 12 years and 3 months, and their average IQ was 77. Some were seriously defective, and, in spite of their age, were still in elementary classes.

Group C. 20 boys who had more or less serious disturbances of character, and scholastic disabilities. Some had difficult relationships with their parents; some had psychiatric traits; some had nocturnal enuresis; some had emotional instability; and some had defective intelligence. Their average age was 14 years and their average IQ was 117.

The results of the Colour Pyramid Test, used as a test of colour preferences, showed that the average frequencies for choices of colours were as noted above for Group A. For Group B, those who had low or defective intelligence, the order of preference was red, green, blue, maroon, yellow and violet, orange, grey, white and black.

For Group C, those with emotional and psychiatric disturbances, the order of preference was green, red, blue, yellow, orange and violet, black, maroon, white and grey.

The interesting points are that Group A preferred blue to all other colours; Group B preferred red and Group C preferred green. Other outstanding differences were that Group B had a much stronger preference for maroon relatively to either of the other Groups A or C, and that Group A had a much stronger preference for violet relatively to either of the other Groups B or C.

Another research, in which actual paintings by patients were studied in relation to personality problems, was that of Joan Stapleton (1953).* In this thesis form and colour were studied in the free paintings and crayon drawings of 40 neurotic patients in relation to behaviour, affect and to concepts of the self and of others, and so on. Paintings of 24 of these patients were compared with those of 20 female college students, and 5 males and 5 female control subjects with whom ten patients were matched. Also paintings by 40 children of various ages were studied for their use of colour. Eight colours were used, namely, red, orange, yellow, green, blue, purple, brown and black. In all 800 paintings were analysed.

Two new tests were devised and their procedure standardised:

(a) An illustration of Emotions Test, which was given to 40 patients and ten control subjects;

(b) A Colour Selection Test, which was used in conjunction with word associations and psycho-galvanic responses, and these

---

* The writer acknowledges with thanks the kind permission of Miss Joan Stapleton and the University of Bristol Librarian to include the following abstract of her work, based to a considerable extent on her own summary.

were given to 18 female college students and 30 neurotic patients. From the data collected the following inferences were drawn about colour:

1. Subjects free from neurotic disturbances usually use five or more colours in painting, and not less than three, with a well-balanced palette, and they freely intermingle colours and produce more brilliant than dull paintings.

2. The following characteristics of colour use are indicative of neurotic disturbance:

(a) Monochromatic, combined, or emphasised use of purple, red and black;

(b) Avoidance or infrequent use of yellow, orange and brown;

(c) More dull than brilliant paintings;

(d) Colours in unbalanced proportions;

(e) Persistent overlay of one colour by another;

(f) Rigid and separate placement of colours, although this is associated with adaptive behaviour in the neurotic group.

Other points about the use of colour are mentioned, and the following notes about particular colours are of significance:

Red was associated with aggression, destructively or constructively expressed, with love and the need to be loved;

Blue was associated with control and with mother-centred emotions and attitudes;

Purple was associated with emotional disturbance and conflict, and with sorrow;

Black was associated with morbid states of fear, anxiety, guilt, depression and with neuroticism;

Green was associated with control, joy, happiness, active construction, the growing self, and feelings of joy and peace;

Yellow was associated with joy and love, and there was a strong sexual connotation;

Orange was associated with sexual concepts, with concepts of light and with adaptive behaviour;

Brown was associated with controlled behaviour, but with the anal-aggressive stage of development.

Miss Stapleton considered that the constancy of colour associations is dependent on certain universally experienced phenomena with which each colour is realistically connected.

Neurotics emphasise purple, red and black, although they are not the colours they prefer. The patients use them to express disturbed feelings. Avoidance of yellow, orange and brown is associated with neurotic repression.

In respect of form and space in paintings the following points were mentioned: neurotic patients, as compared with the normal subjects, showed lack of control, scatter of elements and nonspecific form, although they may produce aesthetically satisfying forms. Other characteristics in paintings are the zigzag line, which reflects tension and the inhibition of activity, and is a symbol of aggression, which in free painting reflects neurotic activity.

The combination of writing and painting was characteristic of the neurotic group. Square and rectangular forms were associated with masculinity; circular forms with femininity. Rhythm and expansion were feminine rather than masculine and were used for the illustration of joy and love. Compression and rule were associated with masculinity and were used more by older subjects. They occurred more in the illustration of fear and sorrow. Repetitive rhythm was associated with disturbed emotions and with fear and anger.

In this short summary it has not been possible to do full justice to the complexity and interest of Miss Stapleton's work, which unfortunately has not been published.

In a research on personality correlates of picture preferences Cerbus and Nichols (1962) made three scales each consisting of pairs of pictures chosen by preliminary ratings and selections so that each pair was equivalent on two of three variables of artistic interest, but different on the third. The artistic variables were represented by: (1) The Achromatic-Chromatic Scale (27 items); (2) the Concrete-Abstract Scale (42 items); and (3) the Objects-People Scale (33 items) based on picture content.

Personality correlates of these three variables were sought by the application of these scales for picture preference together with the California Psychological Inventory (CPI) for a sample of 113 college students, the Minnesota Multiphasic Personality Inventory (MMPI) with 106 neuropsychiatric patients and the Multidimensional Scale for Rating Psychiatric Patients (MSRPP) with an additional group of 51 neuropsychiatric patients all of whom had undergone at least four group therapy sessions.

The authors say that correlations of each of the picture preference scales with the sixty-three verbal personality measures and personality ratings involved in the three tests mentioned above yielded results differing little from chance on the Achromatic-Chromatic Scale and the Concrete-Abstract Scale. However, sixteen significant correlations were found with the scale based on picture content, namely the Objects-People Scale. These suggested that the person who prefers pictures showing people to those without people is more outgoing and friendly, and tends to be more expansive, self-confident and happy than the person who prefers pictures of objects rather than of people.

In a further paper, which is a review of some of the literature on personality variables in relation to response to colour, especially the Rorschach Technique, Cerbus and Nichols (1963) say that there is no support for the possible relationship between colour response and impulsivity or related variables, such as assaultiveness or ego-control. They say support is also lacking for the correlation of colour response with suggestibility, although there is evidence for a relationship with response to stimulation from the impersonal environment, colour being a part of this. 'Strong evidence from Rorschach studies for reduced use of color by depressed individuals, the only relationship to emotionality established, is compatible with the above positive finding, for the depressed patient is uninterested in the external environment' (p. 566). Cerbus and Nichols appear to have overlooked or underestimated the evidence of the relationships of certain personality and temperamental traits with colour preferences.

It is interesting that Green and Pickford (1968) showed, by a factor analysis of ratings for nine aesthetic qualities of 25 paintings in an exhibition of schizophrenic art in Glasgow, 1956, made by 42 university students, that two factors adequately accounted for the variance. The qualities most highly correlated with the first or general factor were dynamic effect, emotional expression and impressionistic effect. The qualities most highly correlated with the second or bipolar factor were harmony of colouring and of design, contrasted with negative photographic accuracy and expressive distortion.

These results show that for this group of judges and these schizophrenic paintings, aesthetic judgments were oriented firstly by dynamicism and emotional expression, but only secondly by the contrast of expressive distortion with harmony of colouring and design. In general the experiment showed that for these painters organising influences were less than for normal artists, revealed by similar factorial studies reported in Chapter 6.

Bibliography and References
for Chapter 9

ALSCHULER, ROSE H., and HATTWICK, LA B. W. (1947). *Painting and Personality: A Study of Young Children.* Chicago: University Press, 2 vols.

ANGYAL, A. (1941). *Foundations for a Science of Personality.* New York: Commonwealth Fund.

BARRON, F. (1955). Threshold for the Perception of Human Movement in Inkblots. *J. Consult. Psychol., 19,* 33–8.

BARRY, HERBERT, III (1957). Relationships between Child Training and the Pictorial Arts. *J. Abnormal and Social Psychol., 54,* 380–3.

BURT, C. (1939). The Factorial Analysis of Emotional Traits. *Char. and Pers., 7,* 238–54 and 285–99.

CARDINET, JEAN (1958). *Préférences Esthétiques et Personnalité. Année Psychologique, 58,* 45–69.

CARRUTHERS, MARGARET (1970). *Colour-Form Dominance and Memory for Colour.* M.A. Thesis. Psychology Department, University of Glasgow (unpublished).

CERBUS, G., and NICHOLS, R. C. (1962). Personality Correlates of Picture Preferences. *J. Abnormal and Social Psychol., 64,* 75–8.

CERBUS, G., and NICHOLS, R. C. (1963). Personality Variables and Response to Color. *Psychol. Bull., 60,* 566–75.

CHILD, I. L. (1962). Personal Preferences as an Expression of Aesthetic Sensitivity. *J. Personality, 30,* 496–512.

CHILD, I. L. (1965). Personality Correlates of Esthetic Judgment in College Students. *J. Personality, 33,* 476–511.

CHILD, I. L. (1969). Esthetics. ch. 28 in *Handbook of Social Psychology.* Eds. G. Lindzey and E. Aronson. Reading, Mass.: Addison Wesley.

CONTICELLI, MARIO (1963). 'Un' Applicazione Italiana della "Piramide del Pfister".' *Actes des VIImes Journées Int. de la Couleur* (1963), 292–7. Florence: Assoc., Ottica Ital.; Padua: Instit. Naz. Col.; Paris: Centre d'Information de la Couleur.

CURRIE, KATHLEEN H. (1966). *Colour Preferences and Personality.* M.A. Thesis, University of Glasgow, Psychology Department (unpublished).

DOW, MILDRED, (1933). Playground Behavior Differentiating Artistic from Non-Artistic Children. *Psychol. Monogr., no. 200,* 82–94.

DREPS, H. F. (1933). The Psychophysical Capacities and Abilities of College Art Students of High and Low Standing. *Psychol. Monogr.,* no. 200, 134–46.

EYSENCK, H. J. (1940a). Some Factors in the Appreciation of Poetry, and their Relation to Temperamental Qualities. *Char. and Pers., 9,* 160–7.

EYSENCK, H. J. (1940b). The General Factor in Aesthetic Judgements. *Brit. J. Psychol., 31,* 94–102.

EYSENCK, H. J. (1941). 'Type'-Factors in Aesthetic Judgements. *Brit. J. Psychol., 31,* 262–70.

EYSENCK, H. J., and EYSENCK, S. B. J. (1965). *Eysenck Personality Inventory.* London: University of London Press.

EYSENCK, H. J., and TUNSTALL, OLIVE (1968). '*La Personalité et l'Esthétique des Formes Simples.*' *Sciences de l'Art, 5, i,* 3–9.

FRANCÈS, R. (1968). *Psychologie de l'Esthétique.* Paris: PUF, chapter V.

GREEN, MAURICE, and PICKFORD, R. W. (1968). A Factor Analysis of Ratings of Schizophrenic Paintings. *Proc. Fifth Int. Congress of Aesthetics,* Amsterdam, 1964. Amsterdam: Mouton, pp. 893–6.

KATZ, S. E. (1931). Color Preference in the Insane. *J. Abnormal and Social Psychol., 26,* 203–11.

KNAPP, R. H. (1964). An Experimental Study of a Triadic Hypothesis Concerning the Sources of Aesthetic Imagery. *J. Projective Techniques and Personality Assessment, 28,* 49–54.

KNAPP, R. H., and GREEN, S. M. (1960). Preferences for Styles of Abstract Art and their Personality Correlates. *J. Projective Techniques, 24,* 396–402.

LÜSCHER, MAX (1949). *Psychologie der Farben.* Basel: Test-Verlag.

MCELROY, W. A. (1953). Colour Form Attitudes: An Analogue from Music. *Australian J. Psychol.,* June, 1953, *5, 1,* 10–16.

MCELROY, W. A. (1955). Personality and the Dislike of Shades of Green and Brown. *The Advancement of Science, 12,* 360 (title of paper only).

MCELROY, W. A. (1957). Aboriginal Orderliness in Central Arnhem Land. *Oceania, 27,* 268–9.

OESER, O. A. (1932). Some Experiments on the Abstraction of Form and Colour, Part I—Tachistoscope Experiments. Part II—Rorschach Tests. *Brit. J. Psychol., 22,* 200–15 and 287–323.

PICKFORD, R. W. (1957). Vision. In *Annual Review of Psychology, 8,* 9.

PICKFORD, R. W. (1967). *Studies in Psychiatric Art.* Springfield: Thomas.

PFISTER, MAX (1951). *Colour Pyramid Test. (Der Farbpyramiden-Test).* Bern: Verlag Hans Huber.

PRECKER, JOSEPH A. (1950). Painting and Drawing in Personality Assessment. *J. Projective Techniques, 14,* 262–86.

RAKSHIT, D. P. (1946). Colour Preference of Extroverted and Introverted Individuals. *Indian J. Psychol., 21,* 89–92.

ROBERTSON, J. P. S. (1952). The Use of Colour in the Paintings of Psychotics. *J. Mental Science, 98,* 174–84.

RODGERS, FRANCES (1933). Variation in the Aesthetic Environment of Artistic and Non-Artistic Children. *Psychol. Monogr., no. 200,* 95–107.

ROE, ANNE (1946a). Alcohol and Creative Work. *Quart. J. Studies on Alcohol.*, 6, 415–67.
ROE, ANNE (1946b). Painting and Personality. *Rorschach Research Exchange*, 10, 86–100.
ROE, ANNE (1946c). The Personality of Artists. *Educational and Psychological Measurement*, 6, 401–10.
ROE, ANNE (1946d). Artists and their Work. *J. Personality*, 15, 1–40.
RORSCHACH, H. (1942). *Psychodiagnostics; Text and Plates* (2nd ed.). Bern: Huber.
STAPLETON, JOAN H. (1953). *A Study of the Significance of Colour and Form in Neurotic Patients' Free Paintings and Drawings.* M.A. Thesis, University of Bristol (unpublished).
THOMASCHEWSKI, E. (1935). 'Die Farbe in der experimentallen Charakterforschung.' *Zeits. f. Jungenkunde*, 5, 50–3.
TIEBOUT, CAROLYN (1933). The Psychophysical Functions Differentiating Artistically Superior from Artistically Inferior Children. *Psychol. Monogr.*, no. 200, 108–33.
WALLACH, M. A., and GAHM, R. C. (1960). Personality Functions of Graphic Constriction and Expansiveness. *J. Personality*, 28, 73–88.
WALLACH, M. A., GREEN, L. R., LIPSITT, P. D., and MINEHART, JEAN B. (1962). Contradiction between Overt and Projective Personality Indications as a Function of Defensiveness. *Psychol. Monogr.*, no. 520, p. 22.
WARNER, SAMUEL J. (1949). The Color Preferences of Psychiatric Groups. *Psychol. Monogr.*, no. 301, pp. v and 25.
WHITING, J. W. M., and CHILD, I. L. (1953). *Child Training and Personality.* New Haven, USA; Yale Univ. Press.

10

Art and aesthetics, and future research

In this chapter it is proposed at first to consider some general questions about the relation of empirical aesthetics, art and psychology, in order to see more clearly the limitations of a study such as this book. Then each chapter or part of the book will be mentioned briefly to indicate the relevance of the work which it covers. The most important outcome will be to see how far and in what ways the psychology of aesthetics can be extended in the future. This concluding chapter will be a series of reflections mainly dealing with possibilities for future research, and not a summary of the book. The problems of psychiatric art and the psychology of ugliness will also be mentioned briefly.

Aesthetics, psychology and art

Psychology is an empirical science, and it does not, in the view of the present writer, seek to explain the nature of artistic values although it may do a great deal to interpret and illuminate the conditions, circumstances and mental and social processes involved in valuations. Empirical aesthetics is extremely dependent on psychology, and particularly on experimental psychology, although not exclusively so, because many observational, comparative and historical branches of aesthetics and even clinical aspects cannot be handled experimentally or may not be essentially psychological.

It does not seem satisfactory, or indeed perhaps it is misleading, to speak of empirical aesthetics as a branch of behavioural science. Art, and consequently aesthetics, are fundamentally dependent on conscious perceptions and the experience of emotions and feelings. They would not exist if consciousness did not exist, and they only involve behaviour in the sense that it leads to or is bound up with aesthetic experiences. Certainly much art and many so-called aesthetic choices, judgments and preferences may well be studied as if they were simply forms of learned behaviour and depended on 'experience', in the sense that such learning is due to repeated performance, either aimed directly at art training, or having the effect of the acquisition of habits related to art unintentionally. This, however, would be the least important way of looking at art, the essence of which is concerned with experience in the sense of consciously perceiving, feeling and imagining in certain ways, namely aesthetic ways.

The artist would not be likely to go to the psychologist (or even to the philosopher) of aesthetics to find out what to do. Either he knows what he must do, in so far as creativity is consciously controlled, or, in so far as it is intuitive and 'unconsciously' controlled, he produces his art without foreseeing the result. Often it is a combination of both. In many cases, no doubt, the artist notices a certain scene, object or group of objects and feels or intuits that they would make themselves into a picture. Later on during the work, he may foresee its completion and be able to use conscious judgment in the final steps. Alternatively, he may start with the impulse to make a certain line or patch of colour and then add to it, being as much surprised as anybody else at the outcome. Psychological aesthetics, therefore, does not exist in order to show the artist what to do, but to interpret and understand what is done. It will not lay down principles of creation but it will make generalisations and interpretations of the artist's creations. And experimental aesthetics exists in order to set up certain critical situations to establish differences and make comparisons, while quantitative and statistical techniques are introduced in order to establish precise experimental and comparative procedures and to lead to clear and decisive thinking.

One important point is that the psychology of aesthetics is not to be identified necessarily or only with the study of liking or of pleasure-giving stimuli, objects or situations. Aesthetically valued objects, situations or stimuli may not always be those which give pleasure or most pleasure, even displeasing or ugly objects may be artistically good, and there are many pleasure-giving situations and objects which are not of aesthetic value or interest.

Form perception and aesthetics

The psychological principles of form and depth perception, and the principles of phenomenal regression (Wyburn, *et al.*, 1964; Fieandt, 1966; Thouless, 1932), explained in Chapter 2, play vital parts in visual art and aesthetics. It is clear, however, that to be aesthetically adequate a picture does not have to follow any of the psychological principles of form and depth perception slavishly. If perspective is part of the technique used in a particular art, then the psychology of perspective can help us to understand that art. If not, then the analysis of the departures from true perspective might be just as interesting. Similarly, with the principles of phenomenal regression. If, in a particular work, these principles strongly influenced the artist, then the organisation of that work would be better understood if we saw what had happened. Another work, however, could flout such principles freely and then it could not be condemened as art because it had disregarded them. For such reasons many people think that the study of the psychological aesthetics of form perception in art is a waste of energy, but this is not so, because every time such principles apply they illuminate the art for us, but every time they do not apply, equally they do not give us the basis for adverse criticism, and the reasons for their non-application are illuminating.

The fundamental requirement of form construction in art is that it should be artistically good. This cannot be determined by saying that it must follow certain psychological principles of form perception. The 'good Gestalt' is not necessarily good art. At the same time form remains essential to it and perhaps the best way of expressing this is to say, with Herbert Read, that art is pattern informed by emotion. We still, however, have to say that not every emotionally informed pattern will be aesthetically good, and to the writer it tends to seem more and more true to say, with Clive Bell (1916), that for art we must have 'significant form', and that this is defined as form capable of exciting the aesthetic emotion. Philosophically speaking, it may be objected that this is based on a circular argument, because there is no way of identifying significant form except through the experience of the aesthetic emotion, but also no way of identifying the aesthetic emotion except that it occurs when we perceive significant form. However, it is the primary fact that the experience of the aesthetic emotion is what identifies significant aesthetic form and distinguishes it from other kinds of form, which may often be 'good Gestalten' but are not aesthetically significant. The greatest difficulty for Clive Bell's approach is to identify the aesthetic emotion, and for the writer it seems more and more that the aesthetic emotion is a special experience not to be identified with a synthesis of other emotions, as he at one time thought. Nevertheless, of course, various combinations of everyday emotions also occur in aesthetic perception and are important. Whether it is possible to perceive aesthetic material and experience it purely in a cognitive way as art, without any emotion whatever, is an interesting and difficult question, and the writer has discussed it many times with his friends, colleagues and pupils, but to him it seems to call for a definitely negative answer.*

Lines, figures and shapes

It would be useful in aesthetics if some of the earlier experiments using lines, figures and shapes could be repeated and developed in such a way that progressive construction from simple to complex patterns and forms was studied. Also the influence of sex, age, artistic ability measured by success in art and not only by formal tests, and social group and racial differences, should be taken into account. The differences between pleasingness and unpleasingness on the one hand, and of artistic value and otherwise on the other hand, should be investigated experimentally. The study of personality and temperamental differences is very important and should not be confined to the use of rigidly quantitative psychological tests. Although some workers have made excellent contributions in these directions there is much more to be done.

Perception and art of the blind

The perception and art of the blind has taught us a great deal about the relevance of visual space and form perception to art in general (Lowenfeld, 1939; Révész, 1950; Fieandt, 1966). If it is

* Useful discussions of Clive Bell's position may be found in *The British Journal of Aesthetics, vol. 5, no. 2*, April 1965, pp. 107–44.

assumed that visual art must base its expressivity in precise and accurate perceptual techniques of binocular vision, then we are excluded from appreciating forms of art, both of visual and tactile interest, which are not so based, but which follow haptic principles not corresponding to realistic space perception of a visual kind. The aesthetic judgments and creations of blind, partly blind, blindfold sighted subjects and seeing subjects should be examined much more fully with carefully planned experimental comparisons.

The psychology of colour and colour vision

It is unfortunate that the earlier researches of adults' and children's colour preferences did not, in many cases, take adequate account of brightness and saturation in addition to hue differences. Nevertheless many of them were of very considerable interest. If brightness and saturation are taken into account (not to mention the proper control of the illuminating light sources) then, as seen in the chapters on adults' and children's judgments and preferences, the whole problem becomes very much more complex, and it may be that conclusions are correspondingly more difficult to draw and subject to more qualifying conditions. In such work age, sex, race and cultural differences are most important, and it is clear that the degree of artistic ability or experience of the subjects of the experiments must be taken into account. Although much valuable work has been done, as reported in the relevant chapters of this book, there is still a wide field open for further research. One very important factor which will have to be considered seriously in the immediate future is the effect of changing fashion and convention. This might be handled to some extent by a careful repetition of key experiments of the past in order to find out how far similar results are now obtained, and to what causes any differences might be attributed.

An important point in dealing with colour is that the most significant problems about colour for the empirical aesthetician are concerned with the use of colours in combination and in relation to designs, forms and representations of scenes and objects. Single colours and simple combinations such as pairs of colours are interesting for experimental psychology, but preferences for them and judgments about them may not tell as much about the actual valuation and use of colours in art. Thus the free use of colours by artists and others, and preferences and judgments about figures and designs which have alternative and interchangeable colour arrangements, will be particularly useful, although experimental results will be complex and may be difficult to interpret. Some experimenters have already used such methods, but there is no doubt that their work should be developed further.

Defective colour vision

The effects of defective colour vision on visual art have been considered and studied from time to time over a long period (Pickford, 1965), but they have not been subjected to anything like enough systematic experimental research. For example we know little or nothing of the extent to which defects of colour vision influence aesthetic judgments about various kinds of coloured pictures. One approach would be possible by setting up what one might call a panel of colour vision defective art judges and comparing their judgments with those of normal people. It would, however, be very difficult to establish groups equivalent in other ways. The possibilities of using changes of lighting, alternative colour combinations in works of art or experimental imitations of them, or colour filters (glass or gelatine), might and should be considered, but unfortunately only some colour vision defects can be imitated by using colour filters, all of which act subtractively.

Experiments with pictures

Many interesting and valuable experiments on aesthetic preferences and judgments concerning pictures have been reported (Pickford, 1955; Child, 1969). A number of significant points have emerged. While it is useful to know that there is a tendency towards a general factor of aesthetic taste or judgment, it is even more important to know, as we do as a result of Child's experiments, that this factor is dependent on the subjects concerned having some knowledge, experience or training in art, although not necessarily of the art in question. The more artistic, experienced in or concerned with art the subjects studied, the more likely it is that there will be a general factor underlying their judgments.

In the writer's view the most illuminating factorial studies are those which reveal the components of the factors concerned, or perhaps we should say those studies which show which kinds of aesthetic qualities are more and which less correlated with the basic factors. These are, of course, colour harmony, form and design, and emotional expression in the principal factor, with qualities of impressionism, photographic accuracy, expressionistic distortion and so on in the second factor.

Many important experiments have made use of sets or pairs of pictures carefully planned on the basis of judgment and selection by experts to differ in respect of some special quality believed to have aesthetic significance. It is better that such experiments should be done with works of gifted and outstanding artists than that suitable pictures should be made for the purpose. Artists who made suitable pairs of pictures would possibly be second rate and their work not so significant for research, or they would not be inspired in these particular works, which would therefore be of less than the desired degree of artistic value. However, such experiments may be used to test the hypotheses that the differences in question have an influence on aesthetic judgments.

This raises the question of agreement with experts. In a lecture to the Scottish Branch of the British Psychological Society in Edinburgh in 1932, entitled, *The Psychological Significance of Recent Paintings by Picasso,* at which the writer was present, Herbert Read, who was then Professor of Fine Art in Edinburgh, said that his students made worse performances on the Maier–Seashore Art Judgment Test after attending his lectures than before. The implication was that they learned to agree with him as an expert, and to differ with other experts. It is well known that many outstanding artists would never have achieved anything unless they had differed with the experts of their time. We cannot define good aesthetic judgment as agreement with the experts, although this agreement may be one aspect of good aesthetic judgment. Disagreement with a particular group of experts might be more important than agreement with them. While the assistance of experts in the planning and construction of experiments is essential, one has to be guarded against the supposition that disagreement with particular experts is necessarily wrong.

It is clear that numerous possibilities exist for further experiments on aesthetic judgments about pictures. Again we have to say that age, sex, national and cultural or racial differences, and comparisons arising from changes of fashion and experience or training, are likely to be of great interest, while degrees of aesthetic ability should always be taken into account.

Cross-cultural studies of aesthetic judgments

Although early cross-cultural studies of colour preferences showed very considerable differences, there was on the whole much agreement. This was emphasised by Eysenck, who pooled the results of 26 studies, including 12,175 white and 8,885 non-white subjects. McElroy, however, showed that there was a correlation in ordering ten colours for preference, between Whites and between Australian Aborigines, but not between Aborigines and Whites.

Child and others showed considerable similarities in colour preferences between US and Vietnamese, and between US and Japanese children, but emphasised that there were marked differences. They worked with much more satisfactory materials than had been used before. Osgood showed both similarities and differences in semantic-differential judgments of colours for Navajo and US white subjects. Stewart and Baxter found no differences between Negro, Latin and Anglo groups, and Hogg has emphasised the overall similarities in factors influencing judgments of colours for British and Japanese subjects.

At present it is an open question whether the similarities of preference are due to genetic-physiological factors and the differences to cultural-psychological factors, or the reverse.

The experiments of Thouless on phenomenal regression showed a marked difference between Eastern and Western subjects which might be related to differences in their art, but an experiment by Beveridge, although it confirmed the finding of greater pheno-menal regression for shapes, did not reveal a difference in art judgments to correspond. Jahoda found that children of Accra were subject broadly to the same influences of sex in relation to shapes as Scottish children, although to a lesser degree. McElroy found a modest degree of agreement within a white Australian group and within a group of Australian Aborigines, but no agreement between the groups, in preferences for tartans and polygons. Davis found similarity in the tendency to fit names to shapes, between English and Mahali children of Tanganyika. Monica Lawlor showed a considerable agreement within each of two groups of English and West African subjects in preferences for Gold Coast patterns and designs, but there was no agreement between the groups. Michael showed that there was no difference in the tendency to closure in visual patterns in Navajo and US white subjects. Osgood showed much inter-cultural uniformity in the relationships between words and pictorial alternatives for Navajos, Mexican-Spanish, Japanese and Anglo subjects, but there were also marked differences. Davis showed that the physiognomic quality of rounded and angular shapes was essentially the same for English and for Mahali (Tanzanian) children.

In the research of Betty Lark-Horovitz, it appeared that Negro and white children of Cleveland differed widely in their preferences for subject pictures, and less widely in preferences for portraits, but had essentially similar preferences for textile patterns. However, 18 out of 39 textiles were of Oriental, African or American Indian origin.

Beveridge showed that Western pictures were generally preferred to Oriental pictures by Gold Coast students. McElroy's experiment with Australian Aborigines showed that there were small correlations among Australian Whites in preferences for picture material, and among Aborigines, but little or no correlation between Whites and Aborigines. Child and his co-workers have taken an important step in selecting subjects who may be supposed to have some aesthetic interest, knowledge or experience, and in several researches with picture material showed in general that there was considerable and even impressive agreement between different cultural groups round the world. There was almost always much more agreement within those groups themselves than between groups.

If it is agreed that there is considerable agreement between cultural and/or racial groups, but much more agreement within those groups, how are we to interpret this is an open question. There is no special reason to suppose that agreement over aesthetic choices must be of innate origin and disagreement due to cultural influences, although this may be true. There are innate differences of physique, appearance and therefore of physiology, between different human races, and there is no reason why some differences of aesthetic preference should not be innate as well. This would not imply 'better' or 'worse', but simply tendencies, which might well lead to similarities, where different groups are exposed to the same cultural influences.

In order to test the hypothesis that similarities of aesthetic judgment are probably innate but differences cultural, which many people take for granted, it would be necessary to do experiments in which different racial groups were subjected, from early childhood or even from infancy, some to the same and others to different cultural influences. Such an experimental research would be very difficult to set up and carry out, but it might well be possible to take non-white groups of experts and of non-experts, some of whom had and some had not been dominated by Western influences, and to compare their aesthetic preferences with those of corresponding white groups. It would be difficult to find white groups who had been subjected to a dominating influence by non-white cultures.

The results, however, still support the hypothesis of a general factor for aesthetic judgments, just as there is evidence for a factor of general ability. In the matter of intelligence, those more highly endowed with general ability would be more likely than others to find their way into occupations making demands on that ability, and would agree more frequently among each other, or be correct, in the handling and solution of problems involving it than they would agree with others, even if their agreements were reduced by cultural and racial differences. Similarly, in the field of aesthetic judgments, people concerned with art and occupied with it would be more likely to be selected from those having higher artistic gifts than others, and to agree more among themselves than with others in aesthetic judgments, although agreement where there were the influences of cultural or racial differences would probably be less than where there were no such influences.

Children's art and aesthetic judgments

Child art has been studied largely as a result of the discovery of the child in education (Oldham, 1940; Meier, 1933; Munro, *et al.*, 1942). Much is now known and understood about the great artistic ability of many young children, and how, in many or most children, this ability must have been linked with early painting interests and tends to be repressed or destroyed by the reality demands at and following adolescence. It is not known how far or in what ways a continuance of artistic creativeness could be ensured beyond adolescence in more children or whether, if it were possible, this would include more children with high artistic gifts who are lost for art at present, or whether those who persist in their artistic activities are mainly those with the greatest artistic ability. The whole development of child art should be studied all over again, using more children in detailed studies and more precise and accurate methods of observation and investigation. As in other fields, cross-cultural studies free from the bias of dominant interest in Western art are essential.

Although an independent chapter has been devoted to children's aesthetic judgments and preferences, the comments in earlier chapters dealing with adults apply again here, with appropriate changes. While it is clear from what has been reported of researches on children's artistic judgments and activities that a large amount of very interesting work has been done, most of it could with advantage be revised, planned again and repeated with changes for the better. It is, therefore, desirable that all the earlier and recent or current work on children's aesthetic judgments and preferences should be carefully reconsidered and repeated where necessary. For instance, it is still not clear that the tendency for a change in preferences for reds and long wave colours to give way to preferences for blues does not take place in early childhood, because Child's work (Child, *et al.,* 1968), which seemed to show no such change, apparently did not take account of children of a sufficiently early age. In other fields of child art and children's aesthetic judgments and preferences, it seems that very often the most illuminating studies have not always been the most scientifically adequate. It often happens that so-called scientific rigour tends to be substituted for psychological illumination. This is very unfortunate, however, and it is urgently important that both requirements should be fulfilled together.

Influences of temperament and personality

It is very clear from what has been said in the relevant chapter that temperamental and personality factors are tremendously important, and should be investigated very much more thoroughly. This is now being done very cleverly by various workers (Child, 1969). While the use of quantitatively exact and standardised tests and experimental methods is very important, a large body of psychologists agree that the use of case-history and descriptive methods is essential, together with the biographical, clinical and psycho-analytic approaches. Personality problems in relation to creative art can hardly be understood adequately without their help. The problem is not to eliminate such methods, but to make them more adequate.

Psychiatric art

The problems of psychiatric art have received much fuller study than the problems of the relationships of temperament and personality with aesthetic judgment. This is because of the great interest in the art of patients from the points of view of diagnoses and art therapy. These problems have been treated in many works (Jakab, 1968 and 1969; Volmat and Wiart, 1969) and rather briefly in Chapter 9. The study of the aesthetic value and quality of psychiatric art or, as it may be named, psychopathological expression, has not been explored in this book. It is, however, clear that psychiatric art is not necessarily bad art, and that so-called normal and good art is not necessarily unrelated to psychiatric and personality problems (Pickford, 1967). The latter point has been fully dealt with in works on psychoanalysis and the artist. What we want to understand more fully is the depth-creative process in the artist's personality.

The problems of the aesthetic valuation and judgment concerning works of psychiatric art have been little dealt with in research, although some beginnings have been made (Main, 1969). It would be worth while to carry out studies with psychiatric pictures and works of art compared with works of normal artists, using groups of normal artistic and non-artistic subjects and comparable groups of non-artistic and artistic psychiatric patients. In this way similarities and differences between patients and normal person's judgments could be elucidated, and also the differences and similarities in their art. We should like to find out how far and in what ways psychiatric art really differs from and is inferior to normal art, if it is inferior.

Problems of ugliness

The psychology of ugliness is a subject which deserves considerable attention, but has received little hitherto, except in the general aesthetic psycho-analytically oriented works (Pickford, 1969). From the point of view of personality, feelings and judgments of ugliness should be examined experimentally in relation to the results of personality and temperamental studies of the subjects in question and age and sex factors should be taken into account. Experimental studies of feelings of ugliness should be made and investigated in relation to liking and disliking, and judgments of aesthetic merit and various aesthetically interesting qualities. It is unfortunate that 'ugliness' was not included as a variable quality in some factorial studies. Many of these points are being dealt with by a colleague of the writer's, Miss Gillian Paul, in a research on the psychology of ugliness being carried out with the help of art experts. The interrelationships of the three dimensions beauty/ugliness, liking/disliking and good/bad aesthetic quality will be elucidated in this research.

Bibliography and References
for Chapter 10

BALL, VICTORIA K. (1965). The Aesthetics of Colour. A Review of Fifty Years of Experimentation. *J. Aesthet. and Art Criticism, 23,* 441–52.

BELL, CLIVE (1916). *Art.* London: Chatto and Windus.

BURT, C. (1933). The Psychology of Art, ch. 15 in *How the Mind Works,* Ed. C. Burt, London: Allen and Unwin.

Brit. J. Aesthetics (1965). vol. 5, no. 2, pp. 107–44 (for studies of Clive Bell's theory).

CHILD, I. L. (1969). Esthetics. Ch. 28 in *Handbook of Social Psychology* (2nd ed.), Eds. Lindzey, G. and Aronson, E. Reading, Mass: Addison Wesley.

CHILD, I. L., HANSEN, J. A. and HORNBECK, F. W. (1968). Age and Sex Differences in Children's Color Preferences. *Child Development, 39,* 237–47.

DAVIS, R. (1961). The Fitness of Names to Drawings. A Cross-Cultural Study in Tanganyika. *Brit. J. Psychol., 52,* 259–68.

FIEANDT, KAI VON (1966). *The World of Perception* (especially ch. 16). Homewood, Ill.: Dorsey Press.

JAKAB, IRENE (1968 and 1969). *Psychiatry and Art.* vols. 1 and 2. Basel: Karger.

LOWENFELD, V. (1939). *The Nature of Creative Activity.* Tr. O. A. Oeser. London: Kegan Paul.

MAIN, A. N. (1969). A New Look at Empathy. *Brit. J. Aesthet., 9,* 60–72.

MEIER, N. C. (1933). Studies in the Psychology of Art. Ed. N. C. Meier. *Psychol. Monogr. no. 200,* pp. i–ix and 1–188.

MUNRO, T., LARK-HOROVITZ, BETTY and BARNHART, E. N. (1942). Children's Art Abilities: Studies at the Cleveland Museum of Art. *J. Exper. Educ., 11,* 97–184.

OLDHAM, HILDA W. (1940). *Child Expression in Colour and Form.* London: John Lane.

PICKFORD, R. W. (1955). Factorial Studies of Aesthetic Judgments. Ch. 37 in *Present-Day Psychology,* Ed. A. A. Roback. New York: Philos. Library.

PICKFORD, R. W. (1965). The Influence of Colour Vision Defects on Painting. *Brit. J. Aesthet., 5,* 211–26.

PICKFORD, R. W. (1967). *Studies in Psychiatric Art.* Springfield, Ill.: Thomas.

PICKFORD, R. W. (1969). The Psychology of Ugliness. *Brit. J. Aesthet.*, *9*, 258–70.

RÉVÉSZ, G. (1950). *Psychology and Art of the Blind.* London: Longmans, Green & Co.

THOULESS, R. H. (1932). A Racial Difference in Perception. *J. Soc. Psychol.*, *4*, 330–9.

VALENTINE, C. W. (1962). *The Experimental Psychology of Beauty.* London: Methuen.

VOLMAT, R. and WIART, C. (1969). *Art and Psychology.* Amsterdam: Excerpta Medica Foundation.

WYBURN, G. M., PICKFORD, R. W. and HIRST, G. (1964). *Human Senses and Perception.* Edinburgh and London: Oliver and Boyd; Toronto: University Press. Ch. 7 and pp. 227–31.

Conclusions

This book has been an attempt to delineate the various phases and aspects of visual aesthetics, mainly from the point of view of the experimental psychologist, since Fechner published his first work on the subject in 1871. It is not intended as a history of the subject. In the writer's view a history would be aimed at outlining and following the various trends and influences which had been at work and their interaction, whereas this book, although its subject-matter has been handled in an historical manner, has been aimed chiefly at putting the reader in possession of the various researches and experiments which were carried out, giving him enough information to see what problems were raised, what methods and techniques were used in attempting to solve them, and what degree of success was achieved. A full enough list of references for each chapter is given to enable the more serious research worker to link up his own aims and methods effectively with those of the past. Thus the whole subject has been treated in a sectional way and each section handled in a separate chapter.

The writer is very much aware that research is progressing apace, and that many interesting and important developments are taking place at the time of writing. It is, however, necessary to bring the compilation of material for a book to a stop at some point, and that has been approximately mid-1970 for this book.

It looks at the present time that many problems, especially those relating to personality differences and unconscious influences in aesthetic preferences and judgments, and perhaps in creativity, may be more efficiently handled than seemed likely ten years ago. The problems of the interrelations of culture and race remain extremely baffling, and equally baffling are those between physiological and hereditary bases and environmental influences or education. If, for example, we ask questions about why a generally 'grotesque' style dominated pre-Columbian art, how it came to be adopted, whether it was valued or appreciated in an 'aesthetic' way by those for whom and by whom the art objects were made, whether, if we see 'aesthetic' value in such a style, it is the same as theirs, what were the interrelationships between art, mythology and religion, and the physiological or racial peculiarities of the peoples in question, and so on, we are going to be left with conjectural answers. Most problems of this kind do not seem open to efficient study by the methods of experimental or social psychology today, although the writer would be the last to suggest that such problems are not worth attention by other methods. It does not help us to give a psychologically oriented answer that the 'grotesque' in art is exciting because it is a more than usually direct expression of unconscious influences (for some people). We still want to know what unconscious influences, what people, and how and why the excitation of these influences on these people mediates aesthetic valuation for them.

If, in conclusion, the book could be summarised in any way by a simple statement, it would be that the psychology of experimental aesthetics has contributed a very great deal to our approach to the problems of understanding art in the last hundred years, provided that we do not assume that experimental aesthetics is the only worth while approach to art.

Index